Developing
Retail
Entertainment
Destinations

Second Edition of
Developing Urban
Entertainment Centers

D1611122

Principal Authors
Michael D. Beyard
Raymond E. Braun
Herbert McLaughlin
Patrick L. Phillips
Michael S.Rubin

Contributing Authors
Andre Bald
Steven Fader
Oliver Jerschow
Terry Lassar
David Mulvihill
David Takesuye

**Urban Land
Institute**

About ULI–the Urban Land Institute

ULI–the Urban Land Institute is a nonprofit education and research institute that is supported by its members. Its mission is to provide responsible leadership in the use of land in order to enhance the total environment.

ULI sponsors education programs and forums to encourage an open international exchange of ideas and sharing of experiences; initiates research that anticipates emerging land use trends and issues and proposes creative solutions based on that research; provides advisory services; and publishes a wide variety of materials to disseminate information on land use and development. Established in 1936, the Institute today has more than 16,000 members and associates from more than 50 countries representing the entire spectrum of the land use and development disciplines.

Richard M. Rosan
President

Project Staff

Senior Vice President, Policy and Practice
Rachelle L. Levitt

Vice President, Real Estate Development Practice
Gayle Berens

Project Director
Senior Resident Fellow
Michael D. Beyard

Director, Book Program
Nancy Stewart

Managing Editor
Eileen Hughes

Manuscript Editor
Sandra F. Chizinsky

Art Director
Betsy VanBuskirk

Book Design
Dever Designs

Associate Director of Publishing Operations
Diann Stanley-Austin

Executive Assistant
Ronnie Van Alstyne

Recommended bibliographic listing:
Beyard, Michael D., et al. *Developing Retail Entertainment Destinations.* Second Edition. (First Edition Title: *Developing Urban Entertainment Centers.)* Washington, D.C.: ULI–the Urban Land Institute, 2001.

ULI Catalog Number: D103
International Standard Book Number: 0-87420-849-1
Library of Congress Catalog Card Number: 2001087642

Cover photograph: The Block at Orange, Orange, California; courtesy of The Mills Corporation.

Acknowledgments

Many people contributed their time and talent to this effort, and to each one of them I say a heartfelt thank-you. I particularly wish to thank my coauthors, Ray Braun, Herb McLaughlin, Patrick Phillips, and Mike Rubin. Without their exceptional breadth of knowledge, experience, and insight into this topic, the book would not have been possible. The authors of the case studies—Andre Bald, Steven Fader, Oliver Jerschow, Terry Lassar, David Mulvihill, and David Takesuye—deserve thanks and special recognition for their thorough research and well-written commentary.

I would also like to thank the many project developers, designers, architects, and public officials who spent time with the case-study authors and provided written materials and photographs, often on very short notice. They always seemed to be available for our questions as we double- and triple-checked information, and they were equally accommodating when it came to our demanding production schedule.

Many other people contributed feature boxes and information on specialized topics that added much to the flavor of the book. Special thanks go to Christian Aaen, Gregory Beck, Jill Bensley, Howard Biel, Raymond E. Braun, Donald Bredberg, Dennis B. Carlberg, Cary Chevat, Paul DeMyer, Economics Research Associates, Robert S. Holt, The Hoyt Organization, Jung S. Kim, Eric Kuhne, James Mira, MRA International, Patrick Phillips, James Edward Sved, David Takesuye, Carrie Volkman, Jay D. Wheatley, and Shea Whitney. I also want to thank the members of ULI's Entertainment Council for their ideas and support.

Finally, I would like to thank Dever Designs for creating such a beautiful design and layout for the book and cover; Sandy Chizinsky for her lively and thorough edit of the text; and the ULI staff for its skill and dedication in bringing this book together: Ronnie Van Alstyne for trying to keep me organized, never complaining as the work piled on, and taking care of so many important assignments; Eileen Hughes for managing the editing process; Betsy VanBuskirk for managing the production process; Diann Stanley-Austin for coordinating the book's publication; David Takesuye, Leslie Holst, and Steve Ducham for coordinating and helping to choose the book's photos and graphics; Joan Campbell and Rick Davis for finding answers to specialized research questions; and Gayle Berens and Rachelle Levitt for their unwavering support throughout the book's lengthy development.

To all who had a hand in this work I extend my sincere appreciation and thanks.

Michael D. Beyard
Project Director

Principal Authors

Michael D. Beyard

Michael D. Beyard is senior resident fellow for retail and entertainment development at ULI. His specialties include urban entertainment, shopping centers, and downtown development. In the course of his long tenure at ULI, Beyard has served as author, coauthor, or project director for numerous publications, including *Developing Urban Entertainment Centers, Downtown Development Handbook, Remaking the Shopping Center, Shopping Center Development Handbook, Developing Power Centers, The Retailing Revolution,* and the *Dollars & Cents of Shopping Centers®* series.

A widely quoted and frequent speaker on urban development issues around the world, Beyard spent three years directing ULI's work with the United States Agency for International Development in central Europe; he also created and is the director of ULI's trailblazing conference series on urban entertainment development. Before joining ULI, Beyard was a senior management consultant with Booz Allen & Hamilton. He holds an undergraduate degree in international economics from Rutgers College and a graduate degree in urban planning and development from Cornell University, and he has been honored with membership in Lambda Alpha.

Raymond E. Braun

Raymond E. Braun is senior vice president at Economics Research Associates (ERA), Los Angeles. ERA's clients in the theme-park industry include the LEGO Group, Paramount Parks, Premier Parks/Six Flags, Universal Studios, and the Walt Disney Company; ERA's retail entertainment projects include Mall of America, the MCI Center, Universal CityWalk, and the Yerba Buena Center.

As head of ERA's entertainment and recreation practice group, Braun specializes in leisure and tourism economics and recreation attraction development consulting. He has extensive experience in the United Kingdom, Europe, Australia, Japan, China, Singapore, Canada, and Mexico, and served as planning consultant for the J. Paul Getty Center in Los Angeles. Braun participates in the following organizations as a member, speaker, and publications contributor: International Association of Amusement Parks and Attractions, International Association of Fairs and Expositions, International Council of Shopping Centers, and ULI. He holds a B.A. degree in economics from Claremont McKenna College and an M.B.A. degree from the University of California at Los Angeles.

Herbert McLaughlin

Herbert Mclaughlin oversees design and research at KMD, which has won more than 100 design awards, including 30 awards from the American Institute of Architects. Recently, KMD has won the following international design competitions: Cheil, Seoul; Han Nam Dong, Seoul; International Design Center, Nagoya; Jayaland Master Plans, Indonesia; Kookmin Bank Headquarters, Seoul; Lu Wan Development, Shanghai; Nasan Metro Plaza, Seoul; New Shanghai International Plaza, Shanghai; Panambi, São Paulo; Plaza Merdeka, Kuala Lumpur; Royal Washington, Hiroshima; Turtle Creek, Dallas; and Malaysian Embassy, Washington.

McLaughlin has been a visiting critic or lecturer at Berkeley, Columbia, Harvard, Stanford, the University of Illinois, the University of Wisconsin, and the University of California at Los Angeles. He has lectured at conferences and seminars sponsored by *Architectural Record,* the National Endowment for the Arts, the National Real Estate Development Center, the National Trust for Historic Preservation, NEOCON, the San Francisco Museum of Modern Art, the Smithsonian Institution, the U.S. Department of Housing and Urban Development, and ULI.

Patrick L. Phillips

Patrick L. Phillips is president of Economics Research Associates (ERA), a private consulting practice that focuses on economic and feasibility analysis, strategic planning, and transaction-related services for real estate investors and developers, public agencies, financial institutions, and nonprofit organizations. Recently, the firm has focused on the market, economic, and financial aspects of a new generation of downtown, visitor-oriented projects that combine retail, entertainment, lodging, and other uses.

Phillips, who is responsible for the development and delivery of ERA's services throughout the eastern United States, coordinates the firm's activities in the area of urban real estate and also serves on its board of directors. Before joining ERA, he was a senior manager with the real estate consulting group of Ernst & Young. A frequent speaker on urban development issues, Phillips is the author or coauthor of six books and numerous articles and teaches at the Berman Real Estate Institute at The Johns Hopkins University. Phillips is a member of ULI and is active on ULI's Urban Development and Mixed-Use Council. He holds a graduate degree in public management and finance from Syracuse University's Maxwell School of Citizenship and Public Affairs.

Michael S. Rubin

Michael S. Rubin is president and cofounder of MRA International. A pioneer in the field of entertainment-enhanced development, Rubin originated the concept of urban entertainment centers and was the innovator behind many of the most creative location-based entertainment concepts. His experience includes more than 15 years of consulting and venture creation with diverse entertainment companies, hospitality companies, development firms, and financial institutions. Rubin holds master of architecture and master of science degrees from the University of Pennsylvania and a Ph.D. from the Wharton School of Business. He has been an adjunct professor at the Fels Institute, the Wharton School, and the Graduate School of Fine Arts (architecture and planning departments) at the University of Pennsylvania. A frequent speaker at entertainment- and real estate–industry forums, Rubin has received *Progressive Architecture's* Award for Excellence and ULI's Apgar Award, as well as professional awards from the American Institute of Architects, the American Planning Association, and the U.S. Department of Housing and Urban Development.

Contents

Developing
Retail
Entertainment
Destinations

Second Edition

Preface

The Urban Land Institute is pleased to offer the second edition of its trailblazing book on retail entertainment development. The goal of the first edition was to strengthen understanding of this evolving form of development and to help move the industry forward as it matured. The goal of this volume is no different. Through all-new case studies and the insights of industry experts, this edition documents how the current varieties of retail entertainment projects are being created; identifies critical issues in the industry and describes how they are being resolved; highlights the challenges that still need to be met; and reports on the lessons learned from first-generation projects. Entertainment companies, real estate developers, and public officials—the partners in most retail entertainment projects—will continue to need this information as they explore uncharted territory, creating new projects that meet public as well as private goals.

ULI believes that today, more than ever, retail entertainment development has unusual potential to change how people think about downtowns and shopping centers, resulting in increased economic and social activity and benefiting both project creators and the public. We also believe that retail entertainment development provides an important way for downtowns and shopping centers to reinvent themselves, in order to remain competitive and to meet the rapidly changing demands of the world's consumers.

**CityPlace, developed in downtown West Palm Beach, ▶
Florida, by the Palladium Company, represents the cutting edge
of entertainment-enhanced mixed-use development.**

The Experience Architecture Timeline

Environmental Design + Media Technology + Narrative

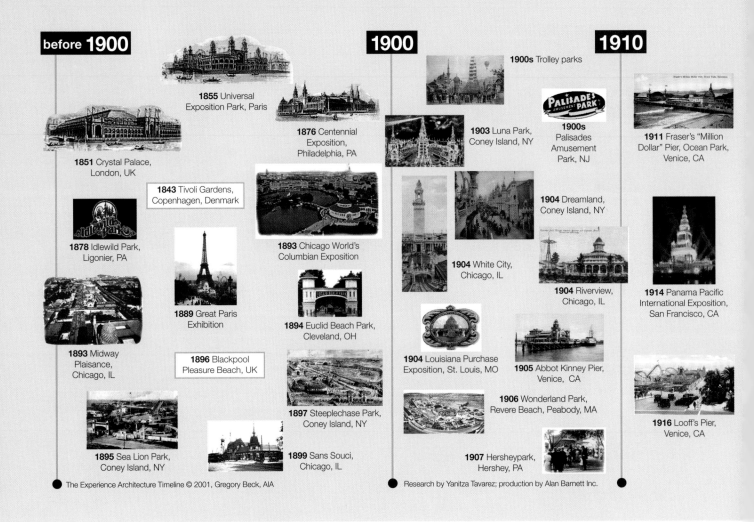

before 1900

1855 Universal Exposition Park, Paris

1851 Crystal Palace, London, UK

1843 Tivoli Gardens, Copenhagen, Denmark

1876 Centennial Exposition, Philadelphia, PA

1878 Idlewild Park, Ligonier, PA

1893 Chicago World's Columbian Exposition

1889 Great Paris Exhibition

1894 Euclid Beach Park, Cleveland, OH

1893 Midway Plaisance, Chicago, IL

1896 Blackpool Pleasure Beach, UK

1897 Steeplechase Park, Coney Island, NY

1895 Sea Lion Park, Coney Island, NY

1899 Sans Souci, Chicago, IL

The Experience Architecture Timeline © 2001, Gregory Beck, AIA

1900

1900s Trolley parks

1903 Luna Park, Coney Island, NY

1904 Dreamland, Coney Island, NY

1904 White City, Chicago, IL

1904 Louisiana Purchase Exposition, St. Louis, MO

1905 Abbot Kinney Pier, Venice, CA

1906 Wonderland Park, Revere Beach, Peabody, MA

1907 Hersheypark, Hershey, PA

Research by Yanitza Tavarez; production by Alan Barnett Inc.

1910

1900s Palisades Amusement Park, NJ

1911 Fraser's "Million Dollar" Pier, Ocean Park, Venice, CA

1904 Riverview, Chicago, IL

1914 Panama Pacific International Exposition, San Francisco, CA

1916 Looff's Pier, Venice, CA

Throughout history and throughout the world, public entertainment, amusements, and cultural facilities have been located in urban centers. The nature of entertainment, however, has evolved rapidly in the past 100 years: the crystal palaces and expositions that were the hallmarks of the Victorian era gave way to the vaudeville houses and amusement parks of the early 1900s; these gave way, in turn, to the "talkies" featured in the great movie palaces of the 1920s and 1930s. Legitimate playhouses and concert halls endured throughout, but by the 1970s, except in a few of our very largest cities, they were the only major forms of entertainment left in most downtowns.

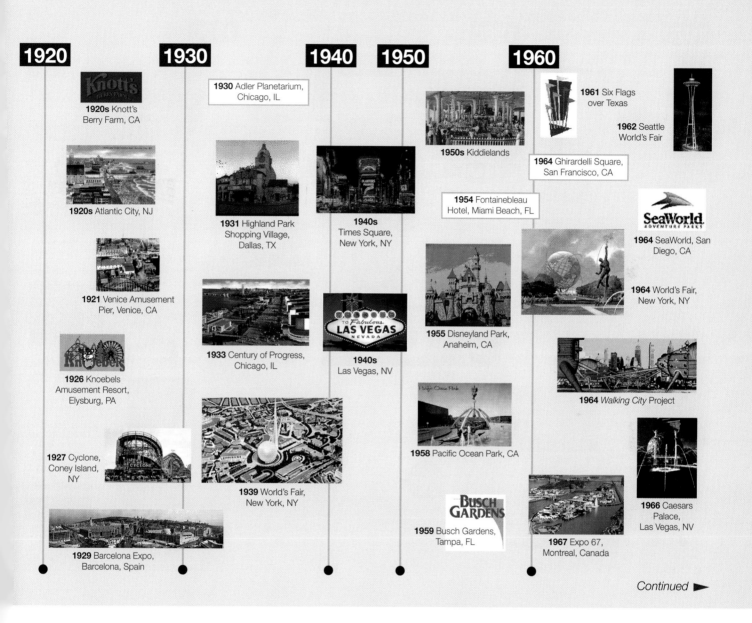

1920

1920s Knott's Berry Farm, CA

1920s Atlantic City, NJ

1921 Venice Amusement Pier, Venice, CA

1926 Knoebels Amusement Resort, Elysburg, PA

1927 Cyclone, Coney Island, NY

1929 Barcelona Expo, Barcelona, Spain

1930

1930 Adler Planetarium, Chicago, IL

1931 Highland Park Shopping Village, Dallas, TX

1933 Century of Progress, Chicago, IL

1939 World's Fair, New York, NY

1940

1940s Times Square, New York, NY

1940s Las Vegas, NV

1950

1950s Kiddielands

1954 Fontainebleau Hotel, Miami Beach, FL

1955 Disneyland Park, Anaheim, CA

1958 Pacific Ocean Park, CA

1959 Busch Gardens, Tampa, FL

1960

1961 Six Flags over Texas

1962 Seattle World's Fair

1964 Ghirardelli Square, San Francisco, CA

1964 SeaWorld, San Diego, CA

1964 World's Fair, New York, NY

1964 *Walking City* Project

1966 Caesars Palace, Las Vegas, NV

1967 Expo 67, Montreal, Canada

Continued ▶

David Nasaw describes this trend in *Going Out: The Rise and Fall of Public Amusements:* "The era of public amusements that was born in the later decades of the nineteenth century has come to an end. We have lost not simply buildings and parks but also the sense of civic sociability they nourished and sustained. Once, [these] amusement spaces defined the city as a place of glamour and glitter, fun and sociability. But they have vanished forever."[1] It is no secret why this occurred: the rapid suburbanization of the post–World War II era; the decentralization of retail activity; the decline of the industrial economy and the rise of a technological and service economy that was not tied to central cities; and the middle-class flight that left central cities devoid of a large and affluent market segment.

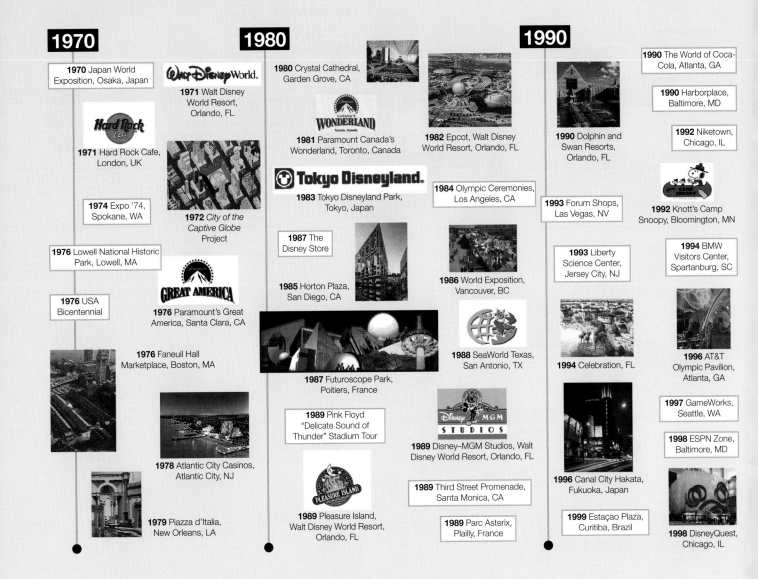

1970

1970 Japan World Exposition, Osaka, Japan

1971 Walt Disney World Resort, Orlando, FL

1971 Hard Rock Cafe, London, UK

1974 Expo '74, Spokane, WA

1972 *City of the Captive Globe* Project

1976 Lowell National Historic Park, Lowell, MA

1976 USA Bicentennial

1976 Paramount's Great America, Santa Clara, CA

1976 Faneuil Hall Marketplace, Boston, MA

1978 Atlantic City Casinos, Atlantic City, NJ

1979 Piazza d'Italia, New Orleans, LA

1980

1980 Crystal Cathedral, Garden Grove, CA

1981 Paramount Canada's Wonderland, Toronto, Canada

1982 Epcot, Walt Disney World Resort, Orlando, FL

1983 Tokyo Disneyland Park, Tokyo, Japan

1984 Olympic Ceremonies, Los Angeles, CA

1987 The Disney Store

1985 Horton Plaza, San Diego, CA

1986 World Exposition, Vancouver, BC

1987 Futuroscope Park, Poitiers, France

1988 SeaWorld Texas, San Antonio, TX

1989 Pink Floyd "Delicate Sound of Thunder" Stadium Tour

1989 Disney–MGM Studios, Walt Disney World Resort, Orlando, FL

1989 Third Street Promenade, Santa Monica, CA

1989 Pleasure Island, Walt Disney World Resort, Orlando, FL

1989 Parc Asterix, Plailly, France

1990

1990 The World of Coca-Cola, Atlanta, GA

1990 Harborplace, Baltimore, MD

1992 Niketown, Chicago, IL

1990 Dolphin and Swan Resorts, Orlando, FL

1993 Forum Shops, Las Vegas, NV

1992 Knott's Camp Snoopy, Bloomington, MN

1993 Liberty Science Center, Jersey City, NJ

1994 BMW Visitors Center, Spartanburg, SC

1994 Celebration, FL

1996 AT&T Olympic Pavilion, Atlanta, GA

1997 GameWorks, Seattle, WA

1998 ESPN Zone, Baltimore, MD

1996 Canal City Hakata, Fukuoka, Japan

1999 Estaçao Plaza, Curitiba, Brazil

1998 DisneyQuest, Chicago, IL

In response to these changes, entertainment shifted from the public to the private realm. By the 1950s, what had once been a very public experience, sought after in the heart of great cities, where all classes of society mingled in close proximity, had begun to take on two different but curiously related forms. On the one hand, the availability of private entertainment in the form of television (and, later, videocassette recorders, home theaters, computer games, and the Internet) meant that Americans could be entertained in the privacy of their own homes—without going out. At the same time, "public" entertainment itself became more private, gradually shifting to the more controlled environments of movies and arcades at regional shopping malls; family amusement parks; ballparks located outside cities; and distant resorts, all of which were far from downtowns and their diverse

1990 Universal Studios Florida, Orlando, FL

1990 Sanrio Puroland, Tama, Japan

1991 Planet Hollywood, New York, NY

1992 Mall of America, Bloomington, MN

1993 Sony Wonder, New York, NY

1992 Disneyland Paris Resort, Paris, France

1992 Expo '92, Seville, Spain

2000

2000 The Millenium Experience, Greenwich, UK

2000 Discovery Cove, Orlando, FL

1993 Universal CityWalk, Los Angeles, CA

1994 House of Blues, Boston, MA

1993 Luxor, Las Vegas, NV

1994 The Trocadero, London, UK

2000 Rose Center for Earth and Space, New York, NY

1994 Sony IMAX Theater, New York, NY

2000 Volkswagen Autostadt, Wolfsberg, Germany

1995 Universal's Port Aventura, Tarragona, Spain

1995 Official All-Star Sports Café, New York, NY

1995 Fremont Street Experience, Las Vegas, NV

2000 Expo 2000, Hanover, Germany

1996 SegaWorld, London, UK

1996 Mohegan Sun Casino, Mystic, CT

1998 UFA Cinema Palace, Dresden, Germany

1997 Newseum, Arlington, VA

2001 Disney's California Adventure, Anaheim, CA

2001 Tokyo DisneySea, Tokyo, Japan

1997 Downtown Disney, Orlando, FL

ANIMAL KINGDOM

1998 Disney's Animal Kingdom, Orlando, FL

2002 Gettysburg National Military Park, Gettysburg, PA

1997 Cirque du Soleil, Orlando, FL

1990s Casinos and resorts, Las Vegas, NV

NBA CITY

2002 Cybercenter, Hong Kong, China

1998 Navy Pier, Chicago, IL

1999 NBA City, Orlando, FL

2002 Swiss National Exposition

1998 Times Square, New York, NY

METREON

2005 World Expo, Aichi, Japan

SUMURCITY

2003 Spaceport Sumurcity, Sumur, Malaysia

1999 Sony Metreon, San Francisco, CA

1999 *Disney Magic*

1999 Universal Studios Islands of Adventure, Orlando, FL

Source: Gregory Beck, AIA, president, Architecture + Entertainment Design.

populations. Nasaw accurately describes—and laments—this trend: "The huge and heterogenous crowds that gathered [downtown] have been dispersed. The audience at a shopping center theater; the spectators at suburban ballparks; and the visitors to theme parks, festival marketplaces, and enclosed shopping malls are, by comparison, frighteningly homogenous."[2]

Can excitement, social inclusion, and interaction be reestablished in America's cities, or are they a thing of the past? The answer is becoming clear: those qualities are indeed being reestablished. The reemergence of entertainment—in the form of galleries, clubs, restaurants, civic and cultural facilities, specialty retailing, sports, and multimedia—has taken root, and, along with alternative living spaces, offers real opportunity for further downtown revitalization.

Developing Retail Entertainment Destinations | **7**

Learning from 150 Years of Experience Architecture

Experience architecture has come of age. What we have learned from a 150-year legacy of world's fairs, expositions, and leisure venues is now being applied to a variety of mainstream design projects. The result? "Entertainment design" is influencing the architecture and real estate development decisions of museums, retail stores, sports arenas, mixed-use urban centers, and Main Streets across the country. The creative and technical prowess of entertainment has escaped the theme park, and now serves an expanding marketplace hungry for experience. Simply said, entertainment values have raised our expectations about the quality and rewards of most places that we visit. Understanding these new priorities is essential to producing successful projects for an experience-based economy.

The field of experience architecture blends environmental design, media technology, and narrative to create compelling "event-places." Every project in the timeline on pages 4–7 distinguishes itself by having a story to tell. Collectively, the projects represent the history of location-based entertainment. Their primary mission is to deliver content, to communicate ideas and emotional substance in a public forum. They are often simultaneously entertaining, educational, and cultural—thereby confounding (and then liberating) our preconceptions about building types and human nature. What these special venues have been trying to tell us is now considered strategic insight: uses can be mixed, learning is pleasure, and storytelling creates culture. What are the lessons from experience architecture that will shape the places we make tomorrow?

The first lesson is that form is not content. The projects of experience architecture create their value by placing content first. They offer packets of ideas and experiences wrapped in a narrative—and often temporary—envelope. They are not about style or "synthetic environments." They are intended as information for public consumption, and they compete for our attention by offering both new and timeless insights into our world. Every design and investment decision conspires to deliver meaningful, accessible, and repeatable experiences. While the media of experience architecture may change, the message is the message.

By celebrating popular culture and emphasizing narrative expression over building form, entertainment design projects chafe against many architectural beliefs. Here the designer's role is as an interpreter, and a script—often written by others—informs the designer's vocabulary. This devotion to content is made possible when many creative disciplines are focused on a common story: it is not about individuals making form-based decisions.

The second lesson is that entertainment is more than theming. Experience architecture teaches us the importance of—and demonstrates the market for—guest-centered experiences. From the portfolio of these projects we have learned architectural techniques for environmental storytelling, and perfected ways to engage large groups of people through compelling ideas. These projects exemplify the social tradition of making places that are designed to remove us from everyday life. They show us the value of appealing to both visceral and intellectual interests. And they remind us of the universal pleasures of relentless curiosity, of stepping into alternative realities, and of making connections in an often chaotic world.

The third lesson is that brands are the new world's fairs. The past decade has seen corporate interests grow to dominate the location-based entertainment industry. As companies rapidly transform their products and services into "brand environments," these new attraction types are becoming a commercial form of the world's fairs and expositions that no longer seem relevant in the 21st century.

World's fairs and their corporate affiliates were initially viewed as the lofty sponsors of new ideas: the projects were a kind of civic offering. As energy companies led us through rainforest dioramas and appliance manufacturers transported us into kitchens of the future, the messages were ideological (and were sometimes thinly veiled advertisements). Nevertheless, the projects often yielded wonderful design work: just think of the seminal Futurama exhibitions sponsored by General Motors at the New York World's Fairs of 1939 and 1964.

But by the 1980s, a growing appetite for mainstream entertainment architecture and a dramatic rise in the sophistication of personal and mass-media technologies made traditional corporate "message-events" far less noteworthy. Today, retail stores are theatrical occasions, entertainment centers revitalize lonely downtown districts, and specialty-format theaters are common destinations on the first date. The bar has been raised—and corporations have the stories to fill the vacuum.

Product and service brands have always represented stories, and the techniques of entertainment design are now allowing them to communicate with renewed clarity and relevance. Brand association is now seen as a lifestyle component, molded to individual needs yet connected to a larger world of values. In contrast with themed settings, which highlight fictional characters or places, brand environments seek to connect commercial ideas with emotional values. Corporate investment now dominates the location-based entertainment industry with attraction types that range from brand attractions to entertainment centers and corporate museums.

The fourth and final lesson is that the future is in retreat. Experience architecture has always thrived on innovation— and supported concepts that promote a social contract between environments and progress. World's fairs typically hosted offerings with futuristic themes, and expositions showcased industrial—and then technological—leaps forward. Many aspects of 20th-century design culture, from architecture to film, have been busy imagining the future. It is, after all, a great story. Then, several years ago, having exhausted a search for architectural characteristics that could express "the future," Disney's Tomorrowland attraction famously turned back the clock, returning to the comfortable era of Jules Verne, when "tomorrow" was a more romantic version of the (then–art deco) present. Today the future seems to both exhilarate and anesthetize us. We can't imagine the look and feel of what's ahead. If we are "experiencing the future" now, what will be our inspiration for the next generation of location-based entertainment venues?

The potential of entertainment design coincides with what can best be described as our growing "future-now" condition. Simply put, the future isn't cool anymore. What we have only imagined can now be experienced. Of the dreams we had postponed in search of technology, much—perhaps too much—is available today. Location-based entertainment feeds, and is nourished by, this emphasis on the present. We should not be misled to judge the "now" as easy: it's probably the most difficult design problem of all. The goal for experience architecture is to fully express the moment, to be a tool chest for helping the culture to communicate. ●

Source: Gregory Beck, AIA, president, Architecture + Entertainment Design.

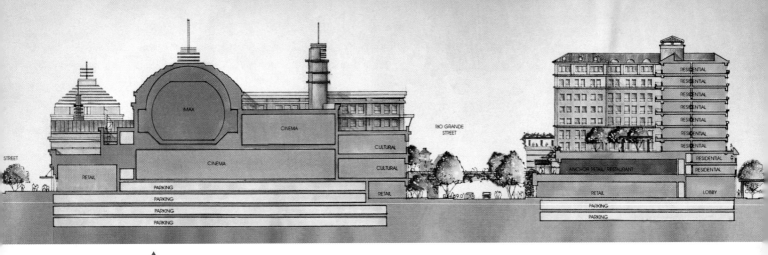

▲
The Gateway, a multiblock, mixed-use destination in downtown Salt Lake City, Utah, will serve as the central gathering place for the 2002 Olympics.

Several generations of Americans have now grown up in a largely homogenous suburban environment, and they are looking for something more. For consumers who have been everywhere, seen everything, and done everything, the old entertainment options simply will not do. People are becoming blasé about the technological wizardry that is available to them at home and at work. And the old-style shopping mall, the epicenter of suburban culture and entertainment, is dull when compared with the promise of a spectacular collection of new, out-of-home retail and entertainment options that, if creatively bundled and executed, can capture the interest of the most jaded guest.

Downtown and well-positioned suburban markets are being targeted for the largest and most ambitious retail entertainment centers. ULI sees these locations as having the identity, image, access, and (in most cases) related cultural activities that are the key requirements for successful large-scale retail entertainment developments. Since the publication of the first edition, entertainment-enhanced development has even begun to spread to secondary locations and strip centers.

ULI defines a retail entertainment development as a new form of shopping destination that, at a minimum, contains three basic components: at least one "pure" entertainment attraction, usually a new-generation cinema complex; theme restaurants (although this term is used loosely); and entertainment-oriented shops in a coordinated, intensely sociable environment that draws large numbers of diverse patrons who activate the space throughout the day. Many retail entertainment developments also include other land uses and activities to complement and reinforce their role as destinations. Although there may be gated attractions within these developments, gated amusement parks and attractions are fundamentally different from retail entertainment centers, where customers are under no obligation to spend any money and must pay only for those attractions that they are interested in.

Retail entertainment often requires some form of public/private partnership to be successful. ULI strongly supports these partnerships, which offer an efficient way to achieve both public and private goals. From the public perspective, revitalizing downtowns and reenergizing suburban centers generates a wealth of positive effects, including increased tax revenues, employment rates, and residential development. From the private perspective, high development and operating costs, particularly in downtown locations, mean that retail entertainment developments are rarely possible without public sector assistance. And links with public facilities such as museums, performing-arts centers, sports facilities, and convention centers greatly enhance the prospect that retail entertainment developments will be successful.

Retail entertainment projects require higher visitation levels than traditional shopping centers because their construction and operating costs are higher and because customers spend less per capita for entertainment than they do for the more essential goods sold by traditional retailers. This requirement highlights the challenge that the industry faces as it tries to determine what locations, mix of activities, financing structures, and partnerships will make the concept work.

Chapter 1, which explores why retail entertainment development is taking off not only in North America but around the world, describes the confluence of forces that are driving retail entertainment development and suggests how these forces will shape its future. Chapter 2 describes what retail entertainment destinations are, the types of activities they encompass, and the configurations they take. Chapter 3 describes how retail entertainment centers are put together in a business sense, including project positioning, programming, financing, and execution. Chapter 4 describes the unique planning and design issues that must be addressed.

Chapter 5 consists of case studies of projects that have opened since the first edition of this book was published. The projects, which include freestanding retail entertainment centers, a retail entertainment district, and shopping centers that have been infused with entertainment amenities, all have an operating track record. Where figures were available, information was included on project economics: construction and operating costs, rents, and sales per square foot.

Chapter 6 describes where the retail entertainment industry is heading and offers some predictions about future directions and opportunities.

Collective wisdom continues to evolve, and this edition is far from the last word on the development of retail entertainment centers. The volume does provide, however, a comprehensive look at the latest of these developments from a real estate perspective, along with the most practical, up-to-date information on how these projects have been conceived, planned, designed, programmed, structured, and financed. The lessons learned from these second-generation projects will be invaluable to the entertainment and development industries and to the public sector as they work together to create the next generation of retail entertainment projects.

Notes:
1 . David Nasaw, *Going Out: The Rise and Fall of Public Amusements* (New York: Basic Books, 1993).
2. Ibid.

◀ **The Venetian hotel and casino, in Las Vegas, is a fantasy retail and entertainment environment designed to evoke the real Venice.**

Forces Driving Retail Entertainment

Retail entertainment developments emerge when a variety of players bundle together entertainment, dining, and retail components to create synergistic leisure destinations. The proliferation of destination developments, which began in the 1990s and continues today, resulted from the convergence of trends in real estate development, retailing, entertainment, and the revitalization of cities. Developers are seeking new, strategic real estate models to compete against the burgeoning value-oriented retail sector; entertainment companies are seeking new opportunities to exploit regional entertainment and retail initiatives; and municipalities are hoping to strengthen urban revitalization by attracting suitable developments to downtowns. In large part, destination developments are a response to changing consumer preferences favoring leisure options that are easily accessible and closer to home, and that can be frequently enjoyed.

Interestingly, the development of destination projects can be traced to both positive and negative economic conditions over the past few decades. On the one hand, the prevailing importance of leisure in American society is an expression of the current strong economy. At a time when people of all ages and most economic strata have a significant amount of disposable income, pleasure, indulgence, relaxation, stimulation, and entertainment have come to be seen as inalienable rights. Consumers can afford to buy superfluous merchandise like

Lifestyle destinations afford their patrons closer, more accessible leisure options that can be enjoyed more frequently. The Avenue at White Marsh, in Baltimore County, Maryland, is a Main Street–oriented project serving the 2,000-acre White Marsh master-planned community.
Nottingham Properties ▶

logo baseball caps from NASCAR Café, miniature versions of Frank Lloyd Wright–designed stained-glass windows from The Museum Company Store, and magnetic poetry kits for the refrigerator door. They can also afford gratuitous foods like smoothies and cappuccinos, which they consume not because they are thirsty but because they have a specific craving. Entertainment, too—like a five-minute motion-simulator ride priced at a dollar per minute, or a spin on a human gyroscope—is similarly accessible and justifiable.

Yet the retail entertainment destination also owes its origin to the economic constraints of recent decades, especially the recessions of the 1970s and early 1990s. The strained economy spurred the development of off-price and outlet retailers—shopping alternatives that proved to be stiff competition for shopping malls. Seeking a competitive niche, some malls transformed themselves into destination developments. Meanwhile, economic necessity drove the explosion in the number of two-income, time-constrained families that has largely fueled the growth of out-of-home dining. Similarly, the need to revitalize nation's inner cities is a byproduct of long-term economic conditions.

The Intensity of Retail Competition

A variety of circumstances have created a highly competitive retail environment for malls—regional and super-regional shopping centers. One significant factor is the over-building of retail facilities. At the beginning of the 1980s, retail square footage was between 12 and 14 square feet per capita, a figure that conformed to general guidelines for sustainability; by 1994, however, retail square footage was nearly 19 square feet per capita. Much of that excess space is found in malls. According to the ULI's *Dollars & Cents of Shopping Centers®: 2000,* regional shopping centers have, at 8 percent, the highest vacancy rate of all center types, while super-regional centers have a 7 percent vacancy rate. These rates are about four times the rates of community and neighborhood centers.

The decline in mall performance has been caused in part by the degraded conditions of many of the centers, a large number of which are now 15 to 30 years old. In addition, many of the department store chains that had long served as anchor tenants in these developments have consolidated, closing many of their stores. Yet another factor undermining the success of shopping malls is the recent proliferation of value-oriented retailers, such as stand-alone discount stores and off-price, outlet, and power centers. During the recession of the early 1990s, such facilities—which offer maximum breadth and depth of product lines; a no-frills environment; and high-volume, low-markup sales strategies—underwent explosive growth. According to the National Research Bureau's winter 1997 issue of *Shopping Center Directions,* for every regional enclosed mall that opened in 1996, 17 power centers opened.

The threat posed by value-oriented retailers to regional shopping centers, whose tenants typically cannot match the off-price retailers either in price or scope of product line, is exacerbated by the fact that value-oriented retailers have succeeded in capturing higher-income shoppers as well as the expected lower-income shoppers. According to a Roper Starch Worldwide Study, affluent Americans—those with more than $100,000 in household income—are significantly more likely than the typical American to patronize florists, gourmet food stores, greeting-card stores, jewelry stores, kitchenware specialty stores—and warehouse clubs. And, although the proportion of affluent Americans who had done so is lower than that of the general public, about half of the affluent Americans surveyed had made a purchase at a discount store in the previous month.

Mid-1999 estimates put the proportion of American households online at 45 percent, up from essentially zero at the beginning of the decade. Forecasts call for 70 million households—about two-thirds of all American households—to have Internet access by 2003. Online retailing, similarly, jumped from about $3 billion in 1997 to some $12 billion by 1999; yet even with this phenomenal growth, Internet retailing represents less than 1 percent of total domestic retail sales (though penetration is much higher in certain categories, such as computer hardware and books). There can be little doubt, however, that the Internet has changed the rules of the retail game forever.

Overbuilding, aging facilities, loss of traditional tenants, competition from value-oriented retailers, and Internet retailing have led mall developers to embrace destination projects as a way to remain competitive. In these developments, the addition of enter-tainment and dining amenities and the shift toward entertainment-oriented retailers broaden the realm of commerce from physical commodities—clothing, books, and jewelry, for example—to include those that are experiential—fun, excitement, social interaction, and education.

The Rise of Lifestyle Retailing

People have historically been identified by their trade, even taking it as their surname: Cooper, Baker, and Smith are examples. In recent years, however, people have come to identify themselves by their lifestyle, and even more specifically by their leisure interests: "I'm a skier," "I'm a vegetarian," or "I'm an avid reader." In the current competitive environment, retailers have sought to differentiate themselves by catering to the needs of people with specific lifestyle profiles. In fact, in many cases, businesses are specializing in a particular type of consumer rather than a particular type of product. With the emergence of lifestyle retailing, stores have become more leisure oriented and more experiential—characteristics that are typical of retail entertainment developments. At the same time, the appeal to values and aspirations creates demand for the types of products and activities that are found in the new, entertainment-oriented stores and attractions.

Starbucks, for instance, is forming strategic alliances with retailers in various fields, including Barnes & Noble, Crate & Barrel, and Nordstrom, whose patrons fit the same lifestyle profile as those of the gourmet coffee-bar chain. And by selling private-label coffeemakers, mugs, compact discs, and thermal carafes, Starbucks does not aim to sell coffee to everyone as much as to sell "coffee-drinker" lifestyle products to its upscale target market.

Leading retailers are specializing in a particular type of consumer rather than a particular type of product. The prototype design for Guess stores emphasizes image and lifestyle over product. *Gensler*

As department stores retain only the most profitable services and departments—clothing and home furnishings—specialty retailers are expanding their domain to include new product categories in boutique departments. Eddie Bauer, for instance, has expanded from its emphasis on men's clothing to include women's wear, luggage, housewares, and so forth. What makes these ventures successful is that the firms are leveraging the cachet of their brand name and style. Rather than stock "the universe under one roof," as traditional department stores once did, these specialty stores—acting, in essence, as fashion consultants—stock only those goods that fit their customers' lifestyle profile.

Lifestyle retailing makes patrons more inclined to identify with a particular store, not only because of its products but because there is a growing emphasis among retailers on the integration of experiential pursuits. Some retailers incorporate entertainment-oriented activities within their stores, inducing consumers to spend their leisure time in a retail environment. Gourmet coffee bars, McDonald's Playlands, and live jazz at Barnes & Noble and at Borders Books & Music illustrate this strategy. An extreme example of personal attention is Levi Strauss and Co.'s made-to-order Personalized Pair blue jeans, which are manufactured to the customer's measurements taken at a retail boutique.

Street Retail: Old Wine, New Bottles

Thirty-nine years ago, Jane Jacobs authored one of the most powerful and insightful books ever written on the (then current) efforts of city planning and redevelopment. *The Death and Life of Great American Cities* blasted away at popular theories and practices such as the segregation of land uses (and people), the creation of superblocks, the proliferation of superhighways, and the ever-growing popularity of "standardized suburban chain-store shopping." Instead, Jacobs cried out for urban diversity, mixed uses, vibrant street life, and 24-hour safe places where individuals and families love to live, work, shop, and play.

Only very recently, particularly in the past five or six years, has the pendulum of retail development begun to shift toward the paradigm suggested by Jacobs, principally because of fundamental changes in urban retailing supply and demand. On the supply side, regional malls are approaching saturation, and power centers demonstrate premature vulnerability; on the demand side, the American demographic profile is decid-

edly changing. The proportion of families that fit the "traditional" pattern—suburban father and mother with "two-plus" kids at home—has dropped dramatically, and the proportion of single households, single-parent households, and nonfamily households has increased. Another source of change is the rapid emergence and acceptance of information technology in general, and e-commerce in particular.

In response to these changes in supply and demand—and to consumers' utter boredom with enclosed regional malls and their predictable tenancies, terrazzo, and temperature—the marketplace has rediscovered (Main) Street Retail. Whatever the label (and many of the labels are used interchangeably and often misapplied)—town center, urban entertainment district, location-based entertainment, urban village, edge city, or infill development—there is every indication that properly conceived and implemented street retail development can be successful in a variety of urban American contexts. The keys to success are the skillful calibration of uses, designs, merchandising, streetscaping,

▲
Valencia Town Center in Valencia, California.

and marketing, and the management of public and private building programs that define places where people truly crave to be.

Street retail at Federal Realty Investment Trust was officially born in 1994 with the formation of Street Retail, Inc., a wholly owned subsidiary of the trust. The approach sprang from two sources: first, Federal Realty's strong interest in the evolution of first-quality, metropolitan-area retailing; second, the expressed interest of our best tenants to locate on emerging "great streets" that were central to underserved pockets

with excellent demographic profiles. Rather than compete with a rash of newly formed real estate investment trusts whose bidding wars (fueled by the ample availability of capital) were driving up the price of desirable shopping centers, Federal Realty launched an aggressive program of property purchases in areas where building redevelopment and store remerchandising would yield distinctive value for the trust and its shareholders.

The principal projects in the first phase of Street Retail's history were the Woolworth store, on Greenwich Avenue in

Continued ▶

Greenwich, Connecticut; the Westfield Cinema, on Central Avenue in Westfield, New Jersey; and the Col-Fair building, on Colorado Boulevard in Pasadena, California. To better serve each of their respective host markets, the Woolworth building became Saks Fifth Avenues first Main Street store; Westfield Cinema became Imaginarium and Legg-Mason; and the vacant and deteriorating Col-Fair building was transformed into a Pottery Barn and residential lofts. The lesson of this phase, however, was that economies of scale certainly hold true in this business: while these projects created definite value for the trust, they created even larger marginal value for adjoining property owners, who profited from Street Retail's vision, energies, and speculative investment.

Consequently, the focus in phase two was on purchasing an entire block, rather than individual buildings, on these emerging "Main Streets." For example, Street Retail partnered with local developers in southern California and southeastern Pennsylvania to purchase and redevelop threshold holdings on Fifth Avenue, in the Gaslamp District of San Diego;

on Third Street Promenade, in Santa Monica; and on Main Street in Manayunk, just outside Center City Philadelphia. A great street is more than a collection of national retailers who move *en masse* to a fashionable address; by aggregating more real estate in these selected submarkets, Street Retail was better able to orchestrate a diverse and intrinsically appealing blend of local, regional, and national merchandisers.

It was through our work in our hometown laboratory— Bethesda Row, in Bethesda, Maryland—that we moved into the third and current phase of street retail development. All the necessary ingredients converge at Bethesda Row: the five contiguous blocks are central to an outstanding local marketplace; a short stroll from the Bethesda Metro Station; and transected by the most popular hiking, biking, and roller-blading trail in the Washington metropolitan area. Within a short distance are the vibrant shopping centers of White Flint Mall, Mazza Gallerie, and Montgomery Mall.

The 950-space Montgomery County garage is embedded at the core of our

building program, and a three-story, "urban-style" Barnes & Noble serves as the principal anchor for the redevelopment. But street retail, unlike traditional shopping centers, is not defined by anchors or major stores. Instead, the diversity, variety, and rhythm of retailing rules: shake up uses and sizes and heights and frontages and storefronts and signs and lighting and street furniture and trees and opportunities to turn corners and walk randomly through city space, and you will have defined the street retail substance that successful urban villages—past, present, and future—are made of.

Now in its third year of attracting patronage, Bethesda Row is so much more than a retail street. The offices above merchant stores are highly sought after and always fully occupied. Second-level retail works, too. A 24-hour Kinko's provides round-the-clock traffic and "eyes on the street," to use the phrase that Jane Jacobs coined to describe the additional security that is created when store operations remain open and generate activity late at night. Our restaurants are, for the most part, local businesses, and include ethnic delights from a

great range of cultures; most are modestly priced and enjoy plenty of repeat trade from primary-market residents, workers, and shoppers. And our district has no sharp edges, no heralding signs or banners; we wish to be seamless with surrounding buildings, streets, and neighborhoods, yet serve as the heart of this ever-more-popular urban place.

What was missing from Bethesda Row were the vertically integrated and horizontally interlaced mixed-density residential uses that firmly and finally define the urban village. However, other firms are already constructing living quarters in close proximity to Street Retail's recent enterprise, and we too, are now adding a variety of home types to our emerging village pattern. What's most exciting, both in this project and others, is the tremendous desire of nearby residents to take up residence in planned townhomes, apartments, lofts, mid-rise luxury units, or live-work quarters, in order to share in this reemerging urban lifestyle.

Our street retail work carries us now to Pentagon Row, in Arlington, Virginia, where we are undertaking development of 300,000 square feet of urban-village-style retailing and 1,150 residential units (500 mid-rise apartments above retail, being developed in partnership with Post Properties, and 650 units in two adjacent high-rise towers). We are also moving toward a construction start later this year at Santana Row, in San Jose, California, with 650,000 square feet of street retail and 1,200 units of mixed-density residential development, in addition to a 200-room hotel. And, at MARTA's Lindbergh Station, in Atlanta, we are working in cooperation with Post and others to plan a wonderful urban village consisting of 300,000 square feet of vibrant retail, 1.2 million square feet of office development, approximately 1,000 residential dwellings, and, again, a 200-room hotel.

The success of street retail and urban-village development will be driven by the careful selection of host environments that demonstrate an unambiguous political will to understand and underwrite Main Street repositioning, remerchandising, redevelopment, and ongoing marketing. These are complex, creative, time-consuming, and expensive

enterprises; a public/private partnership is mandatory. Retail catalysts include bookstores (one big, or several smaller); art cinemas (massive multiplexes typically overwhelm the street and district); specialty food stores; abundant and diverse restaurants, taverns, coffee shops, and take-outs; and lifestyle apparel and home-furnishings merchants. What these elements add up to is Urban Entertainment spelled with a small (understated) *u* and *e*.

To cap the story, try to revisit New York as soon as you can. Plant yourself on the Upper West Side; in Carnegie Hill/Upper East; in Chelsea; in the West Village; or on Park Slope, in Brooklyn; and watch—better yet, participate in—the urban ballet. Once you're hooked . . . ●

Source: Howard Biel, president, Palisades Realty & Development, Bethesda, Maryland.

Educational experiences can also link retailers and consumers. Home Depot patrons, for instance, can learn how to lay tile and install plumbing in the store's home-improvement classes. In such cases, retailers assume the role of advocate for, or consultant to, the consumer, passing on their expertise and more-or-less impartial opinion about the goods for sale.

However, the distinction between entertainment and education in the retail setting is often blurred. Sporting goods and music stores offer "play-before-you-pay" or "try-before-you-buy" opportunities that allow consumers to test merchandise in the store before purchasing it. At Bass Pro Shops Outdoor World, in Springfield, Missouri, for example, shoppers can learn how to tie fishing flies and then test them out at the store's indoor trout pond; they can also use rifle and bow ranges. At Oshman's Sporting Goods chain, customers can give athletic equipment a trial run on in-store courts. Similarly, the REI (Recreation Equipment Incorporated) flagship store in Seattle has a 475-foot-long mountain-bike test track, a rain room in which to test waterproof clothing, a faux hiking trail on which to test boots, and a 65-foot-high indoor rock-climbing pinnacle. True, in these instances customers are learning about the merchandise, but because the merchandise is typically leisure related, they are clearly enjoying it as well. The strategy, then, is to increase consumer exposure to the merchandise in anticipation that the goods will sell themselves.

One result of lifestyle retailing is that stores are coming to emphasize the experience as much as the merchandise. In this new breed of retail facility, the store could easily be viewed as an entertainment center that has a store theme—and the merchandise could be

Lifestyle retailing emphasizes the experience as much as the merchandise. The Discovery Channel Store at the MCI Center, in Washington, D.C., is a dramatic, 30,000-square-foot, multilevel store and theater combining merchandising and education.
Gensler/Pompei A.D.; Maxwell MacKenzie

a manufacturer grinds, packages, and sells those same beans in a grocery store . . . the price to a consumer jumps to between five and 25 cents per cup. Brew the beans in a run-of-the-mill diner . . . and that service now sells for 50 cents to a dollar per cup. Serve the same cup in a five-star restaurant or espresso bar, where the ordering, creation, and consumption of the cup embodies a heightened ambience or sense of theater, and consumers gladly pay anywhere from two dollars to five dollars for each cup. Businesses that ascend to this fourth level of value establish a distinctive experience that [increases] its value by two orders of magnitude over the original commodity.

It is by offering just such experiences that retailers at destination developments—Virgin Records megastore and the Disney Store, for instance—are able to compete with discount stores like Wal-Mart, which sell many of the same goods. Furthermore, these experiences are being bundled together to create highly synergistic relationships. One recently proposed destination development would have had an IMAX specialty-format film theater showing educational films next to educational retailers like The Nature Company and The Museum Company Store. Meanwhile, sports bars and athletic-gear retailers could be located in their own "jock-oriented" area. Arrangements of this kind bear a striking resemblance to those in theme parks such as Disneyland—where, in the various theme areas (Frontierland and Fantasyland, for example), all components, including attractions, food and beverage outlets, and shops, reinforce the theme.

viewed as souvenirs that commemorate the experience. In *The Experience Economy: Work Is Theatre and Every Business a Stage,* B. Joseph Pine and James J. Gilmore assert that the "experience economy" is upon us, wherein consumers want—and will pay more for—experiences:

> Consider, for example, a true commodity: the coffee bean. Companies that harvest coffee receive a little more than $1 per pound, which translates into one or two cents per cup. When

The Strength of Demand for Out-of-Home Dining

Dining is an essential component of the destination development mix. The current strength of demand for out-of-home dining derives largely from fundamental social changes of the past half-century, including an increase in the number of single-parent and dual-income households, a resulting decrease in the amount of time available to plan and prepare meals at home, and a reduction in family size. While restaurant business constituted 29.7 percent of total food expenditures in 1982, the figure had climbed to 34.6 percent by 1992. In 1997, the National Restaurant Association's *Restaurant Industry Forecast* predicted that the industry would reach an all-time sales high of $320.4 billion, representing a 4.3 percent increase over the previous year.

As the "traditional" family has changed, so has the traditional family dinner. As more and more consumers grab a bite to eat on the run, myriad out-of-home dining options have emerged. The increase in demand, along with the development of new suburban communities offering ripe territory for expansion, has enabled fast-food and casual-restaurant chains to experience rapid growth. Such growth has allowed them to amortize the costs of developing centrally manufactured food products, distribution systems, preparation techniques, and brand identities. Furthermore, these chains have perfected facility designs, menus, and operating systems—such as compact seating, single-person portion sizes, and counter service—that can accommodate single diners or groups of diners paying separately.

These more efficient restaurants are credible corporate tenants that can be located virtually anywhere—in neighborhood, community, and convenience shopping centers; in shopping malls; and in destination developments (frequently within food courts)—as well as in alternative locations like airports and college campuses. Thus, dining out has become a convenient adjunct to other activities, including shopping and entertainment.

At the same time, dining—which is intrinsically pleasurable—has also remained a leisure activity, a role it has played since ancient times. This was confirmed by the 1994 MasterCard *Dining Out Study,* which found that Americans view dining out as the number-one way to unwind and relax. Gourmet coffee-bars, popcorn wagons, frozen-yogurt shops, pretzel carts, fruit-juice bars, and the like illustrate the wide range of indulgence-oriented dining facilities that satisfy consumers' cravings more than their hunger. And theme restaurants, sports bars, jazz clubs, and dinner theaters offer an even higher level of leisure dining that acts, in essence, as entertainment.

Consumers' demand—or willingness—to enjoy food with other attractions is an essential source of the synergy that fuels destination development. For those patrons who visit a destination development primarily to dine, the accompanying retail and entertainment amenities complement their experience. Conversely, customers who visit a destination development mainly for retail or entertainment purposes will find a range of dining

opportunities to satisfy their hunger or to indulge their taste for something special.

The restaurant business has experienced some fluctuation in recent years—mainly because of economic contractions, which promote more conscientious spending patterns; an overabundance of facilities in some markets; increasingly convenient packaged-food items at supermarkets; and the new view of home cooking as fashionable—but the long-term trend is strong for out-of-home dining. The trend is further buttressed by the fact that Generation X is the first to have been raised eating restaurant food on a regular basis. Critical social phenomena, like dual-income households and single parenthood, are likely to continue to exert their influence as well.

The Ubiquity of Entertainment

A combination of sociological and technological developments have spurred ubiquity in entertainment. Among them are the domestic constraints that have emerged in the past few decades, altering leisure patterns. Dual-income households, single parenthood, job insecurity, and children's conflicting school schedules have shifted consumer preferences away from costly, infrequent, preplanned, and extended vacations toward leisure pursuits that are brief, easily accessible, economical, flexible, and can be enjoyed frequently. Contributing to the demand for such pursuits is an increase in disposable income among youth, who tend to be predisposed toward discretionary spending on entertainment and have the means to travel to local destinations but are less able to venture outside the region. More than ever, consumers are seeking leisure experiences in convenient doses on a weekly basis, inspiring the development of new regional and community-level retail entertainment destinations.

Dining out is now an essential adjunct to shopping and entertainment. One Colorado, in Pasadena, California, an early prototype of a retail entertainment destination with 25 retail, entertainment, educational, and dining establishments, is a historic redevelopment of a city block with five alleys cutting through it. *KMD*
▼

The repeat visitation pattern typical at these locales is facilitated by refreshed forms of traditional entertainment like cinemas, live-performance theaters, music venues, and sporting events, all of which draw patrons back again by offering ever-changing presentations. At the same time, dramatic new technological advances have brought about unique modes of entertainment like video and virtual-reality games that encourage repeat, interactive play. Meanwhile, new, physically compact, technology-based attractions like motion simulators have emerged. Requiring only a few hundred square feet, these rides fit within the destination's retail-scale environment yet are able to offer a dynamic, theme park–caliber experience on a par with that of a roller coaster. Because many of these attractions use changeable media and software, they tend to be uniquely suited to meeting the destination's need to encourage repeat visits. Many can be installed and removed with ease, and some are even portable, allowing them to be located virtually anywhere. The compact size and widespread appeal of video games, for instance, have long made them an ever-present diversion in places as different as convenience stores, pizza parlors, and student unions.

In part because of consumers' real or perceived "time poverty," there is also a demand for entertainment that supplements or accentuates existing activities, many of which are central to destination developments. Thus, "entertainment value," as a means of quantifying how entertaining something is, has emerged as a competitive factor in everything from restaurants ("eatertainment") to museums ("edutainment"). Retail stores—or, more specifically, entertainment-oriented retail stores—have also embraced entertainment as a value-added commodity and a way to differentiate themselves from the competition. Store design themes, dynamic audio and visual presentations, elaborate visual merchandising displays, interactive "play-before-you-pay" stations, and in-store cafés are some of the ways retailers have transformed shopping into a leisure experience.

Expansion in the Entertainment Industry

Early in their history, companies like Paramount Pictures, under founder W. W. Hodkins and later under Adolf Zukor, understood the power of vertical integration. By pulling the industry's three distinct functions—production, distribution, and exhibition—into a single organization, these innovators were able to exploit fully the value of cinema at each stage, from scripting to screening.

Similarly, in recent years, entertainment companies like Disney, Sony, Time Warner, and Universal Studios have pursued rampant expansion, mergers, and acquisitions to enable them to capitalize on their core assets—the ephemeral intellectual "properties" that are the stories, characters, and brands that they own. To illustrate, in 1955 the Walt Disney Company (then called Walt Disney Productions) described in its annual report its involvement in theatrical production and, beginning that year, distribution;

Entertainment destinations depend on repeat visits. Cinemas, music, and sports venues all offer ever-changing presentations that help achieve this goal. The Egyptian-themed, 24-screen Muvico Paradise, in Davie, Florida, combines movie-going with a range of innovative guest services, such as a children's play-room that allows parents to enjoy the movie in peace. *Development Design Group, Inc.*

television production (in the form of two shows); Disneyland, which opened that summer; and the licensing of characters and music. In contrast, by 1996 the company's activities included film production and distribution; home video; television and cable production, syndication, and broadcasting; radio production, syndication, and broadcasting; music publishing, production, distribution, and licensing; live theatrical productions; character merchandising and licensing; retailing; newspaper, technical, book, and magazine publishing; the development and marketing of multimedia computer products; ownership and interests in theme-park resort developments worldwide, with a cruise-ship line underway; and ownership of and interest in professional sports teams.

The resulting synergy among integrated activities has allowed companies to amortize marketing expenses across multiple product types, achieve higher levels of consumer awareness through multimodal penetration, and insulate themselves from economic downturns in particular business areas. For instance, a rise in oil prices may hurt Disney's destination theme parks but leave box-office earnings unaffected. The converse, however, is that when properties fail—especially when a film "bombs" at the box office, because films frequently introduce other properties— it can hurt the theme parks (which may have

parades and attractions tied to the movie) as well as licensed consumer products and retail stores (which sell products based on the movie). For instance, Disney reported in its 1996 annual report that comparable store sales in its Disney stores were down 2 percent "primarily due to the strength of *The Lion King* [an animated feature film] merchandise in the prior year," which is another way of saying that the follow-up animated film the next year was not as strong a property. Thus, vertical integration makes strong properties all the more critical.

The impact of entertainment-industry expansion on retail entertainment destinations is both direct and indirect. As the prevalence of theme parks in the United States approaches the saturation point, entertainment companies are looking for new opportunities, through regional or community projects, to exploit their intellectual properties and to apply their design and operational expertise.

Disney's involvement in the 42nd Street revitalization effort in New York City's Times Square is an example of the company's participation in the development of a more comprehensive cultural and entertainment district. In 2001, the company opened Downtown Disney, a retail entertainment complex, as part of the expansion of its Anaheim property. The project, which features name-brand and local tenants within a dynamic pedestrian environment, serves to link the Disney hotel complex with Disneyland and the Disney California Adventure theme park, which is situated on what was the parking lot.

In large part, the model for this project is Universal CityWalk, a prototypical retail entertainment destination that Universal Studios Hollywood opened next to its theme park in Universal City, California, in 1993.

In addition, DreamWorks SKG, Sega Enterprises, and Universal Studios have opened the first few of their planned chain of GameWorks centers, each of which will include hundreds of video games; several proprietary game experiences; a compact, counter-service café; a pub; and a retail boutique selling logo items—all distributed throughout a 30,000- to 50,000-square-foot industrial-theme space laden with sensory stimuli. Sony, too, explored the regional entertainment field with its multifaceted complex, Metreon, at Yerba Buena Gardens in San Francisco. Along with a cinema complex similar to that at Sony's Lincoln Square, New York, site, the Yerba Buena Center includes innovative restaurants, retail, and a play facility based on *Where the Wild Things Are,* a book by famed children's author and illustrator Maurice Sendak.

Entertainment-industry retail chains like the Disney Store and Warner Bros. Studio Store have raised consumers' expectations of the retail experience. These stores' extensive design features—intensely themed facades and interiors, projection screens showing film and television properties, and elaborate and evolving visual merchandising displays, for example—are being imitated by the nonessential, fashion, gift, and impulse merchandisers that are typical of destination developments, as such stores come to see experiential retailing as a viable competitive edge over value-oriented, off-price, big-box, and outlet stores.

Urban Revitalization

The drive to revitalize blighted downtowns has created remarkable opportunities for the development of retail entertainment projects. Following World War II, growing families seeking the middle-class luxury of homeownership—aided by government mortgage policies and transportation initiatives—led the movement of America's population to the suburbs, which, after a period of time, left the nation's cities in despair. In the decades that followed, private investment likewise flowed into the sprawling communities that ringed the cities, resulting in new development forms—such as shopping centers and industrial and business parks—that further hastened the obsolescence of many downtowns. While those in the suburbs had fewer reasons to venture into the city, those left behind—primarily disadvantaged residents—found themselves unable to obtain access to education, employment, or services.

Entertainment Company Business Centers

Film and television
Film production and distribution
Television production and syndication
Home video production and distribution
Animation production

Music
Recording, publishing, and distribution
Broadcasting
Network television, cable channels, and radio stations

Publishing
Books, magazines, and newspapers

Theme parks
Design and operation

Consumer products
Licensing and product development
Multimedia
Retail stores and catalogs

Other
Professional sports teams
Cruise lines
Live theatrical shows
Online games and entertainment

Entertainment industry giants have raised consumers' expectations of the retail experience, and retailers have responded with experiential environments to give themselves a competitive edge over value-oriented off-price stores. The flagship Disney Store, on Fifth Avenue in New York City, is one prototype that yielded subsequent imitations, both good and bad.

Realizing that the vitality of the downtown is essential to the economic health of an entire region, governments at all levels have undertaken a spectrum of legislative and economic actions aimed at encouraging redevelopment, revitalization, adaptive use, and infill development. The goals of these revitalization efforts have typically included raising property values and taxes, increasing sales tax revenues, stemming crime, creating employment in the construction industry, creating jobs, improving the civic image, and attracting tourists.

The strategies used to stimulate the private investment that is necessary to accomplish these goals include cash contributions, financing aid, tax abatements, zoning and building code variances, new or improved infrastructure, and the creation of dedicated taxes for physical improvements.[1] Some cities have created business improvement districts as well, which provide street maintenance, security, parking, marketing, and tenant recruitment services in much the same way that shopping centers do.[2]

However, as manufacturing and even professional services have become less reliant on urban locations, cities have reevaluated the types of development that can be sustained in downtowns—and found develop-

ment related to leisure pursuits to be very attractive. As cities seek to accentuate their remaining assets—their geographic centrality; their ability to attract tourists and business travelers; their pedestrian orientation and architectural integrity; and their established symbolic, historic, and cultural role as the heart of the region—they have largely repositioned themselves as leisure destinations. By emphasizing arts and entertainment; dining and retail amenities; and special venues like convention centers, stadiums, and sports arenas, cities have succeeded in transforming themselves into exotic "nearby getaways" for consumers who desire a fleeting escape from the homogeneous suburbs (see the accompanying feature box).

Sometimes urban revitalization efforts revolve around a large retail entertainment complex: E-Walk, on 42nd Street in New York's Times Square; Metreon, in San Francisco, which has been developed by New York–based Millennium Partners and Sony Development, Inc.; and the Gateway District, in Salt Lake City, Utah, which will be the central gathering point for the 2002 Winter Olympics. In other locations, revitalization takes the form of cultural and entertainment districts that arise through public efforts and involve myriad developers, such as in Old Pasadena and in Santa Monica's Third Street Promenade, both in California.

Notes:
1. For an in-depth discussion of these mechanisms, see *Downtown Development Handbook* (Washington, D.C.: ULI–The Urban Land Institute, 1992).
2. For an in-depth discussion of how these districts operate and the types of functions they perform, see *Business Improvement Districts* (Washington, D.C.: ULI–The Urban Land Institute, 1997).

Urban Chic

The emerging popularity of the imagery and ideals of "city life" is fueling the success of urban leisure developments among the generation of consumers who grew up in the suburbs. Music-video portrayals of gritty downtown settings, the popularity of thrift-store apparel, and angst-filled "grunge" subcultures like that of skateboarders are evidence of an "urban chic" aesthetic. While this mode originated as a vernacular expression of Generation X's pessimism about prevailing economic and social conditions—which the deteriorated inner cities amply symbolized—it has since been absorbed by the commercial design, fashion, and media industries. Burgeoning lifestyle retail chains like Hot Topic, Junkyard, and Urban Outfitters, and the GameWorks entertainment centers—which share a dystopian motif of scrap metal, graffiti graphics, dilapidated architecture, and industrial grime—exemplify the surging fashionableness of urbanism.

As this aesthetic both shapes and expresses people's perceptions of "the city," mitigating or capitalizing on it may be part of cities' strategic efforts to attract visitors downtown. For instance, rather than be demolished, old industrial warehouses and abandoned factories may be given new life through adaptive use. Thus, cities retain their historic roots while such structures provide visitors with an "authentic" experience distinct from what they would find in the suburbs. According to the July 1997 issue of the *Entertainment Real Estate Report,* the number of industrial buildings transformed into retail entertainment destinations doubled between 1992 and 1997. One example is the Power Plant, in Baltimore's Inner Harbor, which was converted by the Cordish Company into an entertainment destination with a Barnes & Noble, a Hard Rock Café, and a Starbucks; plus virtual-reality centers, music venues, and other amenities. At the same time, London's Battersea Power Station is reportedly undergoing a $296 million redevelopment by the landowner, Hong Kong–based Parkview International, and United States–based development partner the Gordon Group. The

▲ **The Power Plant, at Baltimore's Inner Harbor.**

60-year-old art deco building will include a 32-screen cinema complex by Warner Bros. International Theaters and Village Roadshow of Australia. Eventually, the center will add theme-park attractions, retail, hotels, and various other commercial and residential amenities.

The interest in "city life" is as much about urban living as urban aesthetics. Consumers crave the functionality of the city: dense, eclectic, spontaneous, pedestrian environments where entertainment, dining, and retail options are in close proximity. Embracing city life also represents a rejection of the sprawling and homogeneous suburbs, which have proven to be not only lacking in character but entirely inhospitable to pedestrians. The city has thus become the model for destination development design.

In some cases, retail entertainment destinations aim to recreate historic or romanticized Old World streetscapes: promenades, piazzas, benches, fountains, merchant carts, and kiosks. CocoWalk, for example, a successful 138,000-square-foot destination project in Miami's Coconut Grove district, features brick pavers, potted flowers, colorful awnings, and a central plaza. In other cases, and with revitalization in particular, there may be an attempt to restore the original flavor of an area. The design guidelines for the revitalization of 42nd Street in New York, for instance, call for oversized billboards, tacky facades, and "vulgar heterogeneity" by architect Robert A. M. Stern. ●

Source: Patrick Phillips and Jay D. Wheatley, Economics Research Associates (ERA).

CHAPTER 2

What Are Retail Entertainment Destinations?

Attempting to define retail entertainment destinations is a thorny task, as the definition is destined to be either uselessly broad or myopically focused. From small, shopping-center–scale complexes like CocoWalk, in Miami's Coconut Grove, to expansive revitalized urban districts like California's Old Pasadena, the projects that fall under the destination development banner are widely diverse in size, content, and context. This comes as no surprise, however. With a multitude of participants working to put these projects together—property developers, entertainment companies, and local governments—there is no shortage of strategies or creativity.

To each of these participants, destination developments are likely to mean something different. Retail developers may see them as new-wave shopping malls; entertainment companies may view them as next-generation theme parks; and local governments are apt to regard them as fresh takes on urban revitalization. The truth is that destination developments can be all these things. Yet that does not suggest that these diverse aspects have nothing in common. There are, in fact, characteristics that link destination developments and that can serve to describe—if not define—what they are.

Tenant spaces in Universal CityWalk, one of the first retail entertainment ▶ destinations, are individually crafted to create a lively and entertaining environment for shopping, amusement, and public gathering.
Stephen Simpson

Tamboré, in Tamboré, Brazil, 20 kilometers west of São Paulo, will take advantage of its riverside location to provide a waterfront-based destination for its retail and entertainment activities.
KMD

The Trinity of Synergy

In general, destination developments tend to offer a combination of entertainment, dining, and retail—the "trinity of synergy"— within a pedestrian-oriented and multiuse environment. That these amenities act independently but in a complementary way, drawing visitors from a variety of overlapping markets, is what distinguishes destination developments from other forms of retail development. In a destination development, the cinemas, for instance, will attract patrons from an area that is three times as large as the "film zone" of a stand-alone community movie theater; food courts and restaurants may draw the employees of nearby businesses at lunchtime or after work; and, depending on the regional competition, the development as a whole may pull in visitors from an hour or more away. In addition, the development will often count a number of tourists among its visitors, particularly if it is located in an area such as Orlando or Las Vegas.

Although there is greater emphasis on evening activity at destination developments than at shopping malls, visitors at destination developments tend to stay for a few hours and to return regularly, in a pattern that more closely resembles that found at shopping malls than at theme parks. Destination developments are not restricted to downtowns; they are located wherever there are enough people, including the suburbs and tourist spots. Nevertheless, no matter where the project happens to be, typical urban qualities—the density, the vitality, and the eclectic choice of amenities—are essential.

Types of Destination Developments

Destination developments generally fall into two broad categories: districts and complexes, the second of which includes a variety of notable subtypes. These categories are distinguished by the processes and players responsible for their development as well as by differences in form, operation, and location.

Characteristics of Cultural and Entertainment Districts

	Typical	**Third Street Promenade**	**Times Square**
Location	Downtown districts, many of which were formerly blighted	Third Street between Broadway and Wilshire Boulevard in Santa Monica, California	New York City's famed Times Square
Players	Property owners; retail developers; entertainment, restaurant, and retail companies; municipal and state agencies	Various property owners; cinema, restaurant, and retail companies; city of Santa Monica	Disney; Forest City Ratner; Tishman Urban Development Corporation; Urban Development Corporation of the state and city of New York; entertainment, restaurant, and retail companies
Size	One block or more in length	Six blocks in length, with positive effects on adjacent streets	Thirteen acres
Features	Theme and brand-name restaurant and retail tenants; a megaplex cinema or other destination entertainment venue, such as a stadium or arena; hotels, offices, or other complementary uses	Cinema complexes; restaurant and retail tenants, including brand-name chains; megaplex cinema; live performances	Hotels; live-performance theaters; other entertainment venues; E-Walk, a 200,000-square-foot entertainment complex with theme and brand-name restaurants and retailers
Summary	Cities see cultural and entertainment districts as a way to revitalize downtowns and attract business activities that have been lost to the suburbs during recent decades. Successful development of such districts requires involvement by public and private participants.	Formerly an underperforming pedestrian promenade, the area was revitalized in three distinct phases: several cinema complexes moved in and spurred the development of restaurant business, which in turn fueled retail business.	New York State condemned 52 properties on blighted 42nd Street and initiated redevelopment. Developers were awarded rights to develop entertainment-oriented projects.

Source: Economics Research Associates (ERA).

Cultural and Entertainment Districts

Cultural and entertainment districts are urban areas that have been revitalized or repositioned as leisure destinations through the development and renovation of properties and public spaces and the attraction of desirable tenants. For the most part, the urban structure of streets, sidewalks, and buildings remains intact, yet sometimes a street is closed to vehicular traffic and transformed into a pedestrian promenade, either permanently or during the evening. Examples of projects in well-defined areas include Old Pasadena and Santa Monica's Third Street Promenade, both in California, and Times Square, in New York City. Examples of more dispersed districts include Baltimore's Inner Harbor, Chicago's River North, and Denver's Lower Downtown (LoDo).

In major metropolitan areas, the "anchor" for such redevelopment may take the form of regional destinations—stadiums; arenas; convention centers; and cultural centers, such as museums and performing-arts centers. In smaller communities, smaller-scale amenities (such as cinema complexes), which draw from a smaller market area, are sufficient to spur rejuvenation.

Although cultural and entertainment districts can emerge organically, as businesses are drawn to other businesses in a synergistic interaction, in most cases they owe their existence to municipal efforts to revitalize blighted areas. The authority and economic resources that governments may employ in such initiatives are varied and potent. Through such means as cash contributions, financing aid, tax abatements, zoning and building code variances, new or improved infrastructure, and the creation of dedicated taxes for physical improvements, cities can create highly attractive development environments. The public benefits of revitalizing urban areas can be phenomenal: increases in property values, inner-city employment levels, and sales and property tax revenues; a decrease in crime; and an improved civic image, to name a noteworthy few.

Destination Development Complexes

The principal difference between a cultural and entertainment district and a destination development complex is that instead of involving numerous autonomous property owners and developers, complexes are cohesive, managed properties with tenants, not unlike traditional retail centers. Complexes can thus be located outside urban areas—on "greenfield" sites in the suburbs or at resort locations, for instance—as well as in the city. Not surprisingly, complexes have emerged as natural components of cultural and entertainment districts. Examples are the two cornerstones of the 13-acre Times Square redevelopment in New York City: Tishman Urban Development Corporation's 200,000-

Characteristics of Destination Development Complexes

	Typical	Ontario Mills	Universal CityWalk	Irvine Spectrum Center
Location	Highly populated urban and suburban areas; tourist destinations	Near the juncture of Interstates 10 and 15 in Ontario, California	Outside the gates of Universal Studios Hollywood, Universal City, California	Near the juncture of Interstates 5 and 405 in Irvine, California
Players	Entertainment companies, retail developers	The Mills Corporation	Universal Studios, Inc.	The Irvine Company
Subtype	Regional retail, entertainment destination, or freestanding	Retail destination (off-price mall)	Entertainment destination (theme park)	Freestanding
Size (square feet)	150,000 and larger	1,700,000	222,000 (Phase I) 90,000 (Phase II)	260,000 (Phase I) 150,000 (Phase II) Phase III in planning
Features	Theme and brand-name retail and restaurant tenants; megaplex cinema; high-tech game centers and other entertainment venues	Off-price and brand-name retail tenants; food court; megaplex cinema; specialty-format theater; GameWorks; Dave & Buster's; American Wilderness Experience	Retail and restaurant tenants, including theme and brand-name chains and unique local businesses; megaplex cinema; motion simulator; live performances; humorous California theme	Retail and restaurant tenants, including theme and brand-name chains; megaplex cinema; live performances; exotic Moroccan theme
Summary	New-generation leisure development. Destination development complexes that draw tourists or regional visitors typically include destination retail or entertainment amenities, while those without such components generally appeal to a limited market area.	A large off-price retail development with nighttime-oriented entertainment amenities. A complete leisure destination, drawing visitors from throughout the Los Angeles and San Bernardino region.	Intended to bridge the existing theme park, amphitheater, and cinema complex. The project capitalizes on the large number of amphitheater and theme park visitors already being drawn to the site.	Originated as an attempt to meet the dining needs of employees in the nearby business park. Entertainment, particularly the cinema, was included to generate nighttime and local resident business.

Source: Economics Research Associates (ERA).

Entertainment ▶ complexes can be components of, or adjacent to, regional entertainment destinations. The 20-screen cineplex is just one of many attractions at the 312,000-square-foot Universal CityWalk, which is itself adjacent to Universal Studios's theme park in Orlando, Florida.

square-foot E-Walk, and, directly across the street, Forest City Ratner's 335,000-square-foot retail entertainment destination.

Like retail centers, destination development complexes are typically developed by a retail or multiuse developer acting independently or in partnership to construct a new facility or adaptively use an existing building, such as a factory. With respect to operations, many of the same landlord-tenant relationships found in retail centers are found in entertainment complexes. Management is usually responsible for utilities, systems, and services; insurance; marketing; the upkeep of structures, parking facilities, and common areas; ensuring adherence to design codes; scheduling uses and entertainment for common areas; mediation of intertenant disputes; and recruitment of suitable tenants. In compensation, tenants pay charges—such as common-area management fees—in addition to rent. Charges tend to be higher than at typical shopping malls, largely because destination developments tend to have higher

design quality, to occupy more costly real estate, and to support more extensive common-area entertainment.

However, destination development complexes do differ from traditional retail centers in several ways. First, the tenant mix has a greater emphasis on entertainment, dining, and entertainment-oriented retail. Second, to maintain excitement, destination developments require a higher level of reinvestment in and refreshment of amenities. In particular, common-area entertainment and marketing will usually require greater effort and investment than is typical for retail centers. The long-term success of a complex depends on management's ability to attract tenants that create the synergistic relationships characteristic of destination developments. Finally, the retail and entertainment components are often mixed with other land uses, including residences, hotels, offices, and cultural facilities.

Among destination development complexes are a number of notable subtypes:

- Those attached to regional entertainment destinations (theme parks, sports venues, resort-hotel casinos, and cultural or public institutions, for example)
- Those that are freestanding
- Those that are part of urban or suburban mixed-use developments or town centers
- Those that are located in downtowns.

Retail Destinations. Competition from value-oriented retailers and the increasing demand for local leisure options have prompted a growing number of developers and operators of retail centers to turn to the destination development approach. In contrast to retail centers, which focus on selling tangible merchandise, destination developments bundle entertainment, dining, and retail to create a multifaceted leisure experience. At such large-scale retail developments as Ontario Mills in Ontario, California, and Mall of America in Bloomington, Minnesota, the inclusion of unique entertainment and dining amenities was planned from the beginning.

Meanwhile, owners of existing centers—many of which date from the 1960s and 1970s and are in need of rejuvenation—have elected to transform them into destination developments. Through the addition of entertainment, dining, and entertainment-oriented retail amenities, these facilities seek to expand their market area, extend visitors' length of stay, and extract more spending per capita by offering a wider range of spending opportunities. Eventually such additions may fill the spaces formerly occupied by anchor department stores, many of which have been shut down because of consolidations by their parent chains. In 1995, for instance, down-town San Diego's Horton Plaza bolstered its entertainment appeal by filling the space vacated by a Robinsons-May department store with Planet Hollywood and a Sam Goody store, and by expanding the existing United Artists theater to 14 screens.

Entertainment Destinations. Destination development complexes are often developed adjacent to, or as components of, "pure" entertainment destinations. Theme parks, like Universal Studios Hollywood; sports venues, like the MCI Center arena, in Washington, D.C.; resort-hotel casinos, like the Aladdin Resort and Casino, in Las Vegas; and cultural and public institutions, like Yerba Buena Gardens, in San Francisco (which is home to the city's museum of modern art as well as to the Moscone Convention Center) have all emerged as potent anchors for destination developments. Adding dining and retail amenities to a major entertainment venue is not unlike infusing a retail site with entertainment and dining, as described in the previous section. In either case, the goal is to capitalize on the drawing power of a destination, lengthen patrons' visits, and broaden their spending profile.

Freestanding Destinations. Examples of freestanding destination development complexes include Irvine Spectrum Center, in Irvine, California; and CocoWalk, in Miami's Coconut Grove. Because they lack the drawing power of regional retail or entertainment facilities, these projects tend to rely on frequent visits from a tight resident market, which makes particular types of amenities more, or less, appropriate. In general, regardless of whether the principal amenity is entertainment, dining, or retail, it must generate a high level of repeat visits. Cinema complexes, video-game arcades,

Types of Destination Entertainment

Destination Venues

Type	Description	Examples
Casinos	Casinos with games of chance and/or skill	Aladdin, Caesars Palace, MGM Grand, Luxor, New York–New York, Hilton LV, Bellagio, Venetian; all in Las Vegas
Educational facilities	Museums, aquariums, halls of fame, hands-on exhibits, extension classrooms	National Sports Gallery, MCI Center, Washington, D.C.; UCLA Extension, Universal CityWalk, Los Angeles
Indoor theme parks	Full-sized rides; shows and attractions; food and beverage facilities; souvenir shops	Camp Snoopy, Mall of America, Minneapolis; Galaxyland, West Edmonton Mall, Alberta, Canada
Live-performance theaters	Scheduled live shows with theater seating	Country music theaters of Branson, Missouri; New Amsterdam Theater, Times Square, New York City
Sports venues	Stadiums, arenas	Camden Yards, Baltimore; Coors Field, Denver; MCI Center, Washington, D.C.
Cultural centers	Museums and performing-arts centers	Yerba Buena Gardens, San Francisco; National Aquarium, Baltimore

Components

Type	Description	Examples
Cinema complexes	"Category killer" complexes with up to 30 screens	AMC 30-screen cinema at Ontario Mills, Ontario, California; Edwards 21-screen cinema at Irvine Spectrum Center, Irvine, California
Dinner theaters	Complete meals accompanied by a live performance	Caesars Magical Empire, Caesars Palace, Las Vegas; Medieval Times, Orlando
Family entertainment centers	Traditional mix of games and attractions on a pay-as-you-go basis, often with concession stands and party rooms	Coney Island Emporium, New York–New York Hotel and Casino, Las Vegas
High-tech game centers	Off-the-shelf and proprietary technology-based games in an enclosed center; often accompanied by a café and a retail boutique	Dave & Buster's; Jillian's; DisneyQuest; GameWorks
Nightclubs	Alcoholic beverages in conjunction with performances or interactive activities	Hard Rock Live!, Orlando; Universal's Escape; Wildhorse Saloon, Walt Disney World; House of Blues
Specialty-format film theaters	Large-format, domed, 360-degree, or 3-D film presentations; films with computer-controlled seating linked to on-screen action	Sony Theatres 3-D IMAX, Lincoln Center, New York; 3-D IMAX Entertainment Center, Irvine Spectrum Center, Irvine, California

and nightclubs—unlike novelty experiences, such as motion simulators—are highly effective at creating repeat visits. Similarly, one-time-only dining facilities such as dinner theaters and exotic theme restaurants should be eschewed in favor of brand-name casual restaurants and fast-food outlets with broad appeal. Appropriate retailers include "big books" stores like Barnes & Noble and "big music" stores like Virgin Records megastores, which cater to a broad demographic range, including tourists and residents, rather than "studio stores" and niche specialty shops.

Types of Components

Entertainment, dining, and retail amenities are the subatomic particles—the fundamental building blocks—of the destination development universe. Each represents a distinct mode of consumption. Entertainment, for instance, is an example of experiential consumption: the consumer pays for the opportunity to experience something that is pleasurable yet ephemeral. Dining is literal consumption: the consumer pays to consume food or drink on the spot. And in the case of shopping, consumption takes the form of acquisition: the consumer pays to obtain an object to take home for long-lasting or later enjoyment.

In destination developments, not only are these modes compatible, they are complementary. Theme restaurants like Hard Rock Café have retail boutiques, while Borders Books & Music stores have in-store cafés. Movie theaters sell snacks and beverages from concession counters, while at Planet Hollywood, movie clips projected on the walls evoke Hollywood glamour. Virtual-reality centers like the one within DisneyQuest sell brand-name souvenir merchandise, while the REI (Recreational

Equipment, Incorporated) flagship store in Seattle offers a virtual hiking trail and a rain-simulation room in which to test outdoor gear.

The point is that in destination developments the three components—entertainment, dining, and retail—are intertwined and nested in one another in every conceivable way. This characteristic, of course, means that categorizing components is a somewhat challenging task. For instance, should a dinner theater be classified as dining or entertainment? But it is this sort of dynamic ambiguity that is the soul of the destination development type. Some of the most common components

Freestanding destinations may be retail- or entertainment-oriented but rely on frequent visits from a geographically limited region for continued success. Maasmechelen, a proposed 20,000-square-meter factory outlet center in an entertaining environment, would serve the Brussels, Belgium, market.
KMD
▼

of destination developments are described in the three sections that follow.

Entertainment

Various types of dedicated entertainment can be found in destination developments, each effective in its own way. Ambient entertainment, in the form of festive architecture and free street performances, for instance, is a passive yet powerful tool in engaging patrons and drawing them into the center's leisure focus. Meanwhile, impulse entertainment,

Theme Park Developers and Regional Entertainment

As the market for theme parks in the United States nears the saturation point, companies involved in developing theme parks are seeking new ways to exploit their well-known brands and design and operational expertise while responding to changes in demand that favor closer, more accessible leisure options. One result is massive investment in regional entertainment ventures such as the family-oriented DisneyQuest facilities and the GameWorks chain, both of which are high-tech game centers developed by large and vertically integrated entertainment companies known for their premier theme parks.

DisneyQuest is the creation of the company's recently formed regional entertainment division. During the next ten years, the company plans to build several of the 80,000- to 100,000-square-foot centers in cities worldwide, including sites at existing Disney resorts in Anaheim, Paris, and Tokyo. The first center opened at Walt Disney World in 1998, followed by one in Chicago in 1999.

At DisneyQuest, which will charge a gate fee and use a proprietary Smartcard (a stored-value card system developed by American Express), there will be four distinct theme environments: the

▲
High-profile regional entertainment facilities are often part of retail entertainment destinations; an example is this GameWorks at the 200,000-square-foot Barra Entertainment Center, in Rio de Janeiro, Brazil. *KMD*

Explore Zone, a virtual "Adventureland" where guests will be immersed in exotic or ancient locales; the Score Zone, a city where guests can match their game-playing skills against those of superheroes; the Create Zone, a private "Imagineering" studio for artistic self-expression and invention; and the Replay Zone, a carnival on the moon where guests will experience a "retro-futuristic" spin on classic rides and games. The Wired Wonderland Café, one of the two dining options, will combine indulgent desserts and an Internet-based attraction; FoodQuest will be a quick-service café.

Meanwhile, through a joint venture, Sega Enterprises, DreamWorks SKG, and Universal Studios plan to open as many as five GameWorks centers worldwide over a five-year period that began in 1997;

in that year, sites opened in Seattle, Las Vegas, and Ontario, California, among other locations. Each 30,000- to 50,000-square-foot facility includes top-of-the-line video games by various manufacturers, several proprietary games inspired by Steven Spielberg, an Internet lounge with laptop-equipped easy chairs, food and beverage counters, and a retail boutique selling logo-emblazoned goods. The design theme consists of a grungy "urban chic" aesthetic: rusty metal, exposed brick walls, and grime-covered pipes like those you might see in a gritty MTV video.

Unlike family entertainment centers, which tend to be located along freeways in suburban communities, these high-profile regional entertainment facilities are often part of destination development complexes or urban cultural and entertainment districts. Like

theme restaurants, regional entertainment centers represent extensive investments and must therefore be located in high-traffic or tourist-oriented areas. This is certainly true of the Seattle, Las Vegas, and Ontario GameWorks centers. The Seattle site is located in a burgeoning cultural and entertainment district, within a block of Planet Hollywood, Nike-Town, FAO Schwarz, and a Cineplex Odeon multiplex. The Las Vegas site is within the "Showcase" on the strip. And the Ontario Mills site, outside of Los Angeles, is in a 1,700,000-square-foot, off-price entertainment and retail megamall developed by The Mills Corporation and the Simon Property Group. ●

Source: Raymond E. Braun and Jay D. Wheatley, Economics Research Associates (ERA).

like carousels and rock-climbing walls, provides visitors with opportunities for spontaneous experiences. Finally, destination entertainment, including cinema complexes, live-performance theaters, and sports venues, draws traffic to the center, leading to spillover business for adjoining restaurants, retailers, and other entertainment venues.

Ambient Entertainment. In many respects, ambient entertainment is the fundamental requirement of a destination development.

opment's retailers, restaurants, and providers of impulse entertainment.

Whereas traditional shopping malls built in the 1960s and 1970s tended to be rational and functional in design, in today's destination developments, the unconventional manipulation of design variables such as materials, scale, composition, and context is used to evoke a feeling of excitement, energy, and creativity. Such features as theme architecture; dynamic signage; bold landscaping; unique lighting; and interesting "street" fixtures, like foun-

◀ Free "street" performances are a form of ambient entertainment, replicating the spontaneity and festivity of the archetypal marketplace. At Blackcomb Resort, in Whistler, British Columbia, the developer provides scheduled and impromptu entertainment in the public spaces.

Through design themes and public performances in common areas, ambient entertainment serves to set the mood, establishing the destination development as a leisure destination that is enjoyable to visit regardless of the stores one patronizes. By extending the duration of guests' visits and inducing them to linger and browse, ambient entertainment works to the special advantage of the devel-

tains and kiosks, are part and parcel of the destination development landscape. For instance, the dazzling streetscape of Universal CityWalk combines fantasy architecture, surreal signage—including a towering King Kong scaling a building facade—interactive fountains, and enormous props, such as a

Destination Development Consumption Modes: The "Trinity of Synergy"

Entertainment
Experiential consumption:
Experience that is pleasurable yet ephemeral.

Dining
Literal consumption:
Food or beverages to be consumed on the spot.

Retail
Acquisition consumption:
Objects to take home for long-term or later enjoyment.

Source: Economics Research Associates (ERA).

spaceship crashed into a building facade. This aesthetic is borrowed in part from European streets and piazzas but also from the theme-park industry (an increasing number of theme-park designers and fabricators have become active in the retail sector).

Free "street" performances, another form of ambient entertainment, strive to replicate the spontaneity and festivity of the archetypal, if not mythical, marketplace. Because they are engaging and often interactive, these performances can be highly effective in energizing crowds.

Authentic performances are given by musicians, actors, magicians, jugglers, and others who perform solely for tips and are not formally sponsored by or invited to the development. Such performers are found almost exclusively in public spaces like sidewalks and parks in cultural and entertainment districts. These performers represent the historic archetype upon which all common-area per-

formances are based. Yet, because they work independently, their performances can be unpredictable, making them potentially disruptive to both visitors and tenants. Thus, authentic performances are not commonly allowed on the private property of destination development complexes.

Sanctioned performances resemble authentic performances but are explicitly permitted or even contracted for in the common areas. Although sanctioned performances aim to replicate the liveliness of authentic performances, there are several distinctions. First, they tend to exclude some of the more unusual offerings characteristic of the authentic genre, such as psychics, palm readers, and mannequin imitators. Second, they commonly include performers not typical of authentic performances, such as roaming costumed characters and robots.

In general, the costumes and stage setups for sanctioned performances are of higher quality than those associated with authentic performances. In addition, such performances are often scheduled for specific times of the day and week to target particular groups. For example, costumed characters or magicians that appeal to children would be scheduled during the day, while reggae or jazz bands would be scheduled in the evening.

Programmed entertainment—fashion shows, arts and crafts festivals, traveling museum displays, and opportunities to be photographed with Santa Claus, for example—can occur in common areas or public spaces at destination developments. These events are arranged by complex managers or district associations for the purpose of drawing crowds and fostering rapport with the community. Thus, programmed entertainment can become a temporary form of destination entertainment. It may be financed entirely by center owners or through marketing funds to which tenants contribute.

Impulse Entertainment. Impulse entertainment provides opportunities for guests to pay, on a whim, to engage in spontaneous experiences that fulfill their immediate needs and desires. Attractions like carousels, rock-climbing walls, bungee-trampolines, portrait artists, and human gyroscopes are often located in common areas, where they have the visibility to generate impulse sales. They can also serve as ambient entertainment for nonparticipants who gather to watch and enjoy the experience vicariously. They may be operated by center management or by special arrangement with outside vendors. Other types of impulse entertainment, like motion simulators, virtual-reality attrac-

tions, and video games, are typically operated as dedicated attractions or within entertainment venues such as indoor theme parks, family entertainment centers, or high-tech game centers.

Impulse entertainment experiences have several common characteristics. First, they are of short duration. Second, entry opportunities are frequent or continuous. Third, access—ticket purchase, for instance—can be obtained on site just before entry to the entertainment experience. Beyond these similarities, impulse entertainment attractions can vary in a number of regards. Some, like rock-climbing walls or virtual-reality experiences, are interactive—meaning that the patron's active involvement is essential for the experience to take place—while others, like motion simulators or carousels, allow more passive participation. Some—video

◀ **Impulse entertainment attractions are often located in common areas to generate impulse sales and to enhance ambient entertainment. Wolfchase Galleria, in Eastside Memphis, features a 12,000-square-foot entertainment/food court.**
HOK/Dave Whitcomb

Nesting Entertainment, Dining, and Retail

Entertainment	Dining	Retail
GameWorks	**ESPN Zone**	**Borders Books & Music**
Entertainment: Video games, Internet access, theming	***Entertainment:*** Sports programming, video games, sports theming, live broadcast events	***Entertainment:*** Live jazz, reading chairs
Dining: Pub and brewery, café, coffee bar	***Dining:*** Full-service restaurant, bar	***Dining:*** Café, coffee bar
Retail: Boutique with logo t-shirts, hats, and jackets	***Retail:*** Boutique with logo t-shirts, hats, jackets, and sports items	***Retail:*** Books and recorded music

Source: Economics Research Associates (ERA).

games and motion simulators, for example—accept new media or software that ensure their novelty; others, like carousels, remain unchanged. In addition, attractions like motion simulators and carousels can accommodate a group of participants at once; others, such as bungee-trampolines or portrait artists, can accommodate only one. However, most impulse entertainment experiences are either interactive or accept new media or software, attributes that are essential to ensuring repeat visits. In fact, even the theme-park industry is witnessing a greater demand for these attributes in new attractions.

Impulse entertainment is often highly flexible, allowing new attractions to emerge in response to evolving cultural and technological developments. Moreover, impulse entertainment "facilities" are often portable and leased or operated through a split-revenue arrangement, allowing "fad" experiences to

be added or removed with the ebb and flow of customer interest. For instance, rock-climbing walls, bungee-trampolines, and human gyroscopes are in keeping with the "extreme sports" trend of recent years. So is Seattle's new REI flagship store, which is equipped with a 65-foot climbing pinnacle and other "demonstration stations" that allow customers to test the sports merchandise sold in the store. According to *American Demographics,* the U.S. Bungee Association estimates that more than 7 million bungee jumps have occurred since the late 1980s; the U.S. Parachute Association reported that its membership is growing at 10 percent annually; and membership in the American Mountain Guide Association is skyrocketing at 3 percent per month.

Destination Entertainment Venues.

Destination entertainment venues vary in both physical size and drawing power; consequently, their relationships with destination developments vary as well. Some entertainment venues are relatively small, and are included within a destination development in the same way that a store is located within a shopping mall. For instance, indoor family entertainment centers, high-tech game centers, nightclubs, live-performance theaters, specialty-format theaters, dinner theaters, educational facilities, and even cinema complexes are often included as part of the tenant mix in a destination development complex. Coney Island Emporium, at the New York–New York Hotel and Casino, in Las Vegas; DisneyQuest and House of Blues, at Downtown Disney, in Orlando; and the Edwards Cinema, at Irvine Spectrum Center, in Irvine, California, are all examples of entertainment venues that are included in destination developments.

While entertainment venues included within destination developments rely on a critical mass of other entertainment, dining, and retail facilities to pull adequate traffic to the center, the largest entertainment venues fully earn their "destination" designation. In fact, some destination entertainment venues can draw enough traffic to support them-

selves regardless of whether they have a destination development connected to them. In these circumstances, the destination developments are often intended to benefit from the entertainment venue's economic spillover.

Powerful destination venues include sports stadiums and arenas, convention centers, cultural centers, casinos, and indoor theme parks. Examples are the MCI Center in

▲
Casinos are diversifying their entertainment activities to broaden their appeal to vacationing families. The Venetian Casino Resort in Las Vegas offers gondola rides through its "grand canals of Venice," which are lined with shops, restaurants, and entertainment.
The Stubbins Associates

Acronym Soup

CEC: Children's Entertainment Center

Offers children's games and attractions, with admission charge. Commonly includes soft modular play systems, party rooms, redemption games, arts and crafts, "edutainment" experiences, and concession stands. Operated by a single business entity. Examples include Club Disney, Discovery Zone, Jeepers.

EOR: Entertainment-Oriented Retail

Retail stores with interactive and entertainment-oriented in-store displays and activities, from kiosks to cafés. Often these stores act as brand-building marketing devices for manufacturers and entertainment companies. Examples include Barnes & Noble, Bass Pro Shops Outdoor World, Borders Books & Music, the Disney Store, NikeTown, Planet Reebok, REI Seattle, Warner Bros. Studio Store, and Virgin Records megastores.

FEC: Family Entertainment Center

Indoor or outdoor facility offering a traditional mix of games and attractions on a pay-as-you-go basis. Commonly includes video-game arcades, miniature golf, go-carts, batting cages, and concession stands. Operated by a single business entity. Examples include Exhilarama, Fun Factory, Mountasia, Nickels & Dimes, Putt Putt Golf & Games, Regal Cinemas Funscape, and Q-City.

LBE: Location-Based Entertainment

(1) Any form of commercial out-of-home entertainment. (2) Facilities, such as high-tech game centers, that do not fit within other categories; or, facilities that are dedicated to one type of attraction (in contrast to FECs, for example, which have multiple types). Examples of (1) include CECs, FECs, destination developments, and theme parks. Examples of (2) include American Wilderness Experience, Dave & Buster's, DisneyQuest, GameWorks, IMAX theaters, skating rinks, and virtual-reality parlors.

UEC: Urban Entertainment Center
UED: Urban Entertainment Destination
LEC: Leisure Entertainment Destination
RDE: Retail Dining Entertainment

Offers a synergistic combination of entertainment, dining, and retail. May take the form of a (1) cohesively owned and operated complex with tenants or a (2) downtown district of independent property owners and tenants. Examples of (1) include CocoWalk, Irvine Spectrum Center, Mall of America, and Universal CityWalk. Examples of (2) include Old Pasadena, New York's Times Square, and Santa Monica's Third Street Promenade.

Source: Economics Research Associates (ERA).

Washington, D.C.; Coors Field in the LoDo portion of Denver; many of the casinos of the Las Vegas strip; the cultural installations of San Francisco's Yerba Buena Gardens; and Camp Snoopy theme park, in Mall of America, all of which draw tremendous numbers of visitors and benefit the shops and restaurants attached to them.

Casinos are a form of destination entertainment that can be tremendously profitable for operators and a lucrative source of tax revenues for local governments. During the past ten years or so, casino gambling has expanded outside of Las Vegas and Atlantic City to become a regional attraction. Casinos are now operated by Indian tribes in 27 states; on riverboat casinos in six; and in limited, land-based casinos in three.

In Las Vegas, where entertainment in the form of live shows has long coexisted with casinos, new forms of diversion have appeared that broaden the city's appeal to vacationing families. Some casinos that do not have entertainment are reportedly losing market share to those that do, as the percentage of revenue from gaming declines and the percentage from hotels and entertainment increases. There have been some encouraging successes with retail entertainment. One example is Forum Shops, a 526,000-square-foot retail and restaurant complex, appended to Caesars Palace in 1992, which profitably melded casino gambling with retail, restaurants, and entertainment amenities. Retail sales per square foot at Forum Shops are reportedly among the highest in the nation. Newer examples include Desert Passage, at the Aladdin Resort and Casino, and the Venetian.

Cultural/educational facilities, or "edutainment," has emerged as a unique category of destination entertainment that will likely become more prevalent as the population ages in the coming years. Decades ago, marine, zoological, and botanical parks like the Sea World chain and Busch Gardens Tampa Bay, in Florida, established the potential for educational leisure ventures. Today, cable television channels like the Discovery Channel, A&E (Arts & Entertainment), the History Channel, and Animal Planet illustrate the education boom in another typical entertainment medium.

The possibilities for education-oriented features in destination developments go beyond retail tenants (The Museum Company Store, the Discovery Channel Stores, and Scientific Revolution, for example) and temporary exhibits (like the Smithsonian Institution Traveling Exhibitions—SITES), which are already found in retail centers. Permanent edu-

▲
The Endangered Species Store at Desert Passage is part of the exotic shopping environment at the Aladdin Resort and Casino, in Las Vegas.

cational facilities include the UnderWater World aquarium at Mall of America; Pier 39, in San Francisco; and the National Sports Gallery at the MCI Center. Another destination development site anchored by cultural and educational amenities is Yerba Buena Gardens, which is bordered by the Visual Arts Center, the Performing Arts Center, and the San Francisco Museum of Art on adjacent blocks. Similarly, Baltimore's Inner Harbor features a children's museum, a marine biology exposition, a city life museum, and a visionary art museum.

The experiential focus of destination developments makes them even more suitable than shopping malls for educational amenities. At Universal CityWalk, for example, an extension center of the University of California, Los Angeles, sits side by side with theme restaurants and cinemas. In addition to being a community service, extension classes are a mode of entertainment, offering students an opportunity to meet people, improve themselves, and explore their hobbies and interests. The Disney Institute at Walt Disney World, which offers educational programs in a resort setting, and the worldwide rise of "ecoresorts" are further examples of the viability of educational entertainment.

Indoor theme parks range from 100,000 to 500,000 square feet and can be found within such massive developments as the West Edmonton Mall, in Edmonton, Alberta; Mall of America; and the Circus Circus resort casino, in Las Vegas. They are also increasingly common throughout Asia. These venues feature a higher caliber of attractions than family entertainment centers, including full-sized rides like roller coasters and log flumes. Because of their size, autonomy, and breadth of amenities—attractions, food and beverage facilities, and souvenir shops—indoor theme parks may serve as alternatives rather than as complements to destination developments. In other cases, theme parks may occupy younger visitors, to whom they especially appeal, while their parents patronize more adult-oriented amenities like retail, restaurants, casinos, and shows.

Live-performance theaters, characterized by scheduled, ticketed stage shows and theater seating, are another increasingly popular form of destination entertainment. The success of Branson, Missouri, which draws visitors from hundreds of miles away to enjoy big-name country music entertainers in indoor theaters, has been a great inspiration in this regard. Another example is Disney's renovation of the New Amsterdam theater, on 42nd Street in New York City's Times Square, which serves as a home for the company's Broadway-style productions.

Sports venues as destinations have proliferated in recent years in response to a number of factors. In some cases, such as Baltimore's Camden Yards, Denver's Coors Field, and the MCI Center, sports venues have been part of municipal planners' efforts to revitalize the downtown district. When new sports venues are built, complementary businesses, including restaurants and retail, are often drawn to the area to take advantage of the large game-day crowds. In otherwise blighted areas, such an influx of additional amenities and businesses can spur construction and renovation, job creation, and increased tax revenues.

In other cases, team owners and developers have exploited the traffic-generating abilities of professional sports events to increase their own revenues and to create amenities that will attract off-season users. For example, the MCI Center, home to the Washington Wizards' National Basketball Association and the Washington Capitals' National Hockey League franchises, features a 23,000-square-foot Discovery Channel superstore, a 25,000-square-foot National Sports Gallery interactive museum, and a 19,300-square-foot Nick and Stef's Steakhouse operated by celebrity chef Joachim Splichal.

The demand for new stadiums and arenas has also come from various trends within the professional sports industry: for one thing, the lack of lucrative luxury suites, preferential club seating, and high-revenue concourse activities has rendered many existing stadiums economically obsolete. Other factors include the surging popularity of professional basketball and hockey; the need, through more intimate and nostalgic ballparks, to spark enthusiasm for baseball; and the evolution of professional sports into a true entertainment industry. This last trend is evident in the celebrity status accorded pro athletes; the explosion of team-logo licensing and merchandising; and the increasing ownership of sports franchises by entertainment companies like 20th Century Fox and AOL Time Warner.

Cinema complexes are, without doubt, the quintessential destination entertainment component of destination developments. In fact, it is difficult to find an example of a destination development that does not include a movie theater. Although cinemas have rather modest per-square-foot earnings in comparison with restaurants and retail stores, they have an unequaled ability to attract repeat visitors because they offer a continually refreshed supply of entertainment. In order to exploit cinema complexes' considerable ability to generate traffic, developers are now locating them in prime locations within the shopping center proper rather than on the outskirts of the parking lot, where they were once relegated.

Dinner theaters serve complete, table-service meals, but their main draw is their unique entertainment value. In addition to the classic form of dinner theater, which features live music or dance performed on a stage, many innovative concepts have emerged. For example, performance cooking in open display kitchens or on table-based grills, popularized by Benihana in the 1970s, allows patrons to observe skilled chefs engage in

theatrical knifework. Robotic dinner-theater performances, as found at Chuck E. Cheese, use "audio-animatronic" characters, pioneered by Disney, to enact musical shows at programmed intervals. At Medieval Times and Buffalo Bill's, an indoor arena is the site for a horse-riding spectacle that includes live stunts, costuming, and special effects; diners are divided into groups and encouraged to root for one of several competing teams of

▲
Cinema complexes have an unequaled ability to attract repeat visitors with continually freshened supplies of entertainment. The whimsically themed Star Theatres, in Southfield, Michigan, is Sony's flagship movie house, with 20 screens and four restaurants.
Rockwell Group/Paul Warchol

performers. At Caesars Magical Empire at Caesars Palace in Las Vegas, guests witness enchanting effects firsthand. Yet another type of dinner theater, the murder-mystery dining experience, challenges patrons to solve a crime over the course of a meal. Dinner theaters usually have defined performance and seating times.

Family entertainment centers (FECs), which can range from 20,000 to 100,000 square feet, typically comprise a large number of impulse entertainment attractions which, when combined, create a destination entertainment venue. Typical components of an FEC include video games, redemption games (such as Skeeball), virtual-reality experiences, motion simulators, rock-climbing walls, and batting cages. Because many of the activities are highly participatory—and therefore highly repeatable—they encourage return visits. Certain traditional FEC components that tend to be the most destination oriented— like miniature golf, bumper boats, soft modular play equipment, and go-carts—are too large to fit within the physical constraints of indoor, destination development-based FECs. Nevertheless, FECs have become increasingly popular tenants at shopping malls, often filling vacancies left by anchor department stores.

High-tech game centers are indoor facilities featuring interactive computer and online games, and computer simulations. They range from 30,000 square feet, the size of Dave & Buster's and GameWorks, to 100,000 square feet, the size of DisneyQuest. Along with cutting-edge off-the-shelf and proprietary games, these centers often create broad-based appeal through traditional games such as billiards and darts. High-tech game centers differ from FECs in that they are more oriented to adults and to nighttime activity; they also include sophisticated food and beverage options, from quick-service cafés (à la Cheesecake Factory) to brand-name microbrewery beer and gourmet-coffee counters. In addition, high-tech game centers are often developed as brand-name chains by well-funded entertainment companies and are typically located within destination development complexes or cultural and entertainment districts. FECs, in contrast, traditionally have a suburban, stand-alone format.

Nightclubs are establishments that primarily serve alcoholic beverages in conjunction with performances and interactive activities and that provide table seating as well as standing room. Because these facilities typically revolve around a particular theme, they attract a clientele with particular tastes in alcohol or entertainment. Types of nightclubs include sports bars, country-western bars, "techno" dance clubs, comedy clubs, martini bars, jazz clubs, and piano bars. Gaylord Entertainment's Wildhorse Saloon, the House of Blues at Walt Disney World, and Hardrock Live! (the world's largest Hardrock Café) at Universal CityWalk Orlando are high-profile examples.

Specialty-format films, or large-format films, as the most common versions are called, employ variations in screen size, aspect ratio, seating configuration, sound quality, and

Megaplex, Art House, and Luxury Cinemas

▲ **To enhance the moviegoing experience and draw customers away from the competition, the megaplexes of the Muvico theater chain employ dramatic fantasy environments.** *Development Design Group*

Recent changes in the nature of theater exhibition have accentuated the benefits of cinema complexes as draws for destination developments. Between 1980 and 1996, the number of movie screens in the United States more than doubled, while the number of cinema locations remained relatively stable. The explanation for this phenomenon is the fact that cinemas have been increasing the number of auditoriums per location while reducing the auditoriums' size. At first, large, single-screen movie houses were split to form two auditoriums. Then, in a move pioneered by AMC in the 1960s, new theaters were designed as multiplexes.

The current vogue is for megaplex—or "category killer"—cinema complexes with as many as 20 or 30 screens in a single facility. For patrons, the result is a wider selection of movies—from Hollywood blockbusters to art films—and more frequent showings at a given site. Theatergoing has thus become more convenient for consumers, to the point of allowing movies to function as impulse entertainment.

Meanwhile, a raft of technical advances have improved the cinema experience, making it both more thrilling and more comfortable. Larger screens; steep, stadium seating (which enhances viewing); and direc-

tional digital sound have intensified movies' sensory impact. Wider, more plush seats with higher backs—and with movable armrests that allow patrons to sit "loveseat-style"—have raised the comfort level. Other recent improvements include spacious lobbies with more sophisticated food and beverage options, retail boutiques, and amenities for patrons with disabilities.

Theater chains are also adding specialty-format film theaters to their multiplexes to broaden their appeal. Both Edwards Theaters and Regal Cinemas, for instance, have plans to open 3-D IMAX theaters in upcoming multiplexes. Furthermore, some cinema chains are developing multifaceted, in-house, cinema-based entertainment centers, such as Regal Cinema's Funscape for children and adult-oriented Escape locations.

Meanwhile, other chains are partnering with theme restaurants and entertainment-oriented retailers to create other products. Planet Movies by AMC, among the first of such endeavors, is a joint venture that will combine Planet Hollywood theme restaurants, AMC cinemas, and additional retail and entertainment offerings at sites worldwide. Carmike Cinemas, Wal-Mart, and Ultrazone laser tag are involved in a coventure.

Two other emerging trends in the cinema industry are the development of new art-house theaters and the proliferation of luxury theaters. These trends are both responses to changes in the independent film industry and in the moviegoing audience. The "independent" film industry is increasingly likely to be under the control of major Hollywood studios that produce commercially successful films that blur the line between typical Hollywood films and art films. These films, in turn, attract affluent audiences who are of an age that Hollywood films largely neglect. As the baby boom generation ages, an increasing number of moviegoers prefer high-quality films, a pleasant atmosphere that is attentive to aesthetic detail, and high-quality food and beverages. Angelika Theaters, which has successfully delivered this experience, plans to expand nationwide. Sundance Cinemas, a partnership between the Sundance Institute and General Cinemas, is also expected to develop art-house theaters across the nation.

At the same time, premium amenities—such as larger, reclining seats and expanded food and beverage services—are being incorporated into traditional theaters; such features cater to adult crowds seeking first-class amenities. Until the 1950s, urban movie theaters commonly offered premium seating sections: at a cost that is double the standard movie-admission price, this feature is making a comeback in theaters in the United States and abroad. Exhibitors currently employing the premier-class concept include Loews Cineplex, Virgin Entertainment Group, Pacific Theaters, and General Cinema, which has developed its own line of luxury theaters. General Cinema's Premium Cinemas feature valet parking; bistro lounges; concierge service; a menu ranging from appetizers to entrées; wines, beers, and champagne; wide leather seats; and a table at each seat. ●

Source: Raymond E. Braun and Jay D. Wheatley, Economics Research Associates (ERA).

Bongos, to be colocated with the Miami Heat store, will capture the flavor and imagery of Old Cuba. By day it will serve authentic Cuban food; by night it will be transformed into a Latin dance club.
Rockwell Group

image definition to create a more immersing—and therefore high-impact—theatergoing experience. Exotic elements such as domed screens, 3-D, and 360-degree presentations (in which viewers are completely surrounded by a ring of screens) are examples of the extent of innovation in this genre. Although specialty-format films have long been incorporated into visitor destinations like theme parks, museums, and world's fairs, they have only recently been integrated into cinema megaplexes and retail entertainment developments.

Dining

Dining plays a critical role in destination developments because of two fundamental factors: First, the basic biological need for sustenance throughout the day means that food services are required wherever people spend extended periods of time. Second, because eating and drinking are intrinsically pleasurable, dining and entertainment have enjoyed a long association. (The connection is reflected in the recent coinages *eatertainment* and *dinnertainment*.)

Fast-food outlets, food courts, and casual restaurants exist to accommodate a demand for food and beverages that is motivated more or less by hunger; theme restaurants meet the demand for food coupled with entertainment. Between these extremes are mixed-purpose, "impulse" dining amenities such as portable concession carts, built-in counters, and in-store cafés, which serve to satisfy hunger, the demand for pleasure, or both.

Functional Dining. Functional dining both encourages and capitalizes on the extended length of the visits associated with entertainment and retail centers. The longer visitors stay, the more likely they are to eat on site; by the same token, on-site dining accommodations allow for longer stays. Since maximizing the time visitors spend at the destination development is key to the success of all the development's amenities, dining plays a critical role.

In a destination development, as in a traditional shopping center, food courts may be an effective means of meeting some visitors' dining needs. The rise in popularity of ethnic and specialized foods (fruit smoothies, gourmet coffee, and flavored pretzels, for example) has spurred the growth of a multitude of brand-name chains with tightly focused product lines—Baja Fresh, Auntie Anne's Pretzels, Boardwalk Fries, and Hot Dog on a Stick, to name a few. Food courts are uniquely suited to offer the various and comprehensive choices that attract a diverse market. An added advantage, the physical proximity of the individual food court facilities, allows for efficient use of shared resources such as seating areas and trays.

While brand-name casual restaurants like Red Robin, Bennigan's, T.G.I. Friday's, and California Pizza Kitchen can sometimes be found inside shopping malls, historically most have been located in freestanding "pad" units on outparcels. Casual restaurants have typically chosen sites outside malls for a number of reasons: the restaurant may have a signature building style that is critical to its identity; its hours may differ from those of the shopping center (for instance, the restaurant may have a bar that gets most of its business at night, after the mall has closed); the restaurant may require an allotment or configuration of space that is not compatible with the mall's structure. Finally,

▲
◄ Impulse dining operations offer food that can be eaten while standing or walking. Here, a food court at a recently renovated Los Angeles International Airport terminal offers impulse dining plus sit-down opportunities in an energized and entertaining environment. *KMD*

mall traffic may not be able to support the restaurant, making an in-mall location a liability. However, since destination developments tend to have more leisure-oriented evening business centered around dining, they are generally more suitable than malls as the sites for casual restaurants.

Impulse Dining. Impulse dining operations are often compact—portable carts, built-in counters, and in-store cafés, for example.

Because our eating patterns are dramatically affected by context, the types of food offered by impulse dining facilities tend to exhibit two key attributes. First, in keeping with the leisure orientation of destination developments, the food is generally of the pleasure or indulgence variety: hot dogs, gourmet coffee, popcorn, soda, ice cream, pretzels, and so forth. Second, the food is portable and imme-

diately available, making it suitable for impulse purchase and ambulatory consumption. Impulse dining amenities can be found within various retail and entertainment venues. The French fry counters in the GameWorks centers and the in-store cafés serving espresso drinks and pastries in Barnes & Noble bookstores are examples.

Entertainment Dining. The link between dining and entertainment stretches back to the feasts of ancient times. Today, this combination is represented best by theme and lifestyle restaurants, whose origins most observers trace to the founding, in 1971, of London's rock-and-roll-based Hard Rock Café. This landmark eatery established many precepts that are followed today.

The restaurant features a theme—a unifying motif derived from a pop-cultural genre, medium, industry, or intellectual property. Among the many examples that emerged in the 1990s were Dive!, Fashion Café, Harley-Davidson Café, Marvel Mania,

Motown Café, NASCAR Café, Official All-Star Café, Planet Hollywood, and Rainforest Café. Some of these restaurants did not live up to early expectations, and a new generation of restaurants with themed lifestyle environments has emerged, including California Pizza Kitchen, Il Fornaio, PF Chang's, and Wolfgang Puck.

The theme is expressed through elaborate interior design features, including exotic finishes, props, theatrical lighting, audio effects, video presentations, and museum-style displays of theme-related artifacts.

The development expense—from $5 million to $15 million for a first-generation theme restaurant, depending on size and location—has generally relegated these eateries to densely populated urban or tourist locations. The newer generation theme restaurants have lower development expenses, appeal to a wider demographic segment, and can be sited in more diverse locations.

Their affiliation with cherished pop-cultural themes with which many people identify, along with their tourist appeal (each city's version of a particular chain is slightly different), initially allowed theme restaurants to sell large quantities of logo merchandise at on-site boutiques. There are already unmistakable signs, however, that this trend cannot be sustained.

Demonstrating early theme restaurants' emphasis on the entertainment experience rather than on cuisine, and their efforts to appeal to as broad a market as possible, nearly every one serves the same American fare: hamburgers, chicken sandwiches, pasta, French fries, and so forth. Newer generation theme restaurants have placed a stronger emphasis on the basics of long-term restaurant success: high-quality food and good service.

Corporate Sponsorship

Corporate sponsorship has become an important source of revenue and promotional assistance for any public attraction. In addition to the intangible value that comes from association with—and the implicit endorsement of—nationally known products and services, a professionally developed sponsorship program can provide a retail venue with a number of other benefits, including a low-cost profit center, preferred-supplier status, in-kind contributions, and co-op marketing opportunities.

The three basic goals of a retail sponsorship program are to generate revenue for the development, to enhance the guest experience, and, perhaps most important, to develop regional and national promotions that will generate increased foot traffic. The major advantage of having a national brand as a partner is its ability to leverage promotional resources that can increase awareness of the retail venue and its products—and thereby incrementally increase foot traffic.

For their part, national companies are interested in the themed retail environment for two reasons. The first is the opportunity to affect the consumer at or near the point of sale. A tremendous amount of research shows that for a wide range of products, the choice of a specific brand is made at the point of purchase. Thus, a consumer may be in Circuit City because he or she intends to buy a television—but, more than likely, the consumer has not decided on a particular brand. Having a presence at the point of purchase allows a company to "activate"—which is marketing jargon for *buy*—its products or

services. The second, less tangible, reason is to change consumers' attitudes toward the company's products by integrating the brand into the entertainment experience.

Metreon, the Sony entertainment center in San Francisco, is a good example of both reasons. At Metreon, corporate partners, including Citibank, EDS, Lincoln-Mercury, and Pepsi-Cola, are carefully integrated into the guest experience through a strategy that maintains the creative integrity of the center while at the same time allowing the partners to achieve their marketing goals. For example, Lincoln-Mercury was integrated into David Macaulay's "The Way Things Work" attraction, allowing the car manufacturer to highlight two "brand messages": innovative technology and a family-oriented product. Pepsi-Cola had a more specific goal: to sell more beverages. With a program of promotions, prominent beverage "islands," and strategically placed signage, the company was able to increase beverage sales, which directly affects the bottom line of both Pepsi-Cola and Sony Development, Inc.

Despite its advantages, corporate sponsorship should not be undertaken lightly. The single most important question is how a sponsor will affect the experience of retail guests. For example, a partnership with a credit card company may seem like a simple, win-win situation: the credit card company will want to solicit new card members from among your guests, and it is willing to pay the "host facility" for each application that is approved. However, depend-

ing upon the demographics of your guests and the criteria of the credit card company, a majority of the applications may be rejected—including those of your guests and of your tenant's employees. And some of those guests whose applications were rejected will never shop at the retail venue again.

Retailers who wish to develop a corporate sponsorship program should get professional assistance. Dozens of regional and national sponsorship agencies can solicit, create, and maintain a sponsorship program; however, it is important to check references to be sure that any agency under consideration has experience in marketing venues.[1]

On its most basic level, obtaining sponsorship means selling a corporation access to your core demographic. And when companies pay for such access, their principal concern is how efficiently they can communicate with consumers. Before attempting to establish a corporate sponsorship program, a retailer should undertake a feasibility study to determine what, if anything, the facility has to offer to a national company. In most cases, the study will identify—and quantify—the facility's audience and trading area (e.g., residential, tourist), as well as provide a profile of the typical guests.

The second task is to inventory your "sponsorship assets"— the resources and benefits that are under your control and that will be made available to your corporate partners to communicate with patrons. Assets may include signage, admissions fees, kiosks, databases, special events, retail opportunities, and

special offers. In addition to inventorying the assets, you need to quantify the costs associated with each. If, for example, a sponsorship fee will cover the lost revenues from the lease of a tenant cart, a sponsorship kiosk may displace a tenant cart.

In a sense, sponsorship should be thought of as relationship marketing: the "product" being sold to the sponsor is your relationship with your guests. Thus, over and above the cost of giving a corporate partner access to sponsorship assets is the necessity of investing a portion of the facility's revenues to fulfill the requirements of the partnership contracts: sponsorship relationships are complex, and require full-time management. Nevertheless, for retailers who understand their opportunities and limitations, sponsorships can be useful marketing tools, valuable revenue sources, and, most important, can enhance the experience of guests. ●

Source: Cary Chevat, Sponsorship Resources, Inc.

Note
1. One of the best resources for sponsorship information is IEG, a trade organization in Chicago that tracks the sponsorship industry; for anyone who is interested in learning the basics of sponsorship marketing, IEG also holds an annual conference in Chicago.

Although Hard Rock Café originated the genre, it was Planet Hollywood that fueled the impressive growth of the theme-restaurant industry in the early 1990s. Several theme restaurants aggressively expanded into numerous markets, overextending their brand, diluting the uniqueness of their concept, and straining their financial positions. Overexpansion took them beyond their focus on large tourist havens and into resident-oriented markets, which lowered average expenditures. Finally, many of the theme restaurants "forgot" about food quality and customer service, which are critical components of the overall experience and the keys to generating repeat visits. As a result, the industry is in a state of transition, with several major chains reevaluating their operations and long-term strategies. Still, it is important to keep in mind that innovative theme restaurants, including Planet Hollywood and Hard Rock Café, played an important role in creating the "experience economy." While overexpanded theme restaurants may be retrenching, the idea of making the dining experience more entertaining is expected to increase in importance in the future.

Retail

Unlike traditional retail centers, which attract more dedicated shoppers (49 percent of whom have a specific store or purchase in mind, according to the International Conference of Shopping Centers' 1996 *Mall Customer Shopping Patterns Report*), destination developments attract more leisurely patrons. Stores found at destination developments generally fall within the category of entertainment-oriented retail, which is characterized by functional, leisure-oriented goods such as books, recorded music, and sporting goods as well as by nonessential gifts, novelties, and collectibles. No matter what is being sold, merchandise and stores tend to be highly branded.

Many of these stores are operated by large, vertically integrated entertainment or manufacturing companies. Because these companies have vast financial resources and use the stores as a strategic tool for building their brand and supporting their other corporate divisions, the quality of the store design and the visual merchandising are among the best there is.

In addition to unique designs, many of these retailers offer added amenities like "play-before-you-pay" or "try-before-you-buy" opportunities, in-store cafés, and entertainment—live music, disc jockeys, and video projection screens. These features allow the retailers to link the goods to a pleasurable and memorable experience.

Brand-Name Souvenir Boutiques. The rise of branding has inspired an aggressive new breed of souvenir retailers. Nearly every brand-name eatery or entertainment venue with any degree of exclusivity, from Rainforest Café restaurants to DisneyQuest virtual-reality parlors, offers a line of brand merchandise that includes items such as logo-emblazoned t-shirts, bomber jackets, hats, sweatshirts, and key chains. By purchasing these items, patrons are able to affiliate with the place's cultural cachet—a mix of hipness, sophistication, exoticism, and elitism.

When successful, boutiques selling brand merchandise may have impressive sales by any standard. It has been estimated, for instance, that at a theme restaurant like Hard Rock Café, a boutique that may be only 500 square feet in size can account for as much as 30 percent of the establishment's profits. A contributing factor, of course, is that the markup on merchandise can be upwards of 200 percent. Logo wear is also a highly effective advertising technique, which partially explains why Hard Rock Café is such a widely recognized property even though it

spends virtually nothing on advertising—whereas McDonald's, for example, reportedly spends about half a billion dollars on advertising annually.

Specialty Stores. Independent and chain specialty stores like Dapy, The Museum Company Store, Brookstone, and Glow (which sells glow-in-the-dark novelties in an ultraviolet-lighted environment) are common to destination development complexes and cultural and entertainment districts. These retailers, which tend to focus on a well-defined theme, product category, or lifestyle profile, usually occupy 3,000 to 4,000 square feet of moderately designed space; stores in high-profile locations tend to be more elaborately designed.

What makes these retailers especially suited to the destination development environment is the "browse-ability" of the goods they sell. Because such stores offer a large number of small, unique items, a visit is akin to a treasure hunt; and when shopping companions excitedly show each other the interesting items they discover, exploring the store also becomes a social experience. Instead of being out of reach—behind glass, in boxes, or encased in shrink-wrap, the merchandise is completely accessible, allowing patrons to

Specialty stores are an integral part of large retail entertainment destinations, such as The Museum Company Store in the 192,000-square-foot E-Walk, on 42nd Street in New York City. *Tishman Urban Development Corporation*

experience the items firsthand. Often, these goods actually "do something" or create a sensory effect that can be experienced immediately within the store.

Brand-Extension Stores.

Brand-extension stores are operated by vertically integrated entertainment and media companies that own well-known intellectual or creative properties, primarily characters and logos; examples include the Disney Stores and Warner Bros. Studio Stores. The businesses behind these stores are seeking to exploit their ephemeral assets to the fullest by selling brand goods directly to the public. ESPN—The Store and the chain of stores opened by Discovery Communications, Inc., which operates the educational Discovery Channel, illustrate how the niche focus of cable channels can translate to niche specialty retail concepts. In the future, with the oft-promised 500 channels, the number of cable-to-retail brand extensions is likely to grow.

Brand-License Stores.

Because of the popularity of brand-extension stores and the enormous demand for goods featuring characters and logos in general, a number of specialty stores have emerged that are operated by retailers who have licensed well-known creative or intellectual properties. NASCAR- and NBA-based stores are recent examples of this genre, as are the shops developed by Store of Knowledge, Inc., in partnership with local PBS affiliates nationwide, which sell items related to PBS programming.

The drawback of brand-license stores is the inefficiency of the relationship between the licensor and licensee, which prevents the level of synergy that brand-extension stores enjoy. In a brand-license arrangement, the licensor does not have control over the stores that provide the public representation of its valuable properties, and the licensee has little sway over the "merchandising side" of the development of creative or intellectual properties.

Product-Showcase Stores.

Product-showcase stores—glamorous retail outlets operated by manufacturers of brand-name goods—are as much brand-building devices as revenue generators. The NikeTown stores, with their bold design and dynamic approach to merchandise presentation, best exemplify this type. Planet Reebok and Sony Style, at San Francisco's Yerba Buena Gardens; World of Coke and the M&M store, on the Las Vegas strip; and American Girl Place, in Chicago, are additional examples. Since opening in 1998, American Girl Place has become a destination in itself, attracting an estimated 750,000 visitors and achieving reported sales of $850 per square foot. At these stores—as at world's fair pavilions—selling the brand image is as important as selling the merchandise. With the growth of alternative retail distribution channels like catalogs and online shopping, which make middleman retailers less critical, these flashy product showcases are likely to proliferate. In the near future, shoppers may visit a product-showcase store to try on athletic shoes or examine housewares, then order the items via the Internet, directly from the factory, for next-day delivery.

Leisure-Oriented Category Killers. Leisure-oriented category-killer retail stores offer a wide selection of brand-name leisure-oriented goods like books, recorded music, and sporting goods in a big-box format. Often, these stores are referred to as "big books" or "big music" stores, or as "megastores" or "superstores." Reflecting the current vogue for lifestyle retailing, these large retailers frequently offer patrons innovative visit-extending and intimacy-inducing in-store experiences. To this end, Barnes & Noble and Borders Books & Music use amenities such as in-store cafés and coffee bars, "sitting room" lounge areas with comfortable reading chairs, and live jazz. In Virgin Records megastores, music-listening stations, multimedia audio and video presentations, and in-store disc jockeys perform the same function.

Sporting and outdoor-gear retailers also offer new experiential elements. In Springfield, Missouri, the 170,000-square-foot Bass Pro Shops Outdoor World offers a host of "play-before-you-pay" areas, including rifle and bow ranges and a trout pond for testing fishing flies. Similarly, the 80,000-square-foot REI flagship store features an outdoor mountain-bike test track and an indoor rock-climbing pinnacle, along with a simulated hiking trail and a room for testing rainproof gear. Meanwhile, Oshman's Super Sports USA stores let customers shoot hoops and practice their putting. The link among these retailers is that the merchandise being sold is for leisure use—and customers have almost as much fun giving these goods a trial run in the store as they would going to an entertainment center.

▲
◀ Leisure-oriented category killers are retail stores that offer merchandise in innovative visit-extending and intimacy-inducing environments. The REI flagship store in Seattle, where customers may "test-drive" the company's recreation merchandise in outdoor and indoor venues, is a classic example.
REI/Robert Pisano

CHAPTER 3

Strategic Positioning, Programming, Financing, and Execution

Destination developments—which range from pure urban entertainment centers to leisure time/lifestyle centers—are having a pervasive impact on the retail landscape that is comparable to that of department stores at the turn of the previous century. These projects, whose impact extends far beyond the limited number of developments created so far, are transfiguring the way traditional retail developments are being laid out and programmed. At the same time, shopping, dining, and leisure are undergoing a fundamental transformation that reflects an even larger transition: the emergence of "the experience economy."

As described in the introductory chapter, a number of powerful forces are reshaping the very nature of the places where consumers go to dine, to shop, and to be entertained. Because of the unusual challenges posed by projects that serve as destinations, and the skills required to create such projects, only a handful of developers have undertaken these novel projects. The first wave of projects vary widely in regard to scale, merchandise mix, configuration, "place-making" devices, and character. Nevertheless, these developments share a common characteristic: their environments, tenants, and entertainment features are designed to distinguish the projects as destinations. The difference between traditional retail developments and this new form of development is, in essence, a difference in the scope and impact of the projects—in short, in their ability to perform as

Jersey Gardens, a 1.5 million-square-foot retail entertainment complex in ▶ Elizabeth, New Jersey, developed by Glimcher Realty Trust, was designed by the Rockwell Group as a family-oriented destination where each visitor is anticipated to stay for several hours. *Rockwell Group/Paul Warchol*

destinations. A successful destination development should be able to draw patrons from two to three times the geographic range of a regional mall, achieve an average patron visit of three hours, and appeal to a far broader spectrum of patrons than traditional retail centers.

Throughout this chapter, the phrase *destination development* is used to refer to a range of urban and suburban projects that employ a mix of tenanting, place-making, and entertainment-enhanced strategies to create shopping, dining, and entertainment offerings that are unique to a region or city. More than other retail centers, destination developments require significant innovation with respect to programming, tenant configuration and mix, venue creation, siting decisions, anchoring components, vertical linkages, and execution. Even with the experience gained from the first wave of destination developments, these projects will continue to require a level of innovation and effort that far exceeds that for other forms of retail development. (Indeed, the majority of destination projects have become catalysts for complex, mixed-use developments that may include residential, hotel, and office uses.) What offsets the extra effort required to develop destination projects is their potential performance. Destination developments can significantly exceed the sales and rents generated by top urban and suburban malls.

This chapter addresses the unique challenges of creating destination developments that integrate shopping, dining, entertainment, cultural activities, and other forms of leisure. It does not focus on specific types of destination developments; instead, it examines the benefits and risks associated with destination developments by discussing the four key stages involved in the planning and execution of these projects. A number of examples are provided to illustrate the factors that contribute to successful development.

Strategic Positioning: Evaluating Opportunities and Constraints

From the outset, the assessment of a destination development is far more complicated than the evaluation of a traditional retail opportunity. A destination project, after all, competes against a broad array of competitors beyond regional retail offerings, including a wide range of leisure-time activities. Unbridled enthusiasm for entertainment- and leisure-enhanced projects, combined with a lack of strategic rigor in evaluating competitive and market constraints, has led to the creation of a number of poorly performing properties.

According to MRA e-Ventures, in addition to employing the criteria used to evaluate traditional retail projects, it is valuable to approach the strategic assessment of a destination opportunity across five dimensions of competitive advantage:

■ Distinctiveness

■ Drawing power

■ Depth of penetration

■ Duration of visit

■ Demand-period programming.

Each of the following sections illustrates the importance of one of these dimensions in determining whether a destination opportunity exists in a particular location.

Distinctiveness

Strategic positioning of a destination development begins with an assessment of its potential distinctiveness within a market region. Few cities or regions can support more than three or four destination projects, while less populated areas can support no more than one. Unlike traditional retail projects, destination developments are made up of icon retailers and restaurants that often limit their regional presence to one or two locations. The leisure and entertainment components of these projects are often similarly limited within a particular market. In this regard, it is worth noting that one of the causes of the current crisis in the cinema industry was the saturation of key markets by megaplexes competing for the same patron base.

Additional sources of competition may include regional leisure attractions; concentrated clusters of restaurants; cinema megaplexes; tourist attractions; and nighttime entertainment districts. Strategic positioning, however, sometimes involves turning potential competition into a source of support. For example, Metreon, Sony's retail entertainment complex in San Francisco, was strategically positioned in the Yerba Buena Gardens district to take advantage of the existing museums, restaurants, shops, hotels, and convention facilities that make the area distinctive as a destination for tourists, conventioneers, and local residents. (See the case study on Metreon in chapter 5.)

Distinctiveness also means achieving dominance within a region. While a variety of retail centers within a region may be enhanced by entertainment features and dining venues, a market can support only a limited number of true destination projects. Thus, distinctiveness involves creating a regional identity and product mix that differentiate the destination from other offerings that compete for the leisure time and expenditures of the region's consumer base.

Third Street Promenade, in Santa Monica, has achieved a high level of distinctiveness even in a market with a variety of malls, seaside attractions, and nearby entertainment destinations.[1] The project's distinctiveness was founded on a street-oriented retail environment and an aggressive tenant-subsidy program that attracted a rich mix of restaurants, theaters, and unique-to-the-market retailers. In the case of Third Street, sustaining distinctiveness as a competitive advantage has involved maintaining the project's one-of-a-kind restaurants and shops and its vibrant street environment, while adding nationally recognized signature restaurants and icon retailers.

Achieving dominance also requires evaluating a variety of factors that support a development's distinctiveness, including access, location, and the ability to shape consumers' perceptions of the destination's identity. All these elements must work together if the developer's worst nightmare is to be avoided: the possibility of being intercepted or outmaneuvered by another project with an advantageous location, superior program, or more attractive anchors.

The critical point of a strategic evaluation is to determine whether an opportunity exists to achieve a sustainable competitive advantage by positioning the project as a regional centerpoint for entertainment, dining, and shopping. Timing, particularly in relation to the presence or the introduction of targeted tenants, is of great significance in achieving regional distinctiveness. As noted earlier, icon and showcase stores, signature restaurants, and

entertainment venues often limit their presence in any one region to one or two locations. Being unable to attract key tenants—or losing them to a competitive development—can limit or destroy a project's ability to achieve destination status.

Drawing Power

Typical regional centers rely heavily on nearby population: according to the most recent data available from Stillerman Jones & Company, 56 percent of mall visitors traveled less than 15 miles, and 87 percent came from within a 30-minute radius; moreover, most malls report that only 5 percent of their business is generated by tourists. Destination projects, in contrast, are regional attractions, drawing patrons from across a metropolitan statistical area and acting as a must-see for tourists. Universal CityWalk, for example, draws more than 40 percent of its visitors from residential areas that are more than 30 minutes from the project.[2]

A destination development is designed to attract consumers from a geographic area at least twice the size of that drawn on by a

regional mall. While the range varies according to the region of the country (e.g., larger in the Midwest, tighter in the Northeast) the median draw of a destination development is about 35 miles, compared with the 15- to 18-mile range of a regional mall. That extended drawing power is related both to the unique features and offerings provided by the destination development (i.e., supply) and to various factors that affect consumers' leisure-time decisions (i.e., demand).

From a supply perspective, the destination development needs to provide an itinerary of experiences that are unique to the region and that justify commute times of an hour or more. From the demand perspective, assessing the development's potential to draw consumers requires a solid analysis of current leisure-time and expenditure patterns. Because these patterns vary significantly by region, the analysis must be market specific, taking account of demographics, psychographics, tourism, regional competitors, and other specific locational factors. A destination development should not be undertaken without the confidence that it can capture and dominate its regional market.

Depth of Penetration

Penetration is the percentage of market captured within a primary zone surrounding the site—typically, five to ten miles, depending on the density of the metropolitan area. To succeed, destination developments must penetrate the primary market to a depth that far exceeds that of most other retail projects. Capture rates of more than 100 percent—and up to 700 percent—have been reached when a development achieves broad-based appeal across a range of market segments.

The key to deep penetration of a regional market, however, is a high rate of repeat visits from a core market. For example, more than two-thirds of the visitors to traditional malls are women, but destination projects need a nearly equal percentage of both men and women in order to succeed—and must also achieve a high level of family participation. Universal CityWalk's visitor mix, 51 percent female and 49 percent male, represents the balance sought by destination developments. Easton Town Center, in Columbus, Ohio, is noted for its very high rate of repeat visits from local residents. Mall of America, which draws a substantial number of consumers from a vast 300-mile range, achieves a penetration of between 600 and 700 percent of the 20-mile regional market.[3]

Projects in the new wave of destination developments—such as CityPlace, in West Palm Beach; Easton Town Center; Penn's Landing, in Philadelphia; and Hollywood & Highland, in Los Angeles—are being programmed to take the critical importance of market penetration into account. First, programmable entertainment venues (e.g., megaplexes, ice-skating rinks, live-performance venues, sports venues, cultural attractions, and events facilities) are being designed in attractive public environments to continually renew demand and achieve high rates of repeat visits. Second, to encourage repeat visits, destination developments are using customized research on the psychographics and leisure-time expenditures of consumer segments; on the location of potential consumers; and on the competitive developments that may intercept them. Finally, to achieve market penetration, destination developments must draw on more market segments than do traditional retail projects by offering entertainment, dining, and shopping choices that appeal to a variety of consumers.

Appealing to an array of market segments is important in two respects. First, in order to achieve a reasonable penetration of the regional market, a destination development needs to appeal to a mix of families, young adults, and older adults (e.g., empty nesters). This has been a challenge for projects designed as evening destinations, which often have limited appeal to families and must therefore rely on very deep penetration of adult market segments.

Second, the decision to visit a destination involves trade-offs with other leisure-time activities; because such choices are often made by a group—whether a family of five or two adult couples—they must satisfy the interests of a number of people. The more a project succeeds in accommodating a mix of preferences, the greater its depth of penetration.

Penn's Landing, a 600,000-square-foot destination development being undertaken by Simon Property Group (SPG), illustrates the type of programming required to simultaneously draw a variety of distinct consumers and achieve a high rate of repeat visits among targeted patrons. To draw families, the project will offer a 130,000-square-foot children's museum; a 30,000-square-foot, multilevel FAO Schwarz flagship store; a variety of family-friendly restaurants, such as Cheesecake Factory; and direct links to an aquarium and children's garden via an aerial tram ride across the Delaware River.

To draw regional visitors, SPG worked with the quasi-public Penn's Landing Corporation to create a 4,000-seat waterfront amphitheater and a 10-acre, roof-deck-level festival park, which in combination will provide over 100 days of programming. An AMC megaplex and a variety of signature restaurants further increase the likelihood of repeat visits. To draw tourists, the project was designed around a three-part itinerary linking it to Philadelphia's historic district and an array of waterfront venues on both sides of the Delaware River.

CityPlace

Opened in November 2000, CityPlace may offer the best example of the new generation of destination developments. The mixed-use, $550-million destination began as a far more modest lifestyle and entertainment-enhanced retail project. Developed on a site that had languished as a redevelopment opportunity for over a decade, CityPlace evolved into the urban centerpoint for the city of West Palm Beach and a regional destination for the communities of Florida's Gold Coast.

Developed by CityPlace Partners, a partnership of The Related Companies (New York and Miami), the O'Connor Group (New York), and Ken Himmel (chief executive officer of the Palladium Company), in collaboration with the city of West Palm Beach, the development illustrates many of the principles that distinguish destination projects.

A Dynamic Urban Context

Mayor Nancy Graham and the city of West Palm Beach awarded development rights to CityPlace Partners largely because the partnership's proposal was strongly responsive to the existing pattern of streets, historic buildings, and adjacent development districts. Over a period of two years, these prelim-

inary plans were incrementally refined to ensure that the development fit within the broader urban context; specifically, the goal was to create a downtown district that would successfully integrate an array of otherwise discrete assets, including the Kravis Center for the Performing Arts, the Norton Museum of Art, the planned Palm Beach Opera, and the Clematis Street arts and entertainment district. CityPlace is "context savvy," in that it takes advantage of a number of adjacent amenities and attractions, thereby strengthening its own impact.

Place Making

CityPlace also exemplifies the power of a significant sense of place as the foundation for a destination development. Crafting this sense of place posed a challenge for the developers, who wanted to create a destination that felt indigenous to the region while employing architecture that was consistent with the scale of the project.

Drawing on the vernacular architectural traditions of the middle-tier townscapes of Tuscany, Howard Elkus, of Boston-based Elkus Manfredi, created building blocks with distinct facades that support individual store presentations, but that nevertheless create a sense of an organic, timeless whole. Grilles, balcony balustrades, window

frames, and cornice lines were carefully executed to create consistent patterns that still offer a variety of architectural expression.

The public spaces of CityPlace are "choreographed" according to the principles of Mediterranean and Tuscan townscapes. The streets open up to a semicircular piazza that surrounds a 1926 Spanish Colonial Revival church, which has been restored as the Harriet Himmel Gilman Theater for Cultural and Performing Arts. A grand stair off the piazza provides access to a 20-screen theater designed to resemble an opera house.

One of the goals of the project was to create a destination that was unique to West Palm Beach and that would come to be viewed more broadly as the centerpoint of the Gold Coast. Because Florida's vernacular architecture had already been used extensively in other projects, such as Mizner Park, the developers felt that a design executed in the local vernacular style would not sufficiently differentiate CityPlace. However, the skillful integration of local materials subtly relates CityPlace's more exuberant architectural style to local building patterns, yielding results that are at once exotic and familiar.

Multianchoring

CityPlace used a multianchoring strategy to reinforce its position as a destination. Retail anchors include a new, 110,000-square-foot, resort-oriented concept store by Macy's; a flagship FAO Schwarz (with a bell tower); a 30,000-square-foot, two-level Barnes & Noble; a two-level Restoration Hardware; and a 10,000-square-foot Pottery Barn. Dining is clustered around signature restaurants and local favorites, including Angelo & Maxie's Steakhouse, Bellagio, Cheesecake Factory, Legal Sea Food, Mezzanotte, and Tsunami. Entertainment includes Muvico's 20-screen theater, with a supervised children's playroom, and the arts center. With over 150 events per year, the adjacent Kravis Center for the Performing Arts will also serve as an anchor for the project.

Critical Mix

While the project certainly offers a critical mass of retail, dining, and entertainment (600,000 square feet), CityPlace—like other destination projects—seeks to differentiate itself on the basis of its *critical mix* of offerings. The retail mix is orchestrated to include a variety of icon retailers as well as unique-to-the-market stores. As noted earlier, the restaurants include

▲
To create a sense of place that both supports and absorbs individual tenant identities, CityPlace, in West Palm Beach, Florida, employs an architectural theme based on the design of Tuscan and Mediterranean villages. The 77-acre redevelopment in the heart of the city includes 600,000 square feet of retail and office space and 600 units of housing. The Palladium Plaza Fountain is shown. *Elkus Manfredi Architects*

both local businesses and widely recognized brand-name restaurants.

The developers worked with tenants to create presentations that would be unlike anything else they had done before. Benetton Sportsystem, for example, created a highly experiential store where fashions and sports equipment are displayed in an "immersion" environment that includes amenities such as climbing walls and equipment-testing stations.

The inclusion of a 27,000-square-foot Wild Oats Gourmet Market was part of the developer's strategy to add local institutions that support, as a key part of the mix, regular weekly traffic from local residents.

Authenticity and Amenity

CityPlace balances the vernacular fantasy of its architecture with a sense of authenticity. The icon for the project, for example, is the former First United Methodist Church, restored and retrofitted by the developers—at a cost of $5 million—as a cultural center and community amenity. Restored by local architect Rick Gonzalez, the church—with its open trusses, cypress-wood vaulted ceiling, ornamental screens, decorative plasterwork, and open-air loggias—acts as a grand living room for the city.

The sense of authenticity is also reinforced by the attention to detail in CityPlace's public spaces. The street pavers, the detailed exterior hardware

(including the carefully recreated Venetian street lamps), and the intriguing mix of local palms and imported olive trees combine to create the sense of an abiding local spirit.

Finally, authenticity is perhaps best illustrated by the project's signature fountains, which include a four-tier, 186-jet "show fountain" at the center of the plaza, designed by STO Design Group; a 14-foot, hand-carved fountain on a scrolled base, planned for the southeast corner of the project; and an antique wall fountain of Vicenza stone to be installed west of the central plaza.

Dimensions of Place

Originally conceived as a lifestyle and entertainment destination, CityPlace became more than the spark of a revitalization effort. As the project took shape on paper, it attracted interest from residential, office, and hotel developers, and evolved into a significant mixed-use development with 600 planned residences, including 51 townhomes, 33 condominiums, and 128 luxury rentals. Three office towers totaling 750,000 square feet are also planned; the first, with 14 stories and 240,000 square feet, is scheduled to open in 2002.

This transformation is indicative of the power of place-oriented destinations to create a sense of identity, community, and amenity (largely absent in our cities and towns) that is equally attractive for business, residential, and hotel development.

Public/Private Collaboration

Like the majority of destination projects, CityPlace could not have been undertaken without the financial and administrative resources of the public sector. Acting as an owner, the city of West Palm Beach created a land lease that addressed the developer's risks; stepped up as guarantor of $55 million in tax-exempt bonds to cover infrastructure costs, including the construction of four parking decks; and facilitated the development process while acting as an advocate for community amenities and urban linkages.

The successful execution of CityPlace is as much about the creation of a consistent, detailed process of public/private collaboration as it is a lesson in forging a savvy destination strategy. ●

Source: Mike Rubin, MRA International.

Duration of Visit

Leisure expenditures are correlated with the length of time a patron spends at a location. The duration of a visit is, in turn, related to the variety of choices and the number of linked activities provided as part of the guest experience; these linked activities are referred to in this chapter as an *itinerary*.

Maximum spending is generally thought to occur with a length of stay of three to four hours. To achieve this length of stay, the challenge for destination developments is to successfully integrate both daytime and evening itineraries that appeal to a variety of visitor groups—an often elusive goal. A majority of projects have a pronounced daytime or evening activity pattern. For example, Irvine Spectrum Center, in Irvine, California, has achieved the status of a regional centerpoint for nighttime activity but enjoys only modest weekday activity. A third phase of development focusing on lifestyle retailing is intended to create a compelling daytime itinerary.

Easton Town Center and CityPlace have been programmed around an overlay of daytime and evening itineraries. With 40 percent of patrons visiting Monday through Thursday, Easton, which has now been in operation since 1998, appears to be on the way to achieving the status of both a weekday and evening destination. A second phase, which will double the size of the project and greatly reinforce the retail and dining mix, should further increase repeat visits by extending both daytime and evening itineraries.

When a destination development provides engaging guest itineraries, visitors remain at the site longer, make larger expenditures, experience greater satisfaction, and are more likely to make repeat visits—thereby strengthening overall project performance.

Demand-Period Programming

Evaluating the market also means considering a variety of distinct demand periods. Demand at all retail projects varies according to the availability and motivations of various market segments over various times of the day and week. Destination developments have the potential advantage of being able to attract particular consumer segments during times that are nonproductive in traditional retail settings. However, this dimension of performance is the most challenging to assess and to address strategically. In a strong tourist market, for example, a destination project may be able to increase the typically low productivity of mornings and mid-afternoons by attracting the overnight visitor with daytime entertainment venues or events. In a market with a large base of university students, the productivity of weekday evenings might be similarly enhanced.

Since the theater industry began to develop larger megaplexes with enhanced features (such as stadium seating and digital sound systems), one challenge has been to increase productivity by attracting patrons during low demand periods. As the industry reorganizes, it is likely to more effectively capitalize on these investments by marketing daytime programming to local schools, business groups, and conventioneers. General Cinema Corporation's successful multisite satellite broadcast of motivational speaker Anthony Robbins's three-day Power Walk Program to 60 theaters around the United States represents the type of programming that can improve theater performance and reinforce cinemas' future role as development anchors.

With destination developments, strong performance depends on identifying the programmatic fit between available consumer segments and key demand periods. Insight into daily and weekly patterns can significantly improve performance, allowing the developer to introduce a mix of tenants and venues that match the motivations of key consumer segments.

Capitalizing on these five dimensions—distinctiveness, drawing power, depth of penetration, duration of visit, and demand-period programming—can significantly increase the performance potential of the destination development over traditional retail developments. Achieving this potential involves recognizing market patterns that are unique to destination developments and using that understanding to shape a distinctive offering.

Defining the Product

Destination developments are far less formula driven than are other forms of retail development. To achieve destination status, these developments need, by definition, to provide an offering that is distinct from that of tradi-tional retail environments. The typical super-regional mall, for example, is based on one of two standard configurations, is anchored by three or four department stores, and has an 85-10-5 mix of retail, dining, and entertainment. By contrast, nearly every urban entertainment center, suburban lifestyle development, and sports-linked or tourist-based destination development has been distinctive—that is, reflective of its location, context, and competitive environment.

Lincoln Square, the topic of a case study in the first edition of this volume, is considered one of the first destination developments and reflects the constraints and opportunities of developing in New York's upper West Side. Developed by Millennium Partners, the project is distributed across three blocks along Broadway, with three- to five-story podiums supporting residential towers. The merchandise mix, which is intended to serve both the neighborhood and the residential towers, offers a five-story sports club, a flagship Barnes & Noble, Tower Records, and Loews-Sony theaters (including a 3-D IMAX). Reinforced by the presence of the IMAX and the proximity of Lincoln Center (which is adjacent to the development), these anchors draw patrons from all parts of the city and attract a substantial day-visitor and tourist trade. When Sony (which operates the theaters and IMAX at Lincoln Square) decided to undertake a joint venture with Millennium to build a "prototype" destination development in San Francisco, the location, context, and competitive environment led to an entirely different configuration.

Similar points could be made by comparing destination projects such as Third Street Promenade to CityWalk, Easton Town Center to CityPlace, or Hollywood & Highland to New York's E-Walk. Nevertheless, developers of destination projects confront severe imped-

Multiplex cinemas ▶
have become the
most significant
traffic generators
for evening
activity and repeat
visits. The UCI
Cinemas chain,
in the United
Kingdom, expects
the sleek design
and amenities of
its two-level multi-
plexes to expand
its market share.
RTKL UK

iments in their efforts to craft distinctive offer-ings: financial institutions demand credit ten-ants to carry rent rolls and have been reluctant to provide capital to projects that break with traditional retail formulas; the promise of new forms of entertainment and leisure offerings to support destination development has largely been unrealized, limiting developers' options; the limited number of "icon" credit tenants in the retail and restaurant sectors leads to predictable tenant rosters; and the cost of creating streetscapes, distinctive archi-tecture, and infrastructure programming typi-cally exceeds private financing parameters—requiring public sector participation to render these projects feasible. Indeed, as noted later in this chapter, many cities have recognized the considerable benefits of destination developments and have become actively involved in creative financing and partnering arrangements.

According to MRA e-Ventures, develop-ers of destination projects have evolved a unique set of strategies to distinguish these projects from traditional real estate projects, including the following:

- Multianchoring the development

- Strengthening tenant identity

- Creating itinerary-based configurations

- Gauging scale in relation to a critical mix

- Building the project around public gather-ing places

- Leveraging the distinctiveness of the place through contextual links

- Integrating these elements to create a sense of identity for the development as a regional destination.

Interestingly, these strategies are now also being applied to traditional retail settings as well as to sports complexes, cultural centers, tourist districts, town centers, and mixed-use developments to enhance their appeal and performance.

Multianchoring

Traditionally, large department stores have anchored retail developments, generating the base of consumer traffic that supported a mix of retailers. Destination developments involve a very different approach to anchoring, which is based on the creation of nighttime and day-time activity patterns. The anchors in these

Multianchoring Retail Entertainment Destinations

Type of anchor	Function	Example
Activity generator: Mainly entertainment-based venues	• Draw a broad segment of the consumer market • Extend the development's geographic range • Increase market penetration	• Megaplex theaters • Specialty-format theaters • Games-based attractions (GameWorks, Jillian's) • Sports-based attractions (ESPN Club) • Live-performance venues
Activity extender: Mainly dining venues	• Extend the length of stay • Increase repeat visitation (penetration) • Extend the development's appeal to a range of market segments • Support daytime and evening itineraries	• Signature restaurants (Cheesecake Factory, Il Fornaio) • Theme restaurants (Hard Rock Café, Rainforest Café) • Entertainment restaurants and clubs (BET, House of Blues)
Activity inducer: Mainly icon retailers	• Extend the development's geographic range • Create a shopping itinerary	• Icon retailers (Barnes & Noble, Crate & Barrel, Williams-Sonoma) • Brand retailers (NikeTown, Sony Style Store, Virgin Records)

Source: MRA International.

projects, which take three forms, are designed to create a combined pull on the market that extends the project's geographic reach and penetration. This blend of anchoring elements is referred to as *multianchoring*.

Entertainment as an Activity Generator.

A majority of destination projects use entertainment as a primary anchor and activity generator. Whereas the typical super-regional mall includes only 5 percent of its gross leasable area (GLA) as entertainment, destination projects program from 20 to 50 percent of GLA for entertainment uses. Multiplex cinemas—often consisting of 20 to 25 screens with stadium seating, torus screens, and digital sound systems—have become the most significant activity generators for evenings. Supported by a well-established software engine (i.e., Hollywood) whose new releases allow for weekly changes to the marquee, the multiplex is the foundation for drawing repeat customers, which can significantly boost retail and dining sales within destination projects. At CocoWalk, in Florida's

Coconut Grove, for example, while retail uses account for only 34 percent of GLA, retail sales—averaging more than $700 per square foot—account for 55 percent of total sales.[4] In traditional malls, by comparison, retail space accounts for 80 percent of GLA and 82 percent of sales; and according to ULI's *Dollars & Cents of Shopping Centers®: 2000,* the top 10 percent of super-regional malls enjoy average sales of $323 per square foot.

An excess of dated, unproductive theaters and the overbuilding of new megaplexes in highly contested theater zones have combined to create an industry-wide crisis for the theater business—which has, in turn, sharply affected destination developments by limiting access to a reliable and programmable entertainment anchor. Over the next several years, as the industry consolidates and closes down unproductive properties, an improved product is likely to emerge; in particular, theaters will begin to use digital and satellite technology to enhance and extend nonproductive daytime and weekday evening periods by offering a greater range of programming, including live broadcasts of events, interactive shows and events, and multisite conferences.

Beginning around 1995, entertainment companies and a wide array of entrepreneurs began actively pursuing other forms of enter-

tainment anchoring. Disney, for example, formed Disney Regional Entertainment to develop opportunities to achieve year-round patronage in urban markets, while carefully avoiding any cannibalization of Disney's theme parks. The results have been mixed: Disney's signature entertainment, dining, and retail venue ESPN Zone had a highly successful debut; Club Disney, on the other hand, was a brilliant but ultimately abandoned effort to capture families with children under ten; DisneyQuest, an 85,000- to 100,000-square-foot indoor theme park, is still being tested and redesigned in Orlando and Chicago.

Sony has similarly experimented with company-created venues at its Metreon development and at the Sony Center on the Potsdamer Platz, in Berlin (see the case study in chapter 5). These projects, which were developed through creative collaborations, are unlikely to be rolled out to other locations as anchors or activity generators.

Ogden Entertainment developed two location-based attractions—Tinsel Town and American Wilderness Experience—that were designed to serve as anchoring elements for retail projects and urban districts. Neither of these efforts proved successful, and Ogden has since abandoned this activity as an area of future business.

Entrepreneurial efforts have produced what appear to be far more engaging forms of entertainment and recreation but face the financial hurdles that inevitably greet untested commercial products. What seem to offer more opportunity are ventures undertaken by more established entities with access to capital, such as Club Med World, the House of Blues clubs and performance venues, BET's clubs and restaurants, Cirque du Soleil's new plans for regional venues, and Vans Skate Parks (initially undertaken in conjunction with The Mills Corporation). These projects offer far more limited rollout potential than theaters, however, and would therefore be applicable to only a handful of destination projects.

Dave and Buster's, GameWorks, and Jillian's are wrestling with the right mix of dining and entertainment (video games, arcade games, bowling, billiards, beach volleyball, bocce, simulation theaters, live theater, music) to act as regional activity generators in a wide range of markets. The performance of these projects has varied widely, with some stellar results. But even the best projects generate about half the visits of a megaplex, indicating that while these venues may be supportive of a destination development, they cannot serve as replacement anchors.

The most recent entrants into the realm of entertainment anchoring have been cultural, media, and sports facilities. Cultural venues include children's museums, science museums, and aquariums. As noted earlier, Penn's Landing will be anchored by a 130,000-square-foot children's museum; Navy Pier's primary anchor is the Chicago Children's Museum;[5] Newport-on-the-Levee, just outside Cincinnati, is anchored by a privately operated aquarium. The Smithsonian Institution has publicized its interest in distributing its archives through privately supported regional satellite museums. Hollywood & Highland is, of course, anchored by the Theater for the Academy of Motion Picture Arts and Sciences.

Media outlets, particularly satellite studios, offer another opportunity to enhance the draw and distinctiveness of a destination project. At Palladium's Columbus Circle development in New York, the five-story podium will be supported by Time Warner's working studios and by Jazz at Lincoln Center's new 100,000-square-foot facility, which includes a 1,300-seat concert theater.

Finally, the synergy of sports and retail, dining, and entertainment is being actively pursued, especially with new arena projects

Cultural, media, and sports venues are increasingly used to anchor entertainment destinations. The MCI Center, in downtown Washington, D.C., includes the home court and home ice of the Washington Wizards and the Washington Capitals, professional basketball and ice-hockey teams; an interactive museum and gallery of American sports history; the flagship Discovery Channel Store and Theater; a team sports store that sells logo merchandise; and Nick & Stef's Steakhouse, which is operated by celebrity chef Joachim Splichal. *Ellerbe Becket/Timothy Hursley*

▼

such as the Staples Center, in Los Angeles; the American Airlines Center, in Dallas; and Denver's new Pepsi Center arena. In Dallas, the arena will anchor a 700,000-square-foot shopping, dining, and entertainment district, generating over 200 events over the course of a year. In the Lower Downtown, or LoDo, district of Denver, a 25-square-block area is anchored by Coors Field on one end and the Pepsi Center on the other.

Illustrative Sales Figures
for Entertainment Restaurants

	Average sales per square foot	Percentage of mall-based average
Mall-based restaurants (median)*	$375	100%
Gordon Biersch Brewery	$594	158%
McCormick & Schmick's	$615	164%
PF Chang's China Bistro	$628	167%
Il Fornaio	$646	172%
Cheesecake Factory	$942	251%

Source: *Dollars & Cents of Shopping Centers®: 2000* (Washington, D.C.: ULI, 2000); 1999 financial disclosures for the listed companies.
*The mall-based figure represents median sales per square foot for national restaurants (owned and operated units only) serving liquor in U.S. super-regional malls.

In all these cases, however, the fit between leisure and entertainment, on the one hand, and retail and dining, on the other, is imperfect. The patrons who are drawn to an entertainment or cultural venue may prove elusive to retailers and even to restaurateurs. For this reason, a successful destination project requires multiple anchors, including retail and dining offerings that draw regional activity.

Restaurants as Activity Extenders. The second form of anchoring involves dining—or, more particularly, the clustering of a number of signature restaurants—to create a second draw. Whereas traditional malls allocate an average of 10 percent of GLA to dining, leading destination projects include 20 to 30 percent for restaurants, cafés, and food halls. Dining can be an effective way to generate traffic, but its primary function as an anchor is to extend the length of stay, enhance the visitor itinerary, and increase repeat visits.

The types of restaurants most effective as activity extenders vary by market, but in all cases the key to using dining as an anchor lies in clustering a number of offerings. Clustering provides the consumer with a range of choices, and (in much the same way the multiplex cinema does) minimizes the likelihood of long waits or the need for a great deal of planning. Projects such as CityPlace; Easton Town Center; Irvine Spectrum Center; Third Street Promenade; and Lincoln Road, in Miami's South Beach, illustrate the significance of clustering restaurants to create a regional draw.

The power of clustering is clearly evident in sales performance. According to ULI's *Dollars & Cents of Shopping Centers®: 2000*, isolated restaurants on pads adjacent to super-regional malls have median sales of $387 per square foot; the clustered dining offerings at CocoWalk, in contrast, have sales of $622 per square foot. Sales in signature restaurants in destination projects can exceed $1,000 per square foot (see the accompanying sidebar).

Icon Retailing as an Activity Inducer. The third type of anchor is drawn from a select set of "icon" or "brand" retailers that attract a broad range of market segments. A number of recent entertainment-enhanced projects, overlooking the importance of supportive retail, have focused instead on entertainment—that is, movie theaters—as the anchor. But multiplexes and other entertainment venues do not provide direct support to daytime shopping itineraries. Instead, they support an evening itinerary that includes dining out and other recreational or leisure activities. Preshow shopping and postevent browsing, when stores are often closed, typically have little impact on retail sales unless they create a second, "shopping-motivated" trip to the project. By creating a second daytime and evening itinerary focused on shopping, icon retailers act as activity inducers, drawing customers to the development for a unique shopping experience.

Since the mid-1990s, retailing has undergone a virtual revolution, driven in part by the perceived threats of Internet shopping and in part by a loss of consumer enthusiasm and loyalty. To ensure the recognition of their brands, a number of manufacturers created their own street-oriented presentation stores. Nike, Sony, and Virgin led this trend—and accidentally became sought-after anchors for destination projects.

An even more important trend has been the creation of stores that provide consumers with memorable, repeatable experiences. Stores such as cosmetics icon Sephora; sports retailers Cabela's and Bass Pro; toy stores such

as FAO Schwarz, the Discovery Channel Store, and American Girl Place; fashion and apparel stores such as Tommy Bahama's, Scoop, and Zara; and lifestyle retailers such as Williams-Sonoma and Smith & Hawken have redefined shopping as a participatory and pleasurable leisure-time activity. These stores have become the sought-after anchors that support shopping and daytime activity at a destination. The challenge for the developer, however, is that these types of stores have a limited inventory and are difficult to secure; moreover, lease terms, including tenant demands for improvements, can be financially onerous.

▲
Clustering restaurants provides consumers with a range of choices, minimizing the likelihood of long waits or the need for reservations. Five restaurants are clustered at Denver Pavilions, an entertainment destination on the 16th Street Mall, in Denver, Colorado.
Development Design Group, Inc./Timothy Hursley

Tenant Identity

Retailers have increasingly turned away from ubiquitous, predictable mall stalls in favor of street-oriented, high-ceilinged, multilevel presentations enhanced by facade treatments, interior architecture, and multimedia displays. Among the factors propelling this transition are a desire to reengage the customer, concern about product identity and consumers' brand affiliation, and increased competition from the full spectrum of retail distribution outlets—from catalogs to off-price centers to e-tailing.

The challenge for the developer is twofold: first, to offer tenants the opportunity for the level of customized expression that they seek; second, to do so within an environment that maintains the integrated character that is required to convey a strong sense of place. However, this customized yet cohesive environment is difficult to achieve, both physically and economically.

With 80 to 150 tenants struggling to achieve identity within a project, there is always the danger that the development will disintegrate into a melee of competing signs and facades. Successful developers have enforced a common design vocabulary and

used the powerful place-making devices of traditional cities and towns—including piazzas, grand public stairs, and streets—to create a sense of place that is able to support and absorb individual tenant identities. Easton

Town Center uses the vocabulary of Main Street America to create an environment that can accept the brand identities of stores like Barnes & Noble, Cheesecake Factory, J. Crew, and Virgin without sacrificing the sense of an integral place. Similarly, at CityPlace, where the architecture is based on that of Tuscany and Mediterranean towns, a piazza with a restored church and central fountain and a grand public stair create a distinctive place that can accept a wide range of retail and restaurant icons.

The more challenging issue has been the costs associated with creating these environments. Facade architecture, scenographic effects, lighting, pavement treatments, street furniture, landscaping, and high-quality graphics and signage are required to create a compelling character for a project, but involve costs typically associated with major civic projects undertaken by governments or public authorities. In the vast majority of destination developments, the public spaces, amenities, and infrastructure require an active public sector with both a commitment to the project and the required resources. In turn, as discussed later in this chapter, the participation of the public sector implies that destination developments must often fulfill a public purpose.

Itinerary-Based Configurations

Tenant identity, the guest experience, and project performance are also linked closely with the layout and adjacency of stores. Unlike the straightforward tenant configurations of traditional shopping centers, in which department stores anchor the ends of shopping corridors, configurations for destination developments involve considerable planning and customization. Factors contributing to the complexity include the presence of retail, dining, and entertainment facilities that are multilevel, street-oriented, or both; the necessity of appropriately distributing multiple anchors; and the differing requirements of daytime and evening activity generators.

Given this context, successful programming involves creating tenant configurations that directly support a variety of distinct visitor itineraries. Itineraries provide the framework for addressing the locations of anchor tenants, tenant adjacencies, vertical linkages, and various place-making decisions. While there are no specific rules for accommodating a mix of itineraries, MRA e-Ventures has identified six basic characteristics of successful configurations.

First, daytime shopping is reinforced by streets or streetlike spaces that organize a sequence of exciting stores with distinct identities. Second, the stores are designed to simultaneously contribute to the streetscape and to draw patrons off the street and into the experiential space offered by the various retail environments. Third, in a departure from traditional mall design, patrons are not pulled by anchor department stores on either end of a shopping corridor but are drawn

◀ **Experiential space draws patrons into retail environments. For example, Yokohama Bayside Marina, in Yokohama, Japan, offers a re-creation of a New England fishing village.**
RTKL/Sanae Inada

along by a sequence of icon and brand stores located at various points along the length of the project's shopping streets.

Fourth, dining facilities tend to be clustered around public spaces such as piazzas or squares—or, in the context of a streetscape, at corner locations or "crossroads." Dining often serves to extend all four of the predominant itineraries—shopping, family excursions, evenings out, and tourist visits.

The fifth point concerns the location of entertainment venues—specifically, the challenge of accommodating weekend and evening itineraries. On the one hand, entertainment venues may require some degree of isolation to accommodate peak-period crowding and long

Patrons form itineraries from a sequence of icon and brand stores at various points along the shopping street. Katy Mills, in Dallas, Texas, a regional shopping center with 1.3 million square feet of gross leasable area, provides multiple theme-based itineraries, each including a number of national-brand icon stores. *RTKL/Dave Whitcomb*

Dining is clustered around public ▶ spaces or at "crossroads." Kaleidoscope, in Mission Viejo, California, acts as the community's town square, with dining at the base of the modern-day rotunda and light beacon. *Altoon + Porter Architects, LLP*

lines. On the other hand, these venues also provide an opportunity to enhance retail sales through spillover activity. In vertically oriented projects, one option is to locate theaters and location-based entertainment venues on upper levels, in close proximity to upper-level dining, an arrangement that requires patrons to pass through the retail areas as part of their itinerary. In Pacific Place (see the case study in chapter 5), express escalators speed entertainment and dining patrons to the third level, where there are four signature restaurants and the lobby of a multiscreen theater. On descent, patrons move floor by floor through the retail core along scissor escalators that encourage browsing. In projects that are in urban districts or organized around ground-level streets, entertainment venues are distributed to create an overlay pattern that is in synch with daytime pedestrian patterns. To achieve this effect, entertainment anchors are located adjacent to retail anchors: during the day, the retail anchors serve as activity generators; in the evening, the entertainment venues pull traffic along the same paths.

As a final point, it should be noted that in some street-oriented destination developments, the approach has been to "district" entertainment venues, thereby balancing the need to physically segregate evening activities with the economic imperative of integrating entertainment itineraries with retail activity. At Broadway at the Beach, in Myrtle Beach, South Carolina, a cineplex and IMAX theater are located at one end of the main shopping street and restaurants are concentrated at the other end, creating a flow of activity that provides for spillover shopping. However, a mix of nightclubs and bars, anchored by a Hard Rock Café, is separated from the main promenade by a footbridge. This configuration

allows dining patrons to easily extend their stay to include late-night activities, while nightclub patrons can also gain access to the club district through a separate entry.

◀ Nighttime entertainment facilities must sometimes be segregated from retail facilities to prevent conflict between event and nonevent traffic. Samsung Entertainment Center, in Seoul, Korea, with six levels of entertainment venues interspersed with shops and cafés, uses escalators to handle traffic. Because the escalators feature changing backlit previews of the entertainment offered at the center, the escalator rides become part of the entertainment. *KMD*

◀ Patrons of dining and entertainment venues must pass through retail areas as part of their itinerary. Westend City Center, in Budapest, Hungary, is a 430,000-square-foot project including retail and entertainment, office space, a hotel, and a conference center. The center is connected to a rail station that serves 400,000 passengers daily. *TrizecHahn*

Because a key source of competitive differentiation comes from assembling a unique group of retailers and restaurants that dominate the competition within a region, achieving a *critical mix* of tenants is more important than achieving *critical mass.* Major tenants at The Power Plant, in Baltimore, Maryland, are ESPN Zone, Hard Rock Café, Gold's Gym, Barnes & Noble, and Arthur Andersen, an accounting firm. The glass pyramid in the background is the National Aquarium. *The Cordish Company*

Creating ▶ a sense of place for patrons and a strong presence for tenants is what gives a destination development its distinctive identity. Sony's Star Theaters, in Southfield, Michigan, offer a colorful interpretation of streamlined art deco that is especially inviting at night. *Rockwell Group/Paul Warchol*

In the Victory mixed-use destination project under development in Dallas, concerns over the level of pedestrian and vehicular traffic generated by events at the nearby American Airlines Center led to the use of a districting strategy. A district adjacent to the center supports pre- and postevent activity when events are scheduled and acts as an independent attraction for evening activity on nonevent nights. At the other end of a four-block promenade, plans for an urban shopping and dining district include a theater in a location that allows for separate access and egress, minimizing conflict with attendees at arena events.

Scale: Critical Mix versus Critical Mass

Destination development projects tend to encompass between 250,000 and 650,000 square feet. The scale is driven by three interrelated factors: first, retail, dining, and entertainment offerings have increased significantly in scale relative to the size of traditional malls. A Barnes & Noble bookstore or FAO Schwarz toy store can exceed 30,000 square feet; restaurants as varied as Cheesecake Factory and PF Chang's range between 7,000 and 17,000 square feet; and multiplexes range between 70,000 and 120,000 square feet.

The second factor is the need for tenant diversity, which is achieved, first, by including a sufficient number and variety of core tenants; and second, by infilling with smaller, specialty tenants that are often unique to a particular region. Core tenants may make up as much as 75 percent of net leasable space, but smaller tenants can play a special role, enhancing visitors' experience by adding a more intimate scale and a sense of local authenticity. In larger destination developments, specialty tenants may expand to as much as 30 percent of the program, with a mix of boutiques, specialty stores, small cafés, and concessions. The higher rents charged to specialty tenants are also essential to creating a successful project. The larger the development, the more infill can typically be accommodated in the mix.

The third factor, which is closely related to tenant diversity, is critical mass—preferably thought of as critical *mix*. Critical mix is a strategic concern because a key source of competitive differentiation is domination of the competition within a region. However, domination depends more on assembling a unique group of retailers and restaurants that do not exist in other regionally competitive locations than it does on the overall number of offerings. Thus, the term *critical mix* more accurately communicates the importance of securing a base of competitively advantageous retail, restaurant, and entertainment tenants.

Place Making

In large part, the distinctiveness of a destination development derives from the creation of environments that yield a sense of place for patrons and a strong presence for tenants. In lieu of the predictable interior courts and shopping corridors that characterize malls and retail centers, destination developments have reintroduced the streets, piazzas, esplanades,

and variations in facade that are the *sine qua non* of great cities. Of course, a variety of retail environments that successfully employed street-oriented presentations and emphasized the vitality of public spaces preceded these developments. Examples include village-style shopping centers, such as Sturbridge Village, and the festival marketplaces created by Jim Rouse, as well as developments such as Mizner Park, in Boca Raton; Country Club Plaza, in Kansas City; and Two Rodeo Drive, in Beverly Hills. But these environments have been the exceptions in the mall-dominated retail world of the past four decades.

There is greater complexity in shaping the distinctive environments that define destinations. As noted earlier, developers must address the individual demands of retail and restaurant tenants for a wide variety of presentations that permit streetfront access, strong brand identity, and multilevel spaces. Creating engaging public places and a cohesive overall identity while simultaneously addressing tenants' competing demands requires not only a skillful development team but a whole new approach to design.

Developers of destination projects engage in an interactive design process, modifying plans throughout the predevelopment stage to address community issues, the various and often changing requirements of tenants, and adjustments to programming. Like the hard costs, the soft costs associated with the planning and design of destination projects are considerably higher than those associated with malls and shopping centers. Along with the expenses related to an iterative process is the cost of expanding the design team, which often includes scenographic artists, landscape architects, special-effects designers, festival planners, graphic artists, and branding consultants.

Creating a destination involves leveraging the location's geographic and cultural context. Drawing synergistic energy from its Yerba Buena neighbors and from the cultural strengths of San Francisco itself, the 350,000-square-foot Metreon fills in the missing elements of the cultural and entertainment district by increasing nighttime and family visits. *Yerba Buena Alliance*

Contextual Links

Because a significant part of what makes a project successful may exist outside the development itself, projects designed as stand-alone destinations are at a distinct disadvantage in achieving and sustaining competitive advantage. In a destination development, success is intimately linked to leveraging and bolstering existing activities, attractions, and amenities, which increases the attractiveness of both the project and its surroundings.

When Sony Development, Inc., selected the Yerba Buena Gardens district in San Francisco as the site for its prototype destination development, the importance of existing activities figured prominently in the decision. San Francisco is a destination city with a wide variety of cultural, recreational, shopping, and dining districts, including China Basin, Fisherman's Wharf/Pier 39, Ghirardelli Square, and Union Square. For Sony, the potential advantages of San Francisco as a market had to be weighed against the disadvantages—which included significant competition, seasonal visitation patterns, and the uncertainties associated with a prototype project.

Sony's response was to position its Metreon entertainment center adjacent to the Moscone Convention Center, the San Francisco Museum of Modern Art, two planned museums, a block of gardens above the convention center, and a strong existing base of destination restaurants. Its decision was based on a deep appreciation of visitor motivations. Yerba Buena, with its base of cultural attractions, was seen as a potential draw for families, regional visitors seeking unique dining experiences, conventioneers (who also represent a potential follow-on leisure trip to the city), and tourists staying in nearby hotels. Metreon's 350,000-square-foot development fits within the existing set of assets while introducing missing elements that are designed to increase nighttime visits (cinemas, unique dining experiences) and family visits (specially created entertainment venues, IMAX), as well as to build on existing shopping excursions (unique signature stores) and cultural excursions.

Another example of a strategic fit between a development and its surroundings is Penn's Landing. Located at a waterfront site long isolated from the city street grid by a major interstate highway, Penn's Landing was an effort on the part of SPG and the city of Philadelphia to establish a number of strong physical and programmatic links between the project and

Philadelphia's famous historic district, an adjacent restaurant district, an emerging nightlife district, attractions on the opposite side of the waterfront, and the needs of the surrounding residential community.

Taking advantage of bridges and elevated platforms that link the project to the city grid, SPG and its public partner included a 4,000-seat rooftop amphitheater, a children's museum, and a 10-acre festival park on a manufactured palisade overlooking the river. Recognizing the site's potential as an extension and enhancement of the established visitor itinerary within Independence National Historic Park, the city and SPG are collaborating to create unique programmatic and pedestrian linkages.

The project also incorporates the landing for a dramatic aerial tram that will span the Delaware River, linking the 600,000-square-foot development with a variety of entertainment venues in Camden, New Jersey, including an aquarium, the 22,500-seat Waterfront Entertainment Center, and a new minor-league baseball stadium.

Creating a Destination's Identity

The success of a destination development depends, finally, on creating a place that provides a shared identity for a region. Indeed, a large part of the appeal of destination projects to local governments is their potential to reestablish residents' and visitors' affinity for a downtown or regional center.

Crafting this identity involves consulting a variety of resources to research the culture, history, events, people, and stories that provide the foundation for the distinctive character of a place. The entrance to the cinemas at Pacific Place, for example, a two-and-a-half-story space framed in heavy native timber with stone fireplaces, evokes the great lodges of the Northwest and the traditional woodcrafts of the region's Native American tribes. To revitalize Ybor City—a historic waterfront district in the Tampa–St. Petersburg metro area—Steiner + Associates, the project developers, thoroughly researched the history and individual characteristics of the cigar factories and entertainment parlors that had once given the area its unique character. And in yet another example, TrizecHahn's redevelopment of Hollywood Boulevard borrows from the historic icons and the great movie sets of the 1930s to establish the centerpoint destination that had eluded generations of tourists in their frustrated efforts to find the real "Hollywood."

A "back story" provides a consistent identity for a destination project's activities and motif. The ancient spice routes that provide the back story for Desert Passage are evident in the itinerary-based, 450,000-square-foot retail and entertainment addition to the Aladdin Hotel and Casino, in Las Vegas, Nevada.
RTKL

▼

A technique borrowed from the entertainment industry has also been used to craft an identity for destination projects. Called a "back story," this approach involves creating a distinctive context that is drawn from local history and culture or from a fictional concept. The Walt Disney Company has histori-

cally used back stories to provide a consistent identity for its theme parks and attractions as well as for its more recent retail, dining, and entertainment projects outside the parks. Pleasure Island, Disney's gated nightlife district in Orlando, was originally based on a back story that described the district as a kind of Brigadoon that appeared at twilight and vanished by morning. Subsequent efforts to increase the project's performance were shaped partly by a new back story in which every night was New Year's Eve, and the party flowed from the individual nightclubs and music venues out into the streets.

Evaluating and Enhancing Financial Performance

The financial performance of a destination development differs from that of other retail-based developments in four important respects. First, as noted, the costs associated with the development can be significantly higher than

those associated with comparably scaled regional malls. Second, the calculus of tenant leases is far more complicated than in other retail developments because of multianchoring, the scale and requirements of core tenants, and the risks associated with new tenant concepts. Third, financing presents special challenges because of the actual and perceived risks associated with these still-novel projects and the lack of comparable developments with lengthy performance histories.

With respect to financial performance, the fourth and most significant difference between a destination development and more traditional retail projects is *destination economics:* this phrase refers to the ability of a project to exceed the performance of a traditional retail center by (1) drawing from a much larger market region, (2) achieving deeper market penetration through multisegment appeal and a higher rate of repeat visits, and (3) increasing consumers' expenditures by extending their length of stay. To achieve successful performance, it is essential to make strategic adjustments to take advantage of destination economics.

Destination Development Costs

Destination developments involve a variety of costs that exceed those of traditional malls, particularly those related to public spaces and common areas, facade treatments, tenant fit-outs, and infrastructure.

Developers often face a Catch-22 in their efforts to create a destination project. Citing a lack of comparable projects, financial institutions have been reluctant to accept the potential of destination developments to outperform traditional retail developments. The limited array of existing projects has often been viewed as too novel or too specific to a particular market. In addition, the higher development costs associated with creating a

Strengthening Performance to Achieve Destination Economics

Seven features of destination projects have the potential to increase project performance:

- Multiple anchors whose combined "pull" draws visitors from a broad region
- Programmable venues and broader consumer choices, which encourage repeat visits
- Regionally exclusive offerings to help achieve market dominance
- A variety of consumer itineraries and choices that provide appeal to a broad spectrum of consumers
- Longer visits and increased consumer expenditures per visit
- Entertainment, cultural, and recreational activities that increase productivity during low-demand periods
- A base of overnight and day-trip tourists drawn by a distinctive mix of offerings and by links with established attractions.

Source: MRA International.

distinctive sense of place; the nontraditional tenants required by these projects; the programming requirements; and the use of untested approaches, such as multianchoring, contribute to a perception of compound risks. Financial institutions therefore enforce prerequisite criteria—such as requirements for substantial preleasing of credit tenants—that, while understandable, reduce the project's potential to perform as a regional destination.

The strategic approaches to this dilemma, while limited, include the following four responses:

- Assigning priority to—and funding—those features that are most critical to positioning the project as a destination
- Pretesting rental assumptions with likely tenants—and, ideally, preleasing the majority of the project before financing
- Seeking ways to subsidize development costs
- Partnering with public bodies or strategic partners capable of making investments to benefit the development.

Assigning priority to development features begins with the first cost estimates. Of the many elements that contribute to the project's distinctiveness, the most prominent and memorable are the public spaces that create a unique sense of place. Creating such places within the constraints of the development pro forma may ultimately involve a number of cost-sharing strategies. In developments that involve public sector participation, some of the costs associated with streets, promenades, piazzas, public stairs, and street amenities may be partially defrayed through grants, subsidies, direct investment, or various abatement programs.

Government participation typically focuses on the infrastructure and redevelopment costs that would otherwise render a project commercially infeasible. Parking structures, access improvements, demolition, and site improvements can constitute as much as 40 percent of total development costs. However, given the public nature of a destination development's streets and piazzas, local governments have demonstrated a willingness to help defray these costs. For governments, the decision to invest is tied to both direct benefits—in the form of new sales, property, and income taxes; job creation; and tourist development—and to broader economic development goals, including revitalization and improved public access and amenities. The public spaces in a destination development may operate as commercial common space or as city streets, depending on the particular development. When the Peterson Companies redeveloped the downtown of Silver Spring, Maryland, as a regional centerpoint for dining, shopping, and entertainment, a sense of place was created at the 22-acre site through the preservation of existing buildings and the enhancement of the public environment. Additional funding for the public spaces, provided by the state and county, allowed the creation of larger, more creative public plazas—including landscaping, lighting, fountains, and other features that would not have been possible without public support.

Another approach to cost sharing is to establish design guidelines for tenant facades, signage, and street furniture. Since retail and restaurant tenants in destination developments are interested in strong streetfront identities, the distinctiveness of the project's public spaces can be reinforced through the design and finish of individual stores. Once persuaded of a project's competitive advantages, tenants have demonstrated a willingness to bear such costs. The Caruso Company has developed a number of high-profile lifestyle destinations, including the Commons at Calabasas, in Calabasas, California, in which tenants assumed the majority of the cost for interior and facade improvements.

The retail and restaurant executions sought for destination developments also involve higher levels of investment on part of the tenants—which, in turn, translates into expectations of higher allowances for tenant improvements. Again, recovery of these costs through rental rates and terms is part of the balancing act that a developer must perform. Often, developers will establish a hierarchy of tenant improvement allowances based on the relative significance of various tenants to the development (see the discussion of weighted leases in the next section).

The primary entertainment anchor is often the most challenging tenant. To date, the principal activity generator for all forms of entertainment-enhanced development (outside of Las Vegas and the theme parks) has been a megaplex with 24 to 30 screens and a footprint ranging from 70,000 to 120,000 square feet (which can account for between 15 and 50 percent of GLA). The lease terms for these anchors vary widely by project, tenant allowance, and geographic area, but typically they involve occupancy costs of no more than half of the average cost for retail tenants. Lower rents have led developers to take a number of cost-management steps—principally, to reduce the amount of valuable street-level space given over to this use by locating theaters on the upper levels. As noted earlier, this approach has the added benefit of creating a vertical flow of consumers, which provides the opportunity to lease upper-level spaces to restaurant and retail tenants at better rates. Developers have also worked with exhibitors to create two-level theater operations and, at times, to contain the overall size of theaters.

There is, in addition, a growing concern that megaplexes lack the brand loyalty associated with department stores and are therefore more vulnerable to competitive offerings. Frenetic expansion by exhibitors seeking regional dominance, which was followed by the industry's current financial crisis, has exacerbated these concerns. Nevertheless, with its demonstrated drawing power, the megaplex is considered essential to the success of the majority of destination developments. To date, no other entertainment venue has demonstrated such broad appeal or the ability to generate an equivalent number of annual visits.

Lease Structures in Multianchored Developments

The complexities of this highly customized form of development are reflected in tenant rents and lease terms. Instead of a mix of anchor and infill tenants, the destination development includes a range of tenants, from established icon retailers to new entertainment venues. The greatest leasing challenge with a multianchored project is to properly structure leases to optimize project performance.

One approach, developed by MRA e-Ventures, is to weight leases to achieve a desirable mix of anchors, core tenants, and supportive uses. Weighting involves balancing seven interrelated criteria:

- Location within the project
- Value of the tenancy
- Expectations of tenant performance
- Product life-cycle expectations
- Tenant space requirements
- Regional uniqueness or exclusivity
- Tenant credit.

In its emphasis on leases as the principal source of income, this approach is consistent with that taken in other retail developments. However, weighting leases in a destination development is linked to the unique structure of these projects. For example, the value of spe-

cific locations within a destination development varies significantly from that in retail malls, where anchors, entry courts, and food courts generate a formulaic configuration. In destination developments, the value of tenant location varies according to the following factors:

- Distribution of anchoring venues on both street and upper levels
- Design and location of public spaces
- Location of icon retailers
- Clustering of signature restaurants.

Equally significant is the degree to which performance is optimized through a well-conceived merchandise mix. Thus, the second aspect of weighting involves analyzing the relative value of tenants, which varies according to the competition in the marketplace, the scale of the project, and the demographics and psychographics of the consumer base. For example, in a market saturated with Barnes & Noble and Borders Books & Music stores, the value of a signature bookstore is diminished relative to that of other types of tenants. The bookstore still may be considered an important part of the mix, but it does not contribute significantly to differentiating the project as a destination. The types of tenants selected to draw visitors also vary with lifestyles and buying power in a given region: identical tenant rosters in two locations will yield different tenant values. For the developer, these values form part of the calculus of lease terms, from improvement allowances to location and space allocations.

Another consideration is estimated tenant performance, which relates closely to life-cycle expectations. For example, a "hot" theme restaurant may contribute significantly

A one-of-a-kind presentation sustains a project's distinctiveness. The four-level Discovery Channel Store at the MCI Center, in downtown Washington, D.C., is an example. *Ellerbe Becket/Timothy Hursley*

to project performance during the early years, only to run its course as the development stabilizes. Decisions regarding lease terms and developer participation in tenant allowances require considerable judgment and significant familiarity with the full range of tenant concepts and tenant operating teams.

Space requirements for core tenants have become particularly tricky in configuring destination developments and achieving effective lease-ups. Often, the presentations of icon stores, brand showcases, concept stores, and signature restaurants are ten times as large as those of traditional in-line stores and restaurants. Retail executions of 30,000 to 70,000 square feet and restaurants of 10,000 to

20,000 square feet can present a variety of challenges. While the larger formats assist the developer in reaching preleasing requirements with fewer commitments, creating sufficient "address points" and incorporating multilevel presentations into projects in which high-visibility, streetfront access is a priority requires an unusual level of innovation. The challenges for the developer include positioning icon tenants to enhance the value of secondary locations while simultaneously reinforcing primary zones of activity.

Yet another consideration in weighting tenant value is uniqueness, whether regional exclusivity or one-of-a-kind presentation. In the case of regional exclusivity, a strategic advantage can be gained by attracting a major tenant with either a limited presence or a single location within a market. A variety of brand-name stores and retail showcases are moving in this direction, with rollout plans often based on single stores in priority markets. Nike, for example, limited the rollout of NikeTown to 14 domestic markets. FAO Schwarz has similarly limited its rollout, focusing on flagships designed to serve an entire region. One-of-a-kind presentations can be even more valuable in sustaining a project's distinctiveness. Coca-Cola's showcase in Atlanta; Chicago's 35,000-square-foot American Girl Place; Seattle's REI (Recreation Equipment Incorporated) flagship store; Discovery Channel's flagship store in the MCI Center, in Washington, D.C.; and the Microsoft store in Metreon fall into this category.

Finally, tenant credit is critical to securing financing for a project. Once again, the developer must balance the desire to differentiate the project by securing unique and innovative tenants with the need to ensure that a significant percentage of the leases are secured by strong credit. An aggressive strategy currently being pursued by a number of developers is to mitigate some of the risks of customizing entertainment development by taking on full or partial ownership of entertainment anchors, restaurants, or novel dining venues. Spin-offs of real estate investment trusts represent a new vehicle for such investments.

The Mills Corporation, for example, created a separate entity to identify, facilitate, and invest in new tenant concepts and joint ventures. At Opry Mills, in Nashville, the corporation was able to strengthen the project as a destination by assisting in the financing of unique tenants such as The Gibson Bluegrass Showcase and The Apple Barn, Cider Bar, and General Store. In addition, through a joint venture with the property owner—Gaylord Entertainment Company—the project was linked programmatically and physically to a larger destination that includes icons such as the Grand Ole Opry, the Opryland Hotel, and the General Jackson Paddle Boat.

Risk Profiles of Entertainment-Based Developments

As noted earlier, the developers of destination projects and other entertainment-based developments face a number of challenges in meeting financial investment criteria. These challenges include the novel character of the developments; the customization required to position projects as destinations; the lack of true comparables with relevant performance histories; the additional development costs associated with differentiating the projects; the risks related to entertainment-based anchoring; and concerns over the difficulty of achieving destination status.

To a large extent, the financial sources interested in funding destination projects have a real estate rather than a new-venture orientation and therefore tend to base finan-cial commitments on comparable real estate transactions. Given that the limited number of projects that have achieved destination status are still anomalies—for example, Forum Shops, in Las Vegas, which achieves $1,300-per-square-foot sales—destination economics are understandably held in suspicion. Accordingly, in presenting these projects to potential financers, developers emphasize the features that are most similar to those of recognized retail models and suggest that destination developments follow a retail formula of sorts. The resulting paradox is that while developers have been pressed into creating developments that appear to perform like retail malls, they are struggling to craft destination projects with far more robust performance. These projects are therefore constrained in their quest to achieve destination-level performance. The way out of this dilemma may be found through alternative sources of financing for infrastructure and signature features, through the successful operation of a number of threshold projects, and through the mitigation of several perceived risks. Recently, retail destinations have been integrated into larger, mixed-use developments as a means of recapturing the value-creating and place-making strengths of the mixed-use projects.

Financial institutions' primary concern about destination developments is that they are new and untested, and have been far too reliant on the theater as an anchor. A strategic response to this concern is to focus on a multi-anchor structure, emphasizing the component features that increase performance. Within this mix of activity generators, activity inducers, and activity extenders lies a strong body of proven and demonstrably successful concepts.

While entertainment venues, other than the megaplex, do not have sufficient operating histories to provide demonstrable levels of performance, within the broader matrix of multianchoring the tolerance for risk may be extended.

In the end, the acceptance of more robust performance expectations for destination developments will depend on the existence of an array of successful projects that have achieved these results in a number of markets over time. The next four to five years will be a critical period in which a variety of developments—including CityPlace, Easton Town Center, Hollywood & Highland, Metreon, and Penn's Landing—will establish solid performance records.

Destination developments have considerably greater potential than other forms of retailing to achieve superior performance

levels. As the accompanying sidebar illustrates, there are significant differences in performance expectations for a regional mall and a destination development. Achieving the expected level of performance, however, requires considerable passion, skill, and strategic insight on the part of the development team.

To create the combined pull from entertainment, dining, and retail components that is required to achieve the status of a regional centerpoint requires a deep understanding of consumer segments and of competitive offerings within the market; the ability to secure key tenants (and, often, to push them to create unique executions of their products); and the ability to effectively array anchoring components in a configuration that supports a variety of visitor itineraries. Similarly, using clustered dining to draw a broad spectrum of patrons and to extend the length of stay requires an intimate understanding of how specific restaurants can be effectively combined to increase consumer choices and attract specific visitor segments. Such atten-

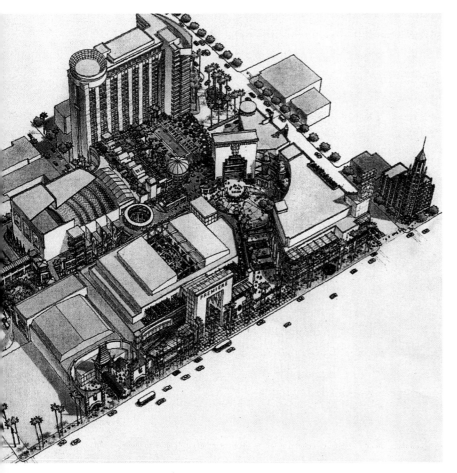

Performance Expectations for a Destination Development and Super-Regional Mall

Performance parameter	Super-regional mall	Destination development
Scale	800,000 to 1.7 million square feet	250,000 to 600,000 square feet
Average sales range per square foot	$225	$500–$700
Top performer's sales per square foot	$450	$1,400
Drawing radius	20 miles	35–40 miles
Repeat visitation	Average of three times per month; penetration of 80–200 percent	Average of two to four times per month; penetration of 100–400 percent
Regional dominance	Achieved through department store anchors, scale, and mix	Achieved through unique-to-region offerings
Multisegment appeal	Limited; visits tend to be focused on shopping trips	Broadened via entertainment and dining offerings
Length of stay	About 1 1/2 hours	About 3 1/2 hours
Demand-period productivity	Distributed across various times of the day and week; affected by season	Concentrated during specific evening and daytime periods; tourist visits and leisure activities improve productivity during low-demand periods
Tourist draw	Limited	Potentially 20–40 percent of visitor base, depending on location

Source: MRA International.

tion to detail begins with the strategic positioning of the destination development, when assessments of the market, demographic and psychographic patterns, competitive offerings, and locational attributes are made. The same level of scrutiny is required in defining the program, the anchoring features, and other project components.

Executing a Destination Development

Successfully defining and executing a development that can perform as a regional destination requires a development team with unique capabilities that often extend beyond those that a single development company has to offer. The most successful developers of destination projects to date have demonstrated an ability to recruit a talented and diverse development team that includes architects, scenographers, branding consultants, leasing agents, and public liaison specialists. The development team must be capable of working successfully with local government and the local community, compelling core tenants to create

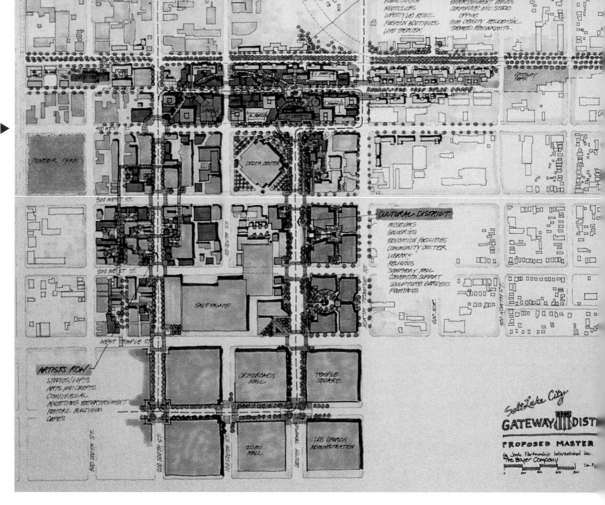

Public sector ▶ **investments in entertainment destinations enhance the performance of cities as visitor centers. The Gateway, in downtown Salt Lake City, is a $375-million mixed-use retail and entertainment destination development that constitutes the first phase of a city-sponsored plan to redevelop 650 acres within its urban core. The project is being developed by The Boyer Company and The Jerde Partnership International, Inc.**
The Jerde Partnership International, Inc.

unique presentations, guiding the planning process toward place making, and creating a satisfying overall guest experience.

Working with the Local Government

The costs associated with executing destination developments typically require the participation of the public sector. Generally speaking, these projects involve infrastructure support—such as improved access, the addition of parking structures, and other enhancements to site capacity. As discussed earlier, public spaces and amenities may also require support from local governments or quasi-public organizations.

Working effectively with local governments involves skills that exceed those required by the public/private ventures of the 1970s and 1980s, which were largely supported by federal programs such as urban development action grants and community development block grants. Funding today relies primarily on local resources and programs such as tax increment financing and community improve-

ment grants, as well as on creative financing instruments (such as sale-leasebacks). Local governments have therefore become far more rigorous in their evaluation and expectations of project investments.

From the local government perspective, returns on investment are judged on the basis of the tax revenues and jobs generated, the public sector's share in project performance, and the potential impact of the development on broader economic development priorities. For a majority of cities, the tourism and leisure industry has risen to the status of an economic generator, equivalent in importance to the service and manufacturing sectors. In large part, the growing importance of the tourism and leisure industry reflects cities' competitive advantage as centers of regional and overnight tourism, which derives largely from their unique sports, cultural, and entertainment offerings. Since the early 1990s, investments in convention centers, performing-arts centers, museums, sports facilities, waterfronts, and parks have been designed to enhance the performance of cities as visitor centers. Within this context, destination developments are also being viewed as important strategic investments.

For the development team, working collaboratively with a local government (often in a development partnership) requires an understanding of public sector goals, capacities, and constraints. Specific areas of collaboration may include incorporating public amenities within the development; accommodating cultural facilities or events; participating in community goal-setting and dialogues; participating in a master-planning effort to integrate the project within a broader development context; structuring development financing to effectively use both public and private investment; and working together over time to achieve destination status for the project.

The principal skill required of the development team in a public/private collaboration is the ability to create and manage a process that effectively deploys the resources of both parties; assigns roles and responsibilities; monitors progress on joint and separate tasks; and supports a working relationship during predevelopment, development, and often operational phases. The greatest challenge often occurs in making the transition from bidding or negotiating for the project (in which the parties are on opposite sides of the table) to collaborating on its execution. A successful partnership requires the best efforts of both parties; nevertheless, the developer's familiarity with project planning and execution may require taking the lead in forging a working relationship.

Master Planning and Urban Development

The context of a destination project is of equal importance to the developer and the local government. From the developer's perspective, supportive activities, amenities, and infrastructure are instrumental to positioning the project as a destination. To the public sector, the destination development is often a means of leveraging cultural and commercial assets near the project or increasing the competitive position of public facilities such as a convention center or sports arena.

To ensure that the goals of both parties are met, the development team often needs to become involved in a master-planning effort that extends well beyond the boundaries of the destination development itself. This has been the case in developments such as CityPlace, Hollywood & Highland, and Penn's Landing.

While regional centers and mixed-use developments also often require developers to get involved in broader master-planning issues, destination developments may require that a far more extensive effort be undertaken to create an integral link between the project and the city's strategic goals as a visitor center.

Community Relations

Closely related to the development team's role in master planning is its role in interacting with residents of surrounding communities. Destination projects can have a significant impact on surrounding areas, attracting more visits per year than the convention and sports facilities of a major city. Community concerns may be centered on traffic and parking, view corridors, impacts on existing businesses, public sector investments, environmental and historic preservation, noise, crime, and a host of other issues.

The development team needs to include professionals who have both broad experience in similar projects that involved community relations, as well as a number of specific skills that range from managing transportation to ensuring security. Like other aspects of the

The guest experience needs to last three to four hours to achieve destination-level financial performance. Penn's Landing, in Philadelphia, Pennsylvania, a waterfront destination project, will offer a high-quality guest experience that will encourage lengthy stays.
Ehrenkrantz, Eckstut & Kuhn Architects

predevelopment process, working with the community requires a series of meetings to identify community concerns and assess means of addressing them; assign priority to issues; provide credible analysis and alternatives for dialogue; and, often, negotiate with community representatives to gain project support. In working with the community, the development team and local government representatives should assume roles that reflect their responsibilities. In some cases the local government will take primary responsibility for working with the community, and the development team's role will be limited to a series of community presentations; in other cases the developer will be the primary point of contact with the community.

When a development serves an outside day-visitor or tourist market, community residents are often concerned about its impact on the local environment and quality of life. However, a well-conceived destination development can make a positive contribution to surrounding neighborhoods as well as boost local real estate values and business performance. A key feature of the development team's interaction with the local community is to identify the potential for community enhancements and to develop a strategy to incorporate them as part of the destination. The Penn's Landing project, for example, involved an extensive series of community meetings: the result was a plan that nearly doubled the scale of public amenities at the existing waterfront facilities.

Collaborating with Core Tenants

Meeting the unique demands of core entertainment, retail, and restaurant tenants in destination developments requires collaborative skills on the part of the development team. However, the scope and focus of the collaboration are different. Working with tenants involves continuous negotiations on venue location, tenant improvements, lease terms, timing, and related issues—all of which need to be effectively managed by the development team while it seeks to achieve mutually successful results. Tenants focus on the performance of their product more than on the project's overall performance.

The development team must reconfigure tenant locations, spatial configurations, and store presentations to satisfy tenant objectives while optimizing the overall potential of the development to perform as a regional destination. The team needs to have a good understanding of core tenants' target markets, presentation concepts, and operations in order to address and balance individual expectations while pushing tenants toward commitments that support the distinctiveness of the project as a whole.

Unlike traditional retail developments, destination projects cannot rely on a leasing plan early in the predevelopment process as the template for tenanting. Changes and adjustments are made well into predevelopment to accommodate customized presentations and to craft a development that optimally addresses the overall guest experience and improves financial performance.

Integrating Entertainment, Retail, and Dining Products

The development team will be involved in integrating entertainment venues within the project and may need to work with core tenants to create customized presentations. TrizecHahn's Hollywood & Highland project required the development team to work closely with Mann Theaters to recreate the majestic theaters of Hollywood's golden age by renovating the historic Chinese Theater and creating the opulent 1,000-seat Babylon Theater.

Similar attention to the details of location, presentation, and operations is also required for core dining and retail tenants. In the end, the development team is responsible for orchestrating a guest experience that is based on the combined effect of a variety of otherwise unrelated entertainment, dining, and retail tenants.

The Guest Experience

Destination development requires skills more akin to those associated with resort development than with typical retail projects. The guest experience must be thought through for each major visitor segment, with a focus on the sequence of activities needed to create a satisfying itinerary. As noted earlier, destination-level performance generally requires that visitors stay three to four hours.

Forum Shops was one of the first projects in which the guest experience took precedence in configuring tenant locations and public spaces. The challenge undertaken by the developers, SPG and the Gordon Company, was to create a centerpoint in a city of extraordinary but often ephemeral attractions. Organized around three public spaces—two enlivened by animatronic statues and special-effects fountains and the third by a re-creation of the sculptural waterworks at Rome's Piazza Navonna—

the Forum creates a sequence of programmed and unprogrammed experiences. The Forum succeeds not only as a must-see attraction but also as the city's centerpoint, attracting both first-time visitors and return guests.

Developments such as CityPlace, Easton Town Center, Hollywood & Highland, and Penn's Landing are also being developed around the guest experience. The challenge for the development team is to recognize the diverse mix of patrons to be accommodated and configure the project to address multiple visitor itineraries.

Brand Development and Identity

The final skill required to execute a destination development is the ability to create a unique identity related to a particular city, town, or context. Given a similar roster of tenants, similar development parameters, and similar performance requirements, this is no mean task. Indeed, the complexities in programming, financing, and executing these projects might favor a more formulaic approach, but the success of a destination project depends in large part on the perception that it offers a unique experience and identity.

The elements involved in creating such an identity include the design of public spaces; the use of architecture and scenographics; the use of back stories or contextual associations; and, at times, the application of brand-development techniques. A variety of developments employ branding consultants to apply the same techniques that are used to create identities for consumer products. Branding has been applied to destination development in the past, as is evident in the strong brand associations consumers have for theme parks and resorts. However, the application of branding to retail environ-

Corporate sponsorships are an increasingly important means of creating value in destination projects. Enron Energy Services, of Houston, agreed to pay the Houston Astros $100 million over 30 years for the right to name the new hometown stadium. *HOK Sport*

ing appeal for the potential visitor by blending the authenticity of a particular place with a sense of fantasy or romance. Cities, like developers, have begun exploring sponsorship as a method of deriving an income stream from the value of enhanced places, facilities, and events.

Toward the Destination Development

The first wave of destination developments faced severe constraints, ranging from the skepticism of financial institutions to the scarcity of high-quality entertainment and leisure venues. The developers who undertook these projects were some of the most skilled and experienced retail developers in the United States. Yet the destination economics that would differentiate these projects and support their broad recognition as a new class of development remains elusive. On the other hand, these developments have had a remarkable and extensive impact. Rarely is a project undertaken today—from a regional mall to a mixed-use development—in which guest experience, facade architecture, and sense of place are not important considerations.

At present there appear to be four directions to the evolution of destination developments. First, there is the continued promise that a number of projects will achieve destination economics, outperforming their traditional competitors several times over. Second, destination developments are demonstrating their value as catalysts in broader mixed-use developments. CityPlace and Easton Town Center, for example, have generated follow-on residential, office, and hotel development. Santa Monica's Third Street Promenade and Denver's LoDo have likewise generated office and residential environments that have brought 24-hour vibrancy to these communities.

ments is new and represents an important skill to be acquired and exercised by the development team.

The potential of branding as a value-creating component of destination projects is demonstrated by corporate sponsors' recent interest in these projects. The Mills Corporation announced the first title sponsorship when its Sugarloaf Mills (25 minutes north of Atlanta) became Discover Mills, following the signing of a ten-year, $10 million agreement with Discover Financial Services. At least a half-dozen similar ventures are currently in development. Industry experience indicates that sponsorship dollars can create an annual revenue stream that strengthens operating performance and can be used to offset a portion of capital costs up front.

Interestingly, the cities that often act as partners in developing destinations have also been turning to branding consultants to define and differentiate themselves as destinations for conventioneers and overnight tourists. These efforts have focused on creat-

Destination developments are often paired with other activity generators, such as sports facilities, to eliminate "dark days" during non-event periods. The proposed Lions Stadium, in downtown Detroit, will be sited next to the new Tigers's baseball stadium, as well as next to 900,000 square feet of entertainment and retail development housed in an old Ford Motor Company warehouse. *KMD*

Third, destination developments appear to offer a new tool for urban revitalization, reinforcing a city's attractiveness as a visitor destination for tourists, conventioneers, and daytrippers. Indeed, cities around the nation have recognized the catalytic effect of these projects. In 2000, over 20 cities—from San Jose, California, to Charlotte, North Carolina—were pursuing destination developments as the linchpin for district-wide redevelopment efforts. Fourth, these projects are increasingly paired with other activity generators, such as sports facilities, to eliminate "dark days" during nonevent periods and create 365-day-a-year activity centers.

Regardless of the various permutations that play out as the first wave of destination developments move into operation, one key factor remains clear. These developments will have an impact on urban real estate that extends far beyond the projects' boundaries. A development vocabulary has been introduced that reapplies lessons from townscapes, city building, resorts, and theme parks to retail and mixed-use environments. Developers who undertake these projects will need considerable skills and perseverance, as well as great passion. There is nothing easy about these projects, but the impact they are likely to have on how we build "place" back into our communities ensures that these developments will be undertakings of lasting cultural significance.

Notes:

1. See the case study on Third Street Promenade in the first edition of this volume.
2. See the case study on Universal CityWalk in the first edition of this volume.
3. See the case study on Mall of America in the first edition of this volume.
4. See the case study on CocoWalk in the first edition of this volume.
5. See the case study on Navy Pier in the first edition of this volume.

Planning and Design

What draws customers to a destination development is as much the desire for personal enjoyment and stimulation as the opportunity to purchase specific goods. Thus, the goal of destination development planning and design should be to create a place that, in addition to including entertainment and retail uses, is in itself entertaining. Successful developments—and the architecture that shapes, defines, and houses them—provide an experience that creates a sense of discovery and excitement, feels continually "new" to the repeat visitor, and does so in a way that is both intimate and energized.

During the years between 1950 and 1990, the design of most shopping environments—particularly large-scale, multilevel shopping malls—became increasingly standardized, while the daily lives of consumers became increasingly varied. Television and films became capable of creating extraordinary special effects; moderately priced leisure travel enabled more people to visit more exotic locations; and restaurant dining not only became more common but more varied and entertaining in its menus, atmosphere, and presentation. These and other changes have created consumers who are attracted to activities and spaces that offer new visual, intellectual, and emotional experiences that surprise, engage, and entertain.

CityPlace, developed in West Palm Beach, Florida, by the Palladium ▶ Company, has been carefully integrated with important downtown anchors, including the Kravis Center for the Performing Arts, West Palm Beach's school for the performing arts, and the city's new convention center.
The Jerde Partnership International, Inc.

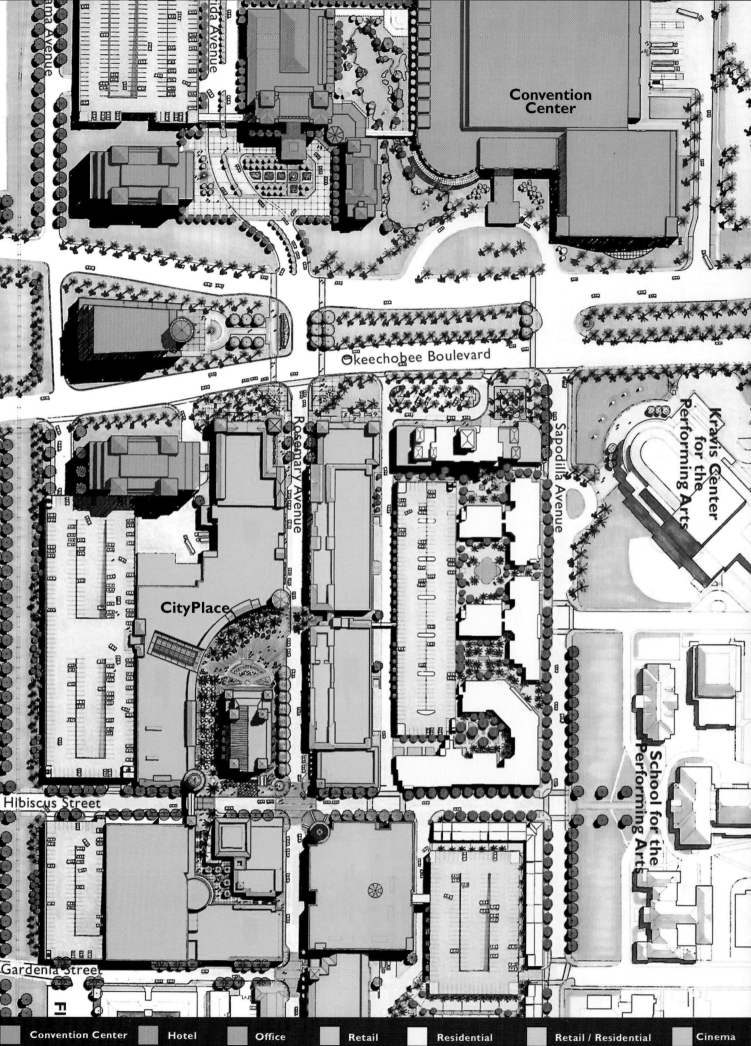

Convention
Center

Florida Avenue

Alabama Avenue

Okeechobee Boulevard

Rosemary Avenue

Sapodilla Avenue

Kravis Center
for the
Performing Arts

CityPlace

School for the
Performing Arts

Hibiscus Street

Gardenia Street

Convention Center   Hotel   Office   Retail   Residential   Retail / Residential   Cinema

▲
Adding the 200,000-square-foot Barra Entertainment Center next to a large regional mall in southern Rio de Janeiro offers an example of an "outparcel" strategy: the new entertainment center extends customers' visitation time by offering customers a wide choice of activities: to dine, see a movie, browse, shop, or perhaps just to see and be seen.
KMD Architects

As Americans have become "plugged in" to a range of electronic devices and media—large-screen televisions, videocassette recorders, digital video disks, Surround Sound audio systems, Nintendos, laptops, cell phones, and the Internet—they have come to expect experiences outside the home to provide an even greater level of stimulation. Through the use of light, color, sound, smell, movement, variety, and detail, destination developments offer spaces designed not so much for circulation as for interaction.

Along with entertaining experiences in entertaining places, consumers want and need broad social contact of a sort that is not available at home. The creation of "people spaces" that are comfortable, safe, and engaging is therefore a critical element in the design of retail entertainment destinations. The food courts in shopping malls were the first attempt to create such places; but destination developments take this effort much further by encouraging contact between people throughout the center.

Another factor influencing the design of destination developments is that people are willing to spend more time there than in traditional retail environments. Instead of buying a few items and rushing home, they come to engage in multiple activities: to dine, to see a movie, or perhaps just to see and be seen. To attract this type of consumer—the recreational shopper who will spend discretionary time at the center, rather than the target shopper who will come and go quickly—destination developments must offer spaces that encourage strolling and browsing while at the same time setting the stage for multiple activities, impulse decision making, and spontaneous interaction.

The architecture of destination developments must respond to a variety of needs. This does not mean that the architecture need be extreme. It does mean that it should have variety, complexity, drama, and texture, and be readily changeable. Visitors should notice new things on repeat visits. The design should encourage visitors to dress up a bit—to be actors on the urban stage. A sense of local heritage and historical continuity can also be important, because the energy of change can be intensified and supported by a distinctive cultural framework.

The basic elements of the tenant mix are discussed in chapter 2; but even if the mix is good, the overall design must provide engaging, attractive public spaces—from alleys to piazzas. Moreover, the energy, excitement, and sense of novelty and adventure must be created within an environment that offers familiarity and security. How and where can this be done? The design strategies depend on the setting.

Design Settings

Destination developments can exist in a number of different settings: within cultural and entertainment districts; shopping malls; large-scale, mixed-use projects; or as stand-

live shop work play

great streets

alone centers. The following sections address the specific planning and design requirements for each of these settings.

Integration of Uses

The mix of experiences and attractions offered by a destination development augments and strengthens surrounding land uses as it attracts more people to the area. Many communities court destination developments to encourage urban revitalization, to generate jobs, and to increase property and sales taxes. Destination developments can be a regional draw, attracting dollars from other communities within a trade area that can extend as far as 30 miles. Large centers often become tourist attractions, drawing out-of-towners who might not otherwise visit.

Because it projects an exciting image of the city to the outside world—an important element in successful urban revitalization—a destination development can become a source of community pride and a focal point for community interaction. This is particularly true of projects sited in the older or historic part of a city, where cultural facilities are concentrated and where the city's unique essence is most powerful.

The integration of public facilities adds local flavor and cultural context to a project, both of which are key to long-term success. Community facilities—such as libraries, university branches, museums, performing-arts venues, sports arenas, and even civic offices—strengthen the mix of activities at destination developments and help differentiate them from similar projects in other cities or at other locations in the metropolitan area. For example, Science City is the centerpiece of a retail entertainment destination in Kansas City's historic Union Station; Metreon is colocated with San Francisco's museum of modern art and its convention center; an extension of the University of California at Los Angeles (UCLA) is housed on the upper levels of Universal CityWalk; the student union at the University of California, San Diego, has a lecture hall that serves as a commercial cinema in the evening; Navy Pier houses Chicago's children's museum and

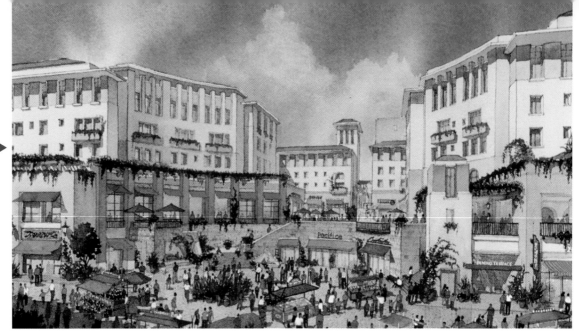

To prevent them ▶ from seeming mall-like, many entertainment destinations are designed with an open-air configuration. Paseo Colorado, in downtown Pasadena, California, in fact replaced an enclosed mall that was torn down as part of a second-generation urban revitalization effort. *TrizecHahn*

Shakespeare Theater; and the MCI Center, a sports arena in Washington, D.C., not only includes a retail entertainment destination within the arena building, but also serves as an anchor for the entire cultural and entertainment district that is emerging between the White House and the Capitol.

Urban Cultural and Entertainment Districts

Destination developments can serve as anchors within larger historic or cultural districts, much as department stores serve as anchors in traditional shopping centers, and they can generate spin-off developments that, over time, can create or revitalize entire districts. The planning, design, and creation of these districts usually involve multiple property owners and some level of public participation. This section describes the creation and evolution of several different types of cultural and entertainment districts in relation to the level of local government involvement required to achieve success.

Limited Government Participation. The success of One Colorado, a small, cineplex-anchored retail entertainment center in the Old Town section of Pasadena, California, demonstrates the vital role that destination developments can play in an urban renewal strategy—and shows how they can some-

times be created with relatively minor government support. One Colorado was privately financed, and municipal aid was limited to bond financing for parking garages that also serve local office buildings. It was not necessary to invoke local government powers to develop the project, and many of the costs of traditional, city-funded redevelopment were avoided.

The design of public spaces within the project was very much a factor in the success of One Colorado—as were the cinemas, convenient parking, and the large floor plates in the remodeled buildings that now accommodate sizeable anchor tenants, including Gordon Biersch and Il Fornaio. But it is the mix of public spaces—from narrow walkways to a generous piazza enlivened by two restaurants—that has made the difference.

Occupying slightly less than a city block, One Colorado has energized an entire neighborhood. In the 12 blocks surrounding the project, the pace of new development has been extraordinary. The project has strengthened the performance of struggling small retail stores on nearby Colorado Boulevard, a wonderfully ample street that is perfect for the annual Rose Bowl Parade but much too wide for the intimate and active scene that shoppers prefer. In addition, a new mixed-use town center, Paseo Colorado, is under construction nearby. It will replace an enclosed mall that failed and provide a new anchor for downtown Pasadena that will strengthen it further as a regional destination for shopping and entertainment.

Moderate Government Participation.
One Colorado is perhaps the most dramatic example of the successful rejuvenation of an urban district with minimal government invention. The equally strong success of Santa Monica's Third Street Promenade, which involved a much higher level of government support, is revealing in a variety of ways. Although the promenade was anchored by a large and prosperous Rouse-owned shopping mall, by the 1980s the merchants of Third Street were not doing well. Recognizing the value of cinemas as a retail draw, in 1986 the city enacted an ordinance limiting all cinema construction to the Third Street district; the street was closed to traffic and relandscaped in 1989. The three new, privately financed cineplexes—and the publicly financed parking garages that were built subsequently—caused an immediate upsurge in business and an influx of new restaurant and retail tenants—which, in turn, created strong demand for offices and hotel rooms in the district. Santa Monica has since become one of Southern California's premier places to shop, visit, and work.

What made Third Street succeed? It was not the closing of the street or its redesigned landscaping; these were relatively minor elements. The city government's clever redevelopment planning, which brought in the cineplex anchors and convenient parking, made the real difference, drawing a supporting cast of entertainment-oriented restaurants and shops.

Why do some entertainment districts succeed and others struggle? The answer seems to depend on whether a city has been able to implement a coordinated public plan to create lively public spaces with strong security, adequate parking, a critical mass of cinemas, and the large floor plates demanded by anchor entertainment tenants.

Larger-Scale Government Participation.
The rejuvenation of New York City's Times Square represents a massive government effort that has transformed, in a remarkably short time, what had become a derelict and dangerous neighborhood into what is once again the world's urban entertainment center. Among the major entertainment anchors on 42nd Street are E-Walk, developed by Tishman Urban Development Corporation on the street's north side at Eighth Avenue; and Forest City Ratner's major cineplex and entertainment center, which is anchored by Madame Tussaud's on the south side.

The rejuvenation of Times Square represents a massive public and private redevelopment that has succeeded, in a remarkably short time, in completely transforming a rundown and dangerous neighborhood into the world's greatest urban entertainment destination. With its dazzling lights and signage, E-Walk, developed by Tishman Urban Development Corporation, is one of the principal anchors on the new 42nd Street.
Tishman Urban Development Corporation

Public/private organizations, including a redevelopment authority and a business improvement district, were established to oversee the transformation. Here are just some of the major public efforts that successfully restored the glitter to Times Square: the city closed the majority of the sex-related businesses and used its powers of condemna-

Coors Field: The Centerpiece of LoDo

In *Cities on the Rebound,* urban commentator William H. Hudnut III observes that downtown sports facilities help "to hold the central core." As focal points of cultural and entertainment districts, they provide a venue for "people to fulfill their gregarious instincts"; and, when bolstered by infrastructure, efficient municipal government, economic development, and revitalized housing, they foster "good cityship."

The 1990s saw a succession of such downtown sports facilities, particularly baseball stadiums, and not just in cities that had major-league teams. Coors Field, in the Lower Downtown (LoDo) district of Denver, is one of the finer examples of a sports facility anchoring a cultural and entertainment district.

Coors Field was completed in 1995, four years after major-league baseball's National League awarded Denver its Colorado Rockies franchise. The ballpark site, once the railroad yard of the Union Pacific Railroad, was selected for its proximity to the LoDo district and to major highways (the interchanges of the north-south I-25 and the east-west I-70 are nearby).

A warehouse and light-industrial district that had historically served the railway and the adjacent downtown business district, LoDo had grown—and then declined—with the fortunes of the railroads. A four-year regeneration was cut short by the national energy crisis in 1983. Then in 1988, LoDo was designated a national historic district, triggering a revitalization that included loft conversions, the restoration of the 100-year-old Oxford Hotel, and an influx of new retail and entertainment businesses.

A true urban ballpark, Coors Field is located right on the street, and one of its greatest strengths is its pedestrian appeal. Although Coors Field seats 50,250, an average capacity among major-league ballparks, the field is sunk about 21 feet below street level, making it feel deceptively small from the street. This design not only allows a smaller street presence but reduces the effects of noise and nighttime lighting on the surrounding neighborhood. The low profile also allows views of the Rocky Mountains and of the Denver skyline from within the stadium.

Unlike suburban ballparks, Coors Field is not surrounded by parking; instead, parking built specifically for the field stretches for 12 blocks along the railroad tracks in a north-easterly direction. Arriving fans park in designated parking areas or in city lots scattered throughout LoDo, then walk or ride shuttle buses to the stadium. As a result, adjacent areas teem with activity on game days, as fans patronize nearby restaurants before and after the game.

In Denver, where water is a super-regional issue, the designer incorporated a 43,000-cubic-foot underground water-storage vault to catch runoff when the seats are washed down after games. Typical ballpark waste (peanut shells and coarse sand, for example) is separated from the water, which is stored and reused for the next stadium washing.

Twelve major-league ballparks, most of them in downtown locations, have opened since 1989. Particularly when the municipality helps to underwrite the cost of the stadium and supporting infrastructure, each new project undergoes increasing scrutiny: as with any real estate development, there is no guarantee that anyone

other than the franchise owner will receive economic benefits. In the case of Coors Field, voters in a six-county area approved a bond issue for a 1 percent sales tax for 20 years, committing $162 million of public money to the project. The owners of the Colorado Rockies added $53 million and received back $15 million for the ballpark naming rights. The sales tax is expected to terminate this year, retiring the debt ten years early.

Has the city, and specifically LoDo, benefited economically? By all accounts it has, even accounting for national and local trends. LoDo had already been on the rise for five years when Coors Field opened in early April 1995, but the introduction of the ballpark accelerated the growth that had already begun, along with changing its character somewhat. Before the opening of Coors Field, sales tax revenue in LoDo had been increasing an average of 22 percent each year; after the ballpark opened, sales tax revenue increased more than 40 percent each year. Twenty-five new restaurants have opened since the field's groundbreaking. Before

▲
Coors Field, in the LoDo (Lower Downtown) district of Denver, offers one of the finest examples of a sports facility anchoring an entertainment district. On game days, the adjacent area teems with activity as fans patronize nearby restaurants before and after the game.
HOK–Sport

the baseball park was built, LoDo had 270 residential units; in 1999, there were 1,302, with another 100 in construction or awaiting permits. In 1990, when Coors Field was still a proposal before the team owners, the chief economist for the Denver Chamber of Commerce projected that the ballpark's economic impact would be $90.5 million: by 1994, the figure had been revised upward to $194.22 million.

The Colorado Rockies led the National League in attendance in the years after the strike-shortened first year of Coors Field, and 3.9 million fans spend their dollars somewhere downtown each year. There were 33 art galleries before the stadium arrived; today there are only 16, indicating that higher rents are driving them out of LoDo. Nevertheless, Coors Field has met Hudnut's test for cultural and entertainment districts: it

has fostered "good cityship" by attracting people to LoDo who would otherwise not have come. ●

Source: David Takesuye, ULI.

Location: Denver, Colorado

Owner/developer: Denver Metropolitan Major League Baseball Stadium District

Size: 1 million square feet (stadium footprint)

Site: 76 acres

Seating capacity: 50,250

Completed: April 1995

Architect: HOK Sports Facilities Group, Kansas City, Missouri

Fashion Island, in Newport Beach, California, has evolved from a traditional mall into a retail entertainment destination with lively outdoor spaces. Visitors enjoy lingering by the fishpond to watch the Japanese koi.
The Jerde Partnership International, Inc.

tion to permit property assembly for redevelopment; granted public subsidies for major projects, starting with Disney's spectacular restoration of the New Amsterdam Theater; undertook public infrastructure improvements, such as the ongoing rebuilding of the massive 42nd Street subway station; passed elaborate new zoning regulations; and created dazzling signage requirements and standards for building design. It is useful to note, however, that on the basis of capital costs per square foot of retail, the New York intervention was much less costly for the city than what many less transitional cities spend to subsidize parking garages for destination developments.

Shopping Malls

The introduction of entertainment can enliven a traditional shopping mall, but it is most effective when the entertainment venues are physically integrated with or connected to the center in a way that creates synergy. The traditional strategy, in use for decades, was to place a few entertainment components—usually cinemas and restaurants—on outpads, either on separate or loosely interlinked sites. Shopping-center developers used this strategy to avoid leasing prime space to tenants—like cinemas—that paid low rent. But this approach fails to bring the cinema customer into the mall itself or the mall customer into the cinema, and it certainly fails to create the synergy that bundled entertainment attractions can.

A second strategy is to use the land adjacent to an existing shopping center to create a complete retail entertainment development—with streets, piazzas, and a mix of tenants—that is functionally connected to the original center and allows pedestrians to move effortlessly from one part to the other. Third Street Promenade, for example, was created adjacent to an enclosed shopping mall, Santa Monica Place, which was reconfigured to encourage customers to move between the two. However, few malls have the amount of land required (ten to 40 acres) for this approach. In some cases, building a parking structure can reclaim the necessary land from surface parking, but this adds a significant cost that may render the project infeasible without financial assistance, such as the public funding at Third Street Promenade.

The third strategy integrates entertainment and entertaining features into the shopping center itself. Fashion Island, in Newport Beach, California, began as a traditional regional mall, but in order to remain competitive with nearby centers, it became more lifestyle oriented and transformed itself into a more entertaining environment. The Beverly Center, in Los Angeles, put cinemas on its third floor, but they were essentially the only entertainment element, and dining choices remained limited. A more extensive and successful version of this strategy was implemented at CocoWalk, in Florida, and at Mall of America, in Minnesota, where the escalator to the third floor has led patrons to a multiplex and a collection of clubs since the late 1980s. Both Mall of America and West Edmonton Mall, in Edmonton, Alberta, have large-scale entertainment attractions in interior atriums that are surrounded by traditional shopping venues. Some of the entertainment attractions at Mall of America are the LEGO Imagination Center, UnderWater World, and Camp Snoopy, an amusement park with a roller coaster; West Edmonton Mall has a wave pool and a submarine. By offering many opportunities to wander and wonder, these places convey a strong sense of vitality: visitors can view others enjoying the entertainment attractions from numerous vantage points on all levels of the shopping center.

The latest examples, which are smaller than these behemoths, include Denver Pavilions, Hollywood & Highland, Metreon, and Paseo Colorado. These shopping centers are carefully integrated with their neighborhoods and rely to some extent on the synergy created by surrounding neighborhoods and attractions. By offering many opportunities to wander and wonder, these places convey a strong sense of vitality: visitors can view others enjoying the entertainment attractions and shopping venues from numerous vantage points on all levels of the shopping center. At each of these developments, the connection to activities and streetscapes beyond the project's edges increases the sense of vitality even more.

A variation of the strategy in which entertainment is integrated into a shopping center involves adding a separate outdoor shopping center, rather than another department store, to serve as a new anchor. In this arrangement, entertainment, lifestyle, and theme-based attractions would lead from the original mall to the opposite end of the outdoor center, where the cinema may be located. An interesting example of this approach is at The Avenue at White Marsh, outside Baltimore, where cinemas; local restaurants; and big-box, lifestyle, and entertainment tenants—all in an outdoor, Main-Street configuration—were added to a successful enclosed mall.

Integrating entertainment into a traditional shopping mall poses several design challenges. Because operating hours for cinemas and other entertainment attractions are often longer than store hours, it may be necessary to provide access to entertainment areas via escalators that can be shut off from the main mall. Care also must be taken that the lines that form at major entertainment venues do not interfere with pedestrian traffic. At the same time, pedestrian links between shopping and entertainment areas must remain easy, open, and visually connected, encouraging natural movement between the two. Finally, to take advantage of the opportunity for synergy, food and beverage services should be readily accessible to entertainment attractions.

Mixed-Use Centers

Entertainment and retail uses can play a vital role in energizing a large mixed-use development and add value to the other land uses. Early examples include New York's Rockefeller Center; Reston Town Center, in suburban Washington, D.C.; and San Francisco's Golden Gateway and Embarcadero Center. Recent examples include the Ayala Center, in Makati, Phillipines (see the case study in chapter 5); the Sony Center, in Berlin, Germany (see the case study in chapter 5); and CityPlace, in West Palm Beach, Florida. Westend Plaza is a mixed-use development proposed for a site in downtown Frankfurt, Germany.

◄ **The plans for Westend Plaza, in downtown Frankfurt, Germany, show how dominant commercial towers can coexist with a retail entertainment village designed on an intimate pedestrian scale.** *Studio 318*
▼

All these projects combine housing, offices, hotel facilities, cinemas, and a variety of retail. The retail entertainment parts of a mixed-use development, even in a dense, high-rise environment, should be designed on an intimate scale, which is not an easy task. Drama, diversity, and attention to detail are critical. In the case of a very large center, some separation between the dominant tower forms—particularly those of office buildings—and the entertainment and retail section allows a "village" to be created on a more intimate scale than is possible when towers, with their large floor plates, are clustered together above the retail component, dominating it with their enormous size.

In all mixed-use developments, vertical integration of uses (that is, offices, residential units, and hotel facilities above the retail and entertainment activities) and horizontal integration of uses (that is, with surrounding neighborhood activities) increase synergistic effects and strengthen the likelihood of long-term project success. At CityPlace, residences have been built above the stores, and clear linkages have been designed to connect the project to the city's major performing-arts center and convention center, both of which are off site. In addition, a public gathering place has been created in front of a restored church that is now used as a performing-arts venue.

Stand-Alone Destination Developments

Development teams are still trying to determine precisely which components, in what combinations, and in what amounts of space are optimal for stand-alone destination developments in different locations and circumstances. Once various types of retail entertainment destinations have established a track record, the guidelines will undoubtedly be clearer. But at this point, only the broadest and most general conclusions can be drawn.

Bluewater

At nearly 2 million square feet, with 320 shops and entertainment facilities, Bluewater is the largest retail and leisure complex in Europe. The project sits on 240 acres of an abandoned chalk quarry, and includes 50 acres of parks and lakes, making it one of the largest parks built in Britain in this century. Bluewater's more than 6,000 seats for catering are nearly double the number at the next-largest center; in the coming year, the total will increase to more than 8,500. In its 12 months of operation, Bluewater has welcomed over 20 million visitors who spent an average of more than £32 per visit (about $48). Sales expectations for the third year—£560 million (about $975 million)—were achieved within the first 12 months.

What makes Bluewater work is the inclusion of over 300,000 square feet of leisure and entertainment, which has extended the stay to more than two and one-half hours (the average stay in the United Kingdom is 45 minutes); increased the frequency of visits; and expanded the radius of the trade area (which extends to two and one-half hours of drive time from the development). Bluewater as a whole enjoys the highest percentage of family visits of any development in Europe, and the leisure facilities have the highest proportion of attendance among men anywhere in Europe.

The inclusion of an extensive civic art program—including epigrams, sculptural panels, and icons at each of the ten gateways into the center, and the largest installation of secular sculpture in 20th-century Britain—has made as much of a contribution to Bluewater's status as a destination as its extraordinary retail offerings have.

Bluewater was developed by Lend Lease Europe, a division of Lend Lease Corporation, of Sydney, Australia. Construction costs were £370 million ($550 million), and the current appraised value of the center is more than £1.25 billion ($1.875 billion). ●

Source: Eric Kuhne, AIA, Eric Kuhne & Associates.

▲
Thanks largely to the extensive use of civic art and the largest collection of secular 20th-century sculpture in the country, the interiors of Bluewater, a regional center in Dartford, England, are characterized by a robust, storytelling quality. *RTKL–UK Ltd.*

The Gateway, in downtown Salt Lake City, Utah, will be a center-point destination that will serve as the central gathering place for the 2002 Winter Olympic Games and as the site for metropolitan civic celebrations. The style and scale will reinforce a sense of heritage and continuity within the strong cultural framework of the city. *The Jerde Partnership International, Inc.*

The maximum size for a destination development has yet to be determined. If Mall of America is one, there is obviously no limit. Even at the smaller end of the scale, however, the trend is toward increasing size, largely because of increases in the standard sizes for cineplexes, restaurants, and retailers.

New-generation theme restaurants, which can occupy between 18,000 and 30,000 square feet, are booming, with an increased emphasis on food quality and service. Entertainment attractions, such as Dave & Buster's and GameWorks, are combining multiple functions—entertainment features plus food and drink operations—that require 60,000 to more than 100,000 square feet of space. Educational, cultural, and civic uses are also increasingly likely to be added to the entertainment mix.

Until recently, cinema complexes with more than 24 screens were being proposed and built in suburban shopping centers as well as in downtown locations, but the spate of bankruptcies in the cinema industry has temporarily halted much of this construction.

The primary question may be how small a destination development can be and still succeed. Judging from the limited number of centers in operation, the minimum size includes 2,500 cinema seats (roughly a 20-plex), 400 restaurant seats, and between 16,000 and 60,000 square feet of general entertainment and retail space. This figure is preliminary and may change over time as more examples become available. Even smaller prototypes are likely to be successful in smaller communities.

Parking ratios are likely to vary widely. In an urban area with existing street and office parking, the ratio may be as low as four per 1,000 square feet of retail space. In isolated suburban projects, particularly those with a large proportion of cinema space, the need may be as high as 17 per 1,000 square feet.

Site Planning

Successful destination developments provide spaces for people to come together to interact with each other and enjoy themselves in ways that have rarely been possible in the United States. Although idealized today, the traditional American "Main Street" was usually so wide, and the retail that opened onto it of such low density, that it fostered relatively little social interaction. The American town square, actually a park, encouraged interaction even less. Successful destination developments, on the other hand, often have spaces and scenes, whether indoor or outdoor, that are similar to those of the ideal small European village, with intricate but active streets and a lively square or piazza whose size, sense of enclosure, and high level of activity developers seek to emulate and improve upon.

Darling Park

Darling Park—Sydney, Australia's, largest waterfront development—has restored the connection between Sydney's downtown and the harbor. Sitting astride six freeways, Darling Park occupies 8.35 acres of the last development parcel in Darling Harbour and offers 1.2 million square feet of facilities, including two 30-story office towers (with provision for a third, 20-story tower), and 110,000 square feet of leisure, retail, catering, and entertainment. A bridge spanning the freeways that were not covered over by the project connects the ground plane of the development with the waterfront.

Built between 1991 and 1999, Darling Park is the largest project Lend Lease Corporation has undertaken in Australia. Construction costs were A$650 million, and the project was 100 percent leased prior to completion.

What makes Darling Park unique in Australia (or the world, for that matter) is that the entire ground plane of the project is accessible to all the residents of Sydney. When the buildings originally on the site were torn down, the new buildings were designed so that all the first-floor spaces would be open to the public. Ten percent of the entire leasable area has been dedicated to civic space, and the terraces, galleries, reception rooms, lobbies, lounges, restaurants, performance spaces, and gardens represent the most comprehensive conversion of tenant space to civic space anywhere in the world. Even though the project sits on the western edge of Sydney's business center, the rents it commands are as high as those for all other Class A office buildings in the central business district—thanks in large part to the development of the leisure, catering, retail, and civic spaces.

▲
Cockle Bay Wharf, the waterfront component of Darling Park, includes 13 of the finest restaurants in Australia, along with two entertainment venues and a small collection of retail shops. *Eric R. Kuhne & Associates*

Cockle Bay Wharf, the waterfront component of Darling Park, includes 13 of the finest restaurants in Australia, along with two entertainment venues and a small collection of retail shops. The roof garden atop the development has three of the top-grossing restaurants in Sydney. The Crescent Garden, the term used to refer collectively to all the public gardens at Darling Park, is the largest corporate garden built for public use anywhere in the Southern Hemisphere. ●

Source: Eric Kuhne, AIA, Eric Kuhne & Associates.

Village Design and Scale

Many destination developments are designed in the style and scale typical of a traditional village. Some, like Third Street Promenade and One Colorado, are largely renovations in which new construction has been designed to fit into the historical context. This strategy is particularly evident at One Colorado, where the one large new building that houses restaurants and cinemas is a close match to the existing red-brick industrial buildings that form most of the streetscape. This technique gives the complex, like a village or city, the appearance of having evolved over time.

The village style reinforces a sense of heritage and continuity within a strong cultural framework that enhances and supports the energy of change. In Universal CityWalk, with its idealized design references to Los

Yerba Buena Center, a cultural and entertainment district in downtown San Francisco, includes Sony's Metreon retail entertainment center, the city's museum of modern art, a convention center, and an extensive park and open-space network. The park, which includes the Martin Luther King Jr. Memorial Waterfall, serves as Yerba Buena's piazza. *Metreon*

Angeles in the 1930s, the design context is recognizable but blended with dramatic and very large scale graphics.

The configuration of the land needed for a stand-alone retail entertainment center is quite flexible, as long as the site will allow for at least 300 feet of pedestrian walkways of various widths and scales to connect the features of the center. The importance of public spaces and their design cannot be overstated: for a destination development to succeed, some form of piazza or town square is essential. In many ways, it is the character and design of retail entertainment centers, even more than the tenant mix, that differentiate them from a traditional shopping mall. The only mall space that even remotely resembles a town square is the food court, and the resemblance is remote. Indoors or outdoors, a piazza provides a place where people can gather to enjoy the passing scene and prolong their stay.

Destination developments function best when their town square is augmented by a variety of pedestrian "streets" for strolling. These can be indoor or outdoor, depending on climate and market preferences. CocoWalk; Easton Town Center, in Columbus, Ohio; the Gateway, in Salt Lake City, Utah; One Colorado; Paso Nicero, in Santa Barbara, California; Reston Town Center, in Reston, Virginia; and Universal CityWalk are some of the best examples of retail entertainment developments with central gathering places and streets for strolling.

In the layout of streets and gathering places, it is important to ensure that the desired mix of large and small tenant spaces can be accommodated without introducing blank walls, inactive spaces, or other gaps in design or activity that would interrupt the continuous stimulus provided by shop windows, marquees, lights, signs, and action. In multilevel retail entertainment projects, each level must be designed so that customers feel visually connected to other parts of the center and are continuously energized by the buzz of other people's activities.

Pedestrian Streets

Ideally, pedestrian streets in retail entertainment projects, whether indoor or outdoor, are rich in detail and used only by pedestrians. Broad avenues and boulevards can indeed be retail successes: the Champs Elysées, in Paris; Fifth Avenue, in New York City; and North Michigan Avenue, in Chicago, are notable examples. But experience at existing retail entertainment developments strongly indicates that for the desired sense of discovery and novelty, the ideal street is one that curves and is 30 to 55 feet wide. In addition, if the street is longer than 200 feet, it should vary in width to avoid visual monotony.

Whether cars should be allowed is a recurring and tricky question. The strategy of closing traditional, relatively wide retail streets to auto traffic, a popular revitalization technique in the 1960s, often met with failure.[1] However, narrow, pedestrian-only streets work well in destination developments when careful attention is given to visual variety and scale, as at The Block at Orange, Universal CityWalk, and Irvine Spectrum Center. At the same time, some very successful new projects, such as

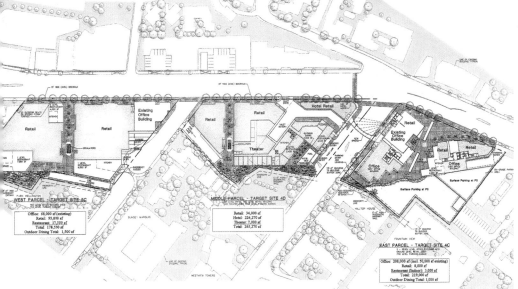

▲
◀ **A pedestrian-oriented hotel, retail, restaurant, theater, and office destination is planned along three blocks of Sunset Boulevard, in West Hollywood, California. The development incorporates existing buildings and seamlessly extends the scale and rhythm of the street by filling in its "missing teeth."** *Gensler*

Valencia Town Center, in Valencia, California, and Easton Town Center, allow automobile traffic: the streets are narrow, curved, or short, to give a sense of enclosure, and must be navigated at low speeds. Although the streets are wide enough to allow for parking, garages and lots accommodate most parking. At Valencia Town Center, parking spaces are angled.

Curved streets seem to enhance pedestrians' experience by increasing their curiosity about what lies beyond the bend. The power of the curve, and of accompanying detail, is exemplified at Desert Passage, at the Aladdin Resort and Casino, in Las Vegas, where the visitor is drawn through the center, along an indoor

pedestrian street, and arrives back at the entrance (or the entrance to the casino) at the end of the visit. The highly detailed environment, which includes individually articulated storefronts and evocative design elements, stimulates the shopper's imagination and creates a sense of intrigue, excitement, and wonder.

The Central Gathering Place

What does the wonderfully evocative word *piazza* mean in relation to a retail entertainment destination? Are there specific techniques for achieving a successful and interactive central gathering place? The answer, perhaps surprisingly, is yes. A KMD research study of the architectural qualities that make

DESERT PASSAGE

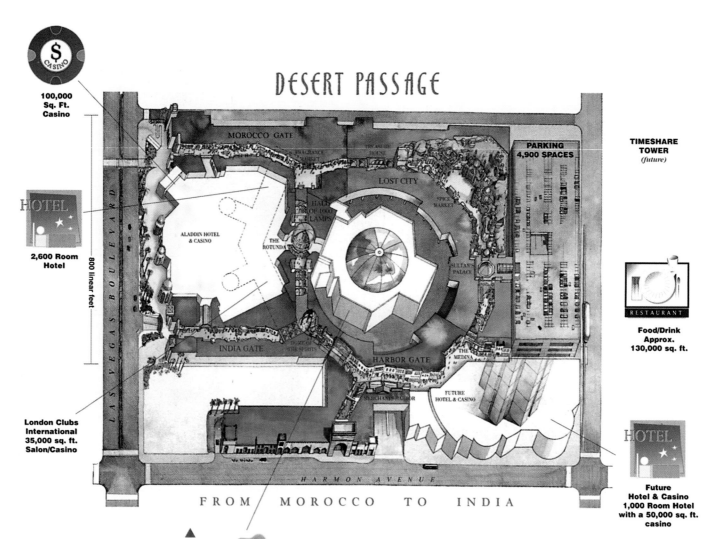

100,000
Sq. Ft.
Casino

2,600 Room
Hotel

800 linear feet

London Clubs
International
35,000 sq. ft.
Salon/Casino

MOROCCO GATE

TREASURE
HOUSE

FRAGRANCE
MARKET

LOST CITY

HALL
OF 1000
LAMPS

SPICE
MARKET

PARKING
4,900 SPACES

TIMESHARE
TOWER
(future)

ALADDIN HOTEL
& CASINO

THE
ROTUNDA

SULTAN'S
PALACE

RESTAURANT

Food/Drink
Approx.
130,000 sq. ft.

INDIA GATE

HARBOR GATE

THE
MEDINA

MERCHANTS HARBOR

FUTURE
HOTEL & CASINO

HARMON AVENUE

FROM MOROCCO TO INDIA

Future
Hotel & Casino
1,000 Room Hotel
with a 50,000 sq. ft.
casino

▲
**Desert Passage, linked to the
Aladdin Resort and Casino, in
Las Vegas, Nevada, employs
curved walkways and varied
setbacks that enhance the
pedestrian's experience by
sparking curiosity about what
lies beyond the bend.**
TrizecHahn

Theatre

7,000 Seat Theater of
the Performing Arts

piazzas work well recommends the following design principles:

- Provide ample public seating in a variety of forms and configurations.

- Provide a clear sense of enclosure, which is particularly important for an outdoor space. Buildings with multistory facades can provide it, but if they are not located on all sides of areas frequented by pedestrians, berms and dense landscaping can substitute.

- Illuminate the space with varied levels of natural and artificial lighting.

- Animate the space with moving water, which provides a focal point, a sense of activity, and soothing background noise.

- Enliven the edges of the space with visible activity, on more than one level if possible.

- Use soft geometric forms. Asymmetrical, irregular, and curving forms seem to increase the chances for successfully animating the gathering place.

- Provide walking surfaces that are varied in level and finish. These variations can be relatively subtle.

- Enliven the space with bright colors and bold graphics.

■ Provide facilities for organized, scheduled entertainment—and, perhaps even more important, for spontaneous interaction among visitors.

Parking and Access

As with any type of retail development, parking must be designed to permit convenient, quick, and safe access. Unless parking is adequate, customers will not return to the center and neighbors will be plagued by overflow cars. Depending on location, configuration, project economics, and local cultural expectations, parking may be provided in surface lots, in structures, or not at all. Universal CityWalk, for example, provides a parking structure, as will Hollywood & Highland; Irvine Spectrum Center provides surface lots and makes extensive use of valet parking. In some dense urban locations—for example, at 42nd Street, in New York City—no parking is provided. Some retail entertainment developments—including Universal CityWalk, Denver Pavilions, and Third Street Promenade—charge parking fees.

Because much of the traffic at retail entertainment projects is generated during evenings and weekends, when residents are at home, increased traffic congestion and the use of residential streets for parking pose potential difficulties. As with other types of commercial development, opposition is less likely if developers are willing to work with the community from the beginning to provide adequate traffic access and parking spaces before problems arise.[2]

The following are general rules for providing parking for destination developments:

■ Choose an appropriate site that does not negatively affect surrounding residential neighborhoods.

The 7th and Collins parking and retail facility, in the heart of the South Beach retail and entertainment district of Miami Beach, features seven exciting retail stores on the ground floor and a four-level, 646-space parking garage above. The exterior is laced with a curved fiberglass trellis that supports irrigated boxes planted with four different varieties of native foliage. The design masks the bulk of the parking garage and creates the illusion that the stores are built into a jungle cliff.

should be articulated and embellished with architectural detail. Retail should be included on the first floor. In addition, the structures should have an open feel; be well lighted, with higher-intensity lighting at and near elevator lobbies; and be well patrolled, so that customers feel secure. With respect to security, above-grade facilities with high visibility into the structure are much more desirable than below-grade facilities. Finally, because they need to be well lighted until the last movie is over and the restaurants are closed, garages should be located away from residential neighborhoods, in order to prevent glare.

Physical Expansion

With the first generation of retail entertainment developments, demand was the great unknown. Nevertheless, the prevailing wisdom—only slightly overstated—was "If we build it, they will come." In fact, in most cases the developers underestimated demand. As a result, within a few years of opening, expansions were planned at Irvine Spectrum Center (Phase II opened in fall 1998), Forum Shops (Phase II opened in fall 1997), and Universal CityWalk (Phase II opened in fall 2000), among others. All three of these centers had allocated space for expansion, and their initial phases were designed in such a way as to make expansion seamless. While not all retail entertainment destinations will be successful enough to justify future expansion, the possibility should be considered during initial project planning.

Designing for expansion must take into account the need for continuity but avoid repeating the same features. New pedestrian streets, for example, should share the variety and interest built into the first phase without creating the feeling that the expansion is either a separate component or a clone.

■ Use siting and landscaping to shield adjacent neighborhoods from parking and potential glare.

■ Direct traffic away from residential neighborhoods by placing entrances and exits on arterials that are wide enough to handle the traffic load.

■ Perhaps most important, provide enough parking spaces so that demand does not spill over into surrounding neighborhoods.

In nonresidential areas, it may be possible to share parking because the timing of demand is different. Offices and college campuses, for example, often require parking during hours that complement the periods of need for retail entertainment centers. In addition, office workers create a built-in customer base for restaurants and entertainment, and students a base for book and record purchases and movies.

If new parking garages are required, they should be attractively designed, since they are often the largest, most bulky, and most visible part of a destination development. Long blank walls should be avoided: instead, facades

Entertaining Iceland

When the Kringlan Mall, in Reykjavik, Iceland, the country's only enclosed shopping center, wanted to expand and add entertainment, conventional thinking was not an option. In this unconventional land, the sun shines at midnight in the summer but barely peeks above the horizon in winter; the landscape is fretted with glaciers and snowy mountains but houses are heated by thermal pools; and the population—the most literate in the world—still believes that elves and trolls wander the countryside.

The initial plan simply involved the addition of two standard mall components— an anchor store and a food court—but the real challenge was how to configure these components as the centerpoint of a retail entertainment development.

The Kringlan shopping center first opened its doors in 1987, anchored by a local supermarket and a general merchandiser. The 310,000-square-foot center prospered from the start by offering a wide variety of retailers and a respite from the elements. A competing shopping center, Borgnar Kringlan, which opened a few years later 50 yards away from Kringlan, was not as fortunate.

Overshadowed by its larger neighbor and unable to carve out a distinguishing niche, it closed in late 1998. Kringlan, meanwhile, which had a waiting list for tenants, was looking to expand. Its owners acquired Borgnar and decided to connect the two shopping centers with a three-level, 100,000-square-foot addition.

Iceland's geographic isolation and small population made it difficult for Kringlan to attract international brand-name stores to anchor the addition. So the owners decided to create their own. They entered a partnership with a local sporting goods store to operate an anchor store featuring outdoor sports equipment and apparel. They named the store "Nanoq," an Icelandic word for polar bear.

The food court would be linked with Nanoq at the pivot point between the two extended mall arcades: Nanoq on the first two floors and the food court on the third. "We saw this as an opportunity to create an urban entertainment center within the mall," said John Cole, the principal in charge of the project for Arrowstreet, Inc. "By linking our two new elements with the

Hard Rock Café Reykjavik, a pub, and a cinema, which were at the ends of the existing malls, we could create a critical mass of entertainment. The synergy would bring traffic for new in-line stores and expand the mall's operating hours."

The challenge, Cole explained, was to break the elements out of their boxes, both physically and imagina-

▲
The developers of Kringlan Mall entered into a partnership with a local store, Nanoq, to operate a lifestyle-oriented anchor featuring outdoor sports equipment and apparel.

tively. One vehicle for this imaginative flight was a three-story basalt climbing structure. Rising majestically between escalators in the anchor court outside the entrance to Nanoq, the column captures the eye

and vertically unifies the three levels. Nanoq staffers who are professional climbers supervise children and adventurous adults who want to climb the stalagmite, which simulates local rock formations. Hundreds of shoppers regularly line the mall's second-level balconies or peer out from tables in the third-level food court to watch climbers strug-

gle to the top. "Everybody wins," said Cole. "By placing the climbing rock into the arcade, Nanoq gets valuable visibility, the mall gets a revenue-producing common

Continued ▶

area (a modest fee is charged to climb the rock), and the food court gets more traffic."

Arrowstreet designer David Schowalter, who earlier in his career developed habitability and space requirements for the National Aeronautics and Space Administration, took on the task of creating a seamless theme-and-merchandising design for Nanoq that would include a logo, graphics, and compelling interiors to complement the store's sports-oriented products. "I brought to the design images of Iceland's rocks, and rivers, and glaciers, and lava fields. And most of all there is the Iceland sky, a color blue you never see anywhere else," Schowalter explained. Schowalter was also captivated by artifacts of the country's social history: turf huts, rusting water towers, and colorful building facades. He decided that the design for Nanoq would combine the physical and the cultural, creating a veritable museum of Iceland's natural and social history.

After pausing at the climbing column, shoppers enter the store and follow a simulated riverbed made of textured glass and holographic images and banked by replicas of smooth washed stones. The

river meanders purposefully from department to department, serving as a guide for shoppers. It flows past abstract turf huts with board-and-batten walls and peaked wooden roof beams bolted in place. It runs past a rusted water tower that hides a modern elevator, past a rope bridge and a salmon-fishing lodge. Overlooking the river is the mezzanine floor, with a huge rock fireplace, lounge chairs, and a library. Throughout the store are stuffed birds and animals, including a ten-foot-tall polar bear positioned as the store's official greeter. Above the merchandising line, the walls and ceiling are painted blue, "the same shade as the Icelandic sky on a summer day," said Schowalter. Also on the walls are pictures of people in robust health engaged in outdoor activities, using equipment and dressed in clothes that are sold in the store. "People reacted very positively to the design, and our merchandising approach," said Thorbjorn Stefansson, chief executive officer (CEO) of Icelandic Outdoors, the company that manages Nanoq. The unique store has become

a destination: 110,000 people have visited the store each week since it opened, and sales are running 15 percent ahead of plan.

The cluster of restaurants and fast-food operators is so distinctive that it had to be given a unique name: Starlight Square. "Calling it a food court just doesn't do it justice," Cole insisted. The design uses the *torg* as a model. "*Torgs* are outdoor community spaces with a lot of activities going on. They have great associations for Icelanders because the weather only allows them to be outdoors for a brief period each year," explained Patricia Cornelison, Arrowstreet's designer for the food hall. "We thought it would be a good idea to bring a *torg* indoors where people could gather year-round. We wanted to evoke the good associations people have with that environment. We made it look like a town square."

In most U.S. malls, the fronts of fast-food restaurants are completely open, but in Kringlan, says Cornelison, "we put each tenant in its own building." The facades of the restaurants resemble historic Icelandic houses, made of brightly colored corrugated

metal and trimmed with intricately carved wood. The tenant mix is also unusual. Half are international fast-food brands—including a McDonald's whose volume is tracking at $6,000 per square foot, ten times the chain's average—and the other half are local vendors.

Among the tenants are two full-service restaurants that attract diners beyond normal mall hours. "These are two elegant, sit-down restaurants, not something you'd see in [most] U.S. malls," said Cole. "But because of Iceland's small population, the restaurants can't be overspecialized. They transform themselves during each day from a coffee shop, to a luncheon bistro, to a white-tablecloth restaurant serving Icelandic delicacies such as reindeer, puffin, and whale."

In conjunction with the Hard Rock Café, a pub, a cinema, and the adjacent city theater, the restaurants give Kringlan an evening entertainment district under one roof that can successfully compete with Reykjavik's downtown nightlife. "The idea is to create a place to be as well as a place

▲
A three-story basalt climbing structure rises majestically between escalators in the shopping center's anchor court. Nanoq staffers who are professional climbers supervise customers who want to climb it.

to buy; a place where people are informed and entertained; a place where they will go without anything particular in mind because they know something will be going on," said Cole. "We set the stage for selling."

"Before, most of our restaurants would close at 4 P.M. on Saturdays," explained Ragnar Gudmundsson, CEO of Kringlan Holding Company, the mall developer. "But now with the restaurants, movies, and the night club, Kringlan has become an evening destination."

A magnificent ceiling deftly unifies and completes the outdoor effect of this indoor *torg/* food hall. In Shakespeare's words, it is a "most excellent canopy; a majestical roof fretted with golden fire." The ceiling is part daytime sky, part nighttime sky. The nighttime sky represents, in fine detail, the northern lights and the star clusters of the Northern Hemisphere; at the center is a spectacular sun. The daytime sky glows brightly and is full of scattered *trompe l'oeil* clouds. Day and night, the fiber-optic lighting is programmed to continuously change color. Sharply angled over the seating area is an oval skylight, which is surrounded by columns in the form of stylized trees. "Whatever time it really is, however unpleasant the weather might really be, in the food *torg* it is a clear summer night," said Cornelison. Like Nanoq's climbing column, the ceiling spills out into the mall arcade to heighten the approaching customers' sense of anticipa-

tion. It is also visible from the exterior through a canted curtain wall that fronts on a public park.

Finally, like a *torg,* Starlight Square has a central space for community performances. Piano recitals and children's programs are frequent fare. "From the beginning, working on this project has been a unique experience," said Cole. "We had to combine traditional mall patterns with contemporary entertainment concepts in a way that appealed to the sensibilities of Icelanders and was respectful of the indigenous architecture."

Gudmundsson says that judging by pedestrian surveys, the design has struck a chord with Icelanders. "With about 40 percent of the country's population coming here each week, it was important to have a design that would bring people back again and again. They feel comfortable here, and they see something new each time they come." ●

Source: James Mira.

Drama, diversity, ▶ and detail should be the guiding principles of entertainment destination architecture, as at Hollywood & Highland, in Hollywood, California. The Grand Stair is shown. *Ehrenkrantz Eckstut & Kuhn Architects*

Architecture

No matter what the setting, the "three Ds"—drama, diversity, and detail—should be the guiding principles of the overall architecture and design of a retail entertainment destination. The creative use and interpretation of these three elements will be key factors in the project's long-term success. Like the facades of a classic shopping street that has evolved over the years, the architecture, signage, and shop windows should be lively, diverse, and visually appealing. The interior layout, finish, and decor of the retail, entertainment, and dining facilities should be similarly distinctive; ideally, they should seem to have been built separately over time.

In the usual planned retail environment, detail is often suppressed in the interests of both economy and uniformity. In a destination development, in contrast, the goal is to create an environment that is more varied and richer in nuance than a typical shopping center. The design of storefronts offers a tremendous opportunity for the creative use of detail. Graphics, landscaping, lighting, and merchandise presentation also contribute significantly to the overall impact of the design. Ideally, facades will be at least 25 feet high to give definition and a sense of enclosure to the pedestrian walkways.

When a destination development is well designed, the shopper becomes an active participant—both an actor in the scene and a consumer who spends time and money enjoying the attractions provided. Active participants want distinct and varied experiences, and they want to wander safely through a friendly environment; at well-designed centers, they can do both.

At a retail entertainment center such as Universal CityWalk, the average income per square foot is reported to be in the range of $1,000 per year—roughly four times that of

The Printworks

The Printworks, an $80 million, 500,000-square-foot urban entertainment development on the site of a former newspaper headquarters, opened in spring 2000 in the heart of downtown Manchester, England. The project was developed by Richardson Developments, a firm based in Birmingham, United Kingdom, and designed by RTKL's entertainment design studio, ID8.

"The Printworks is a focal point of Manchester Millennium's plan to redevelop the city center following the significant damage that occurred in the June 1996 bombing," said David Gester, RTKL associate vice president and project architect for The Printworks. "We are naturally preserving the impressive existing stone facade of the former Mirror Group Newspapers headquarters. The interiors are designed as a streetscape that merges the historic aspects of Manchester with urban cues drawn from movies and actual places to form a Manchester 'street' theater. Planning constraints in England are very strict, but creating a 'street' within the building allows us to blend the visual impact of 21st-century high-energy entertainment with the historic."

Fronting on Exchange Square, the new civic heart of Manchester, The Printworks is designed to be a 24-hour destination offering a wealth of diverse entertainment options. The four-level project encompasses a 110,000-square-foot, 20-screen UCI Cinema with 4,500 seats and a 3-D IMAX theater as well as 250,000 square feet of additional activities—a family entertainment center; a health club; and a variety of restaurants, bars, night

clubs, and specialty retailers. The project also includes a 1,000-space car park and a transport interchange.

The Printworks theme is based on early-20th-century industrial warehouse architecture, updated for modern consumers. The interior spaces are designed with the strolling pedestrian in mind. Restaurants take over public space, luring visitors inside by spilling over onto the covered internal "street." Mezzanines and balconies afford visitors a top-to-bottom view of what is being called the "Entertainment District of Manchester."

To capture the essence of Manchester's heritage and provide the city's residents with a sense of familiarity—and to provide retailers with the opportunity to develop unique

◀ **Printworks was developed on the site of a former newspaper headquarters in downtown Manchester, England.**

interiors—the storefronts and spaces combine traditional and modern materials. Significant floor-to-floor heights enable tenants to develop mezzanines within storefronts. And, in the fashion of the traditional High Street, every unit is directly accessible from the "street." In response to the physical requirements of modern, leisure-oriented tenants, many of the larger units allow internal circulation on three levels. To encourage pedestrian traffic, The Printworks has three entrances, promoting the "permeable city" concept at the heart of Manchester's urban plan. ●

Source: The Hoyt Organization.

a traditional shopping center. Nevertheless, the shopping objectives of visitors to such centers are usually only vaguely defined. For instance, most of the cinema patrons have selected neither a restaurant nor a particular movie starting time before they go. It is a tribute to the attractiveness and special qualities of destination developments that guests visit, planning to spend more than two hours, confident that they will find a film, food, merchandise, people, and events that will make the outing pleasurable.

Styles

Architectural styles at retail entertainment developments vary widely. Irvine Spectrum Center is Mediterranean; University CityWalk is a pastiche of 20th-century Los Angeles icons and oversized graphics and symbols. At Denver Pavilions, along the 16th Street Mall

At Denver Pavilions, along downtown Denver's 16th Street Mall, the architectural styles vary from building to building and incorporate contemporary as well as neotraditional forms. The overall effect is of a destination that has evolved over time and that blends seamlessly into the urban context. *Timothy Hursley*

in downtown Denver, the architectural styles vary from building to building and incorporate contemporary as well as neotraditional forms. The overall effect is of a destination that has evolved over time and that blends seamlessly into the urban context.

Landmarking

Landmarking—that is, identifying a destination development so that it is visible and identifiable from a distance—is very useful. A strong entrance, dramatized by towers or other prominent architectural features and by special lighting and graphics, heightens the attraction and beckons the customer. Most centers have multiple entrances: in an urban setting, from surrounding streets and perhaps from a transit station; in a suburban setting, from parking lots and garages. Ideally, all of these entrances should share a definite character, provided by varied architecture or graphics, to capture the attention, the imagination, and the heart of the consumer. Successful landmarking requires more than just making the center conspicuous: it requires integrating

the building and architectural components, visual themes, and design elements in a way that is fresh and new.

It is especially important to avoid the bleak, blank look that characterizes the exteriors of too many shopping centers. Instead, the center should offer enticing facades both to the surrounding parking lots and to the streets. And regularly spaced openings, enlivened by varied storefronts and signature graphics, should lead from the main pedestrian passage to the parking area.

Horizontal versus Vertical Configuration

Height and mass certainly help landmarking and can contribute to a feeling of enclosure. In suburban settings, the retail entertainment components of destination developments are generally limited to one or two stories because project economics do not justify a higher retail density. In some circumstances, however, housing or offices above retail may be viable, creating the opportunity for greater visual variety and sense of enclosure. In a North American urban setting and in any setting in most other parts of the world, even retail-only shopping centers usually have multiple stories. Regardless of the number of floors, the project's features should be revealed gradually as the consumer moves through the center, and facades should be high enough to provide room for ample detail and enhance the sense of enclosure created by streets, piazzas, and other public spaces. False fronts are one option, but real second floors are preferable.

Because of their height, cinemas—especially modern ones, with stadium seating—create a second-floor facade, and can create an even higher facade if they are positioned on top of a parking structure or some other use (which

The dramatic, contemporary, glass-and-steel canopy entrance to Westend City Center, in Budapest, Hungary, pays homage to the adjacent Budapest train station, which was designed by Gustav Eiffel, of Eiffel Tower fame.
TriGránit Development Corporation

is an emerging trend). However, because cinema exteriors tend to be blank and boxlike, developers must take extra care to effectively disguise their upper level by arranging active uses around them.

Large-scale entertainment restaurants and retailers such as bookstores sometimes occupy two floors. When upper-level retail is not workable, nonretail upper-story uses that complement retail and entertainment uses can contribute to both rental income and the level of activity. For example, cinemas and some nightclubs may be willing to locate on upper floors, and a modest demand often exists for upper-floor retail services such as insurance and travel agencies. A few centers are currently marketing upper-floor space for

outpatient medical facilities—a particularly logical choice since the hours of parking demand for medical facilities complement those of retail establishments. Finally, educational institutions—UCLA at Universal CityWalk, for example—are another highly desirable second-floor tenant, as are offices: Third Street Promenade has become a hot office location.

Stairs should be wide, inviting, and attractive; they should not give the impression of being "too much work" to use, and they should arouse visitors' curiosity about what lies around the bend. Stairs can be designed as a modern sculpture, for visitors to climb on, or to give descending guests the sense that they are making a grand entrance. The staircase at Two Rodeo Center includes a fountain and is designed so that the user turns at each landing, which is only six feet higher than the previous one and is the only one that can be seen by the user. Alternatives to stairs, including escalators, elevators, or ramps, still need to be provided to upper levels.

Enclosed versus Open Design

Many stand-alone retail entertainment developments in warm climates, such as Florida and California, are designed in an open-air configuration. Developers in these areas feel that enclosure is unnecessary, would make the centers seem too mall-like, and involve an unnecessary expense. In climates with a wider variation in the seasons, however, many retail entertainment developments and entertainment components of shopping centers, such as Forum Shops and Mall of America, are designed as enclosed spaces. An exception is Reston Town Center's open-air retail and entertainment space, which has proven to be a popular attraction even in winter.

Since the basic geometry of public spaces in retail entertainment projects is apt to be less regular than that of the usual linear shopping

mall, designing an enclosure is a bit more complex. To provide the necessary spacious feel, the ceiling should be at least 20 feet above the basic walking surface, and it should be at least 20 percent glazed to allow natural lighting to infuse the space. In addition, any interior roof lines longer than 100 feet should vary in design. At Ontario Mills, for example, the roof design is dramatically altered every 150 feet.

Graphics and Signage

Although graphics and signage are valuable marketing tools and add pizzazz to the visual scene, they must be designed with caution: there is some question as to how much pizzazz a repeat customer—usually the main source of demand—will tolerate. An informal survey taken by KMD indicates that for most centers, the use of rich architectural detail and the limited use of dramatic graphics may be the optimal solution. In specialized locations that rely primarily on tourists rather than repeat customers, such as 42nd Street and Times Square, in New York City, signage and graphics will play a more prominent role.

Billboard Architecture

A percentage of the building facades on New York's 42nd Street are now required by ordinance to be masked by massive signage in the tradition of "the Great White Way." Although extreme signage is compelling, this level of "billboard architecture" is designed to suit a very special case, a special tradition, and a special market. Undoubtedly, billboard architecture will be used as an important design element in a few other specialized urban locations, such as Hollywood Boulevard or the Las Vegas strip, but it seems unlikely to make an appearance in most retail entertainment developments, except perhaps in a scaled-down version in centers that cater primarily to tourists. It will be interesting to see if The Block at Orange, a retail entertainment destination in Southern California that actually includes a great many billboards, maintains its freshness several years from now.

Lighting

Exterior and interior lighting is a vital element in design, both to serve users of the center and to create a recognizable identity. The intensity of the lighting should reflect a hierarchy of importance, with the brightest lights identifying focal points. These include project entrances, central circulation areas, water features, major landscape elements, and significant architectural elements, such as those that form the boundaries of the open spaces. The overall intensity of lighting should be secondary to that defining the architectural surfaces that form the boundaries of the open spaces.

Security

A feeling of personal security is critical to the success of a destination development, and visibility—especially of other people—is the most important factor in establishing a sense of security. No matter how well lighted the development is or how many security moni-

The Hibiscus Stairs at CityPlace are wide, inviting and attractive— and, by making visitors wonder what lies around the bend at the top, they succeed in drawing guests to the second level. *C. J. Walker*

The inspiration for the graphics and lighting at Hollywood & Highland are derived from Hollywood glamour and tradition.
Sussman/Prejza & Company, Inc.

tors are provided, visitors need to feel that they are visible to others and that they can see clearly into all parts of any space where they might venture. It may be tempting to create culs-de-sac and small, intimate, or out-of-the-way spaces, but the hazards of doing so are clear. Byways and pathways that will get little use should be avoided not only for safety reasons but also because they do not add to the social energy and interaction that are so vital to all retail entertainment destinations.

Activity Generators

Architecture and design set the stage, but activity generators are required to animate it. As at any commercial development, the principal sources of activity are the customers and the tenants—in the case of destination developments, theme-based retailers, entertainment restaurants, and specialized entertainment attractions. The two previous chapters described which kinds of facilities are most likely to generate activity and how those activities can be bundled to create a synergistic mix. But there are other generators that set retail entertainment destinations apart from traditional retail centers, and that may spell the difference between project success and failure. These include interactive features and events, and cinemas.

Drama, diversity, and detail set the stage for success, but to attract the repeat shopper a retail entertainment project should also provide a range of new experiences and activities with each visit. The design should incorporate a carefully crafted variety of zones, themes, and environments that together transform each shopping trip into a different experience. Visits to a typical destination development are generally defined by seven factors—food, interactive design features, events, retail-related education, films, merchandise, and the ever-changing assortment of people. Continuous changes in each element provide the new experiences that

▲
At the Power Plant, in Baltimore, Maryland, the ESPN Zone provides food, interactive design features, merchandise, and an ever-changing assortment of people.

visitors are looking for: menus change, new features are added, merchandise varies with the season, new events are programmed regularly, new educational experiences are offered, new films are shown, and different people are present on each visit.

Food

Food is one of the greatest activators of retail environments. But at a destination development, the one-dimensional experience of the food court at a typical shopping mall is supplanted by the distinct experiences afforded by a variety of restaurants providing a range of cuisines, often in a theme-based environment. It is absolutely critical that the design of the dining facilities feature strong interaction between the interior and the street and sidewalk, both to draw patrons inside and to activate the public spaces.

Interactive Design Features

Interactive features are a great means of generating activity. The programmable color wall and column at Sony Theaters at Metreon offer a dazzling and constantly changing light show. The computer-controlled fountain at Universal CityWalk is so popular that it has become the basis for a successful concession—photographs taken of both children and adults cavorting in the fountain's irregularly patterned spurts of water.

At the Sony Theaters at Metreon, in San Francisco, the IMAX lobby features a color wall and column made of perforated metals and cold cathode that can be programmed to display different patterns of moving light at set times. *Rockwell Group/Paul Warchol*

Interactive stores and storefronts are a second major activity generator. Window displays need to be intriguing, colorful, educational, whimsical, provocative, and constantly changing, and store interiors must be visible so that customers can browse before entering. Once inside, customers should be greeted by a dramatic environment that presents a strong theme and point of view through merchandise displays, shopping spaces, materials, and interior finishes. Where possible, the interior should incorporate multilevel spaces with intriguing places to explore. The variety and presentation of merchandise should provide an ever-changing visual display. The optimal tenant mix includes local, specialized merchants who sell different and even exotic products as well as the national chains that offer the predictable but nevertheless up-to-the-minute, high-quality goods that have become staples of modern life.

Events

Events constitute the third major activity generator. Seasonal holidays—especially Christmas, but increasingly others, such as Halloween—offer seemingly endless opportunities to create

tie-ins through costuming, displays, ongoing activities, and scheduled events. Events and promotions based on local traditions and cultural attractions are even better because they are, by definition, different from those in other cities. Joint promotions with local performing-arts groups and temporary museum shows can also be a great source of events at retail entertainment centers.

Small-scale activities and events can take place in niches along the pedestrian streets. Mid-sized events—such as festivals, fairs, and outdoor concerts—can be held in the piazza. If possible, spaces large enough for a crowd of 1,000 people should be provided for grander occasions. However, providing this amount of space in the primary public areas may make them oversized in relation to day-to-day use. One possibility is to use adjacent open space, such as a parking lot, provided with special lighting and sound facilities.

While some special events can be costly, the cost of others is negligible. At Universal CityWalk, watching colorfully clad waiters and vendors on the street or gawking at a radio announcer stationed outdoors are free activities. At New York City's Rockefeller Center, there is no charge to use the skating rink or to watch the television shows—such as the *Today Show*—being filmed live every day at the center.

Retail-Related Education

Ours is an information-based society, and learning is an important part of people's lives; it also can be an activity generator in a destination development. Teaching customers about the hottest fashion trends, offering hands-on demonstrations of interactive computer techniques, hosting bookstore discussion groups on a best-selling author, offering

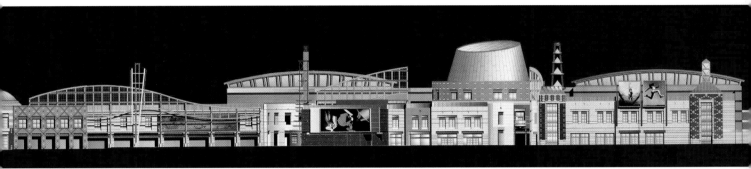

sewing lessons at a fabric store, and offering evening photography classes at a camera shop are all good examples of how education is being used to stimulate retail activity and make it more entertaining.

Whether an interactive display on the roots of jazz will translate into immediate sales of jazz compact disks is debatable, but the fact is that people are interested in gaining knowledge, and they will remember where they gained it: on their trip to the center. When customers are entertained and educated, they are more likely to linger and more likely to come back—and their interest and appreciation may well be sufficiently piqued to provoke a sale: not a bad deal!

Films

Cinemas are blessed because Hollywood pumps out more than 200 films a year, keeping movie houses continuously supplied with new "software." Because there is always something new, there is always a reason to return to a retail entertainment center.

Locating a cinema within a retail entertainment development has become an important issue as the number of screens and the use of stadium seating have increased the height and bulk of cinema buildings. The problem is even more complicated when a special screen, such as an IMAX or Iwerks format, is part of the project. Generally, cinemas should not be freestanding because of

their bulk and the desirability of integrating them with other activities in the center. Except for their entrances and marquees, they should be hidden behind other active uses; otherwise their size and the blankness of their walls can be overwhelming—and visually deadening.

As noted earlier, cinemas can often be successfully placed on upper levels: they are such a powerful draw that patrons will not hesitate to go to the top of the center to see a movie, then filter down to the lower levels afterward, stopping at the stores and restaurants along the way. This overflow activity may justify the higher construction and operating costs of putting cinemas on the upper levels, where other uses may not be appropriate.

In all cases, the relationship of the cinema entrance to the town square or main pedestrian street is critical. The cinema lobby should be designed to enhance the public place but not to dominate it visually.

Merchandise

Merchandise in retail entertainment destinations is sold not only in stores but also in the theme restaurants and entertainment attractions described in detail in chapter 2. Because most of the merchandise represents discretionary purchases, such as brand-name products, impulse goods, and other specialty items, merchandise displays should create

▲
Learning is an important part of people's lives. Star City, in Birmingham, England, located on the site of an old power plant, uses the potent mix of industry and leisure to offer educational, interactive, and experiential places and uses in an innovative environment. *The Jerde Partnership International, Inc.*

Designing Cinemas in South America

The continuing excitement over South American entertainment development is spurred by the fact that most countries are "underscreened," and cinemas can therefore serve as strong anchor attractions. For example, in 1998, Chile had only one screen per 150,000 people, compared with one screen per 9,000 in the United States. It is anticipated that by 2002, Chile and neighboring Argentina will be in the one-per-30,000 range. Most of these new screens will be associated with cinemas in retail environments such as malls and power centers.

South American consumers are enthusiastically embracing new entertainment opportunities. Retail developments in urban areas are incorporating cinemas and other entertainment components into their projects at a rapid rate. The current development trend focuses on dense and complex urban infill sites, which are made up of a variety of small adjacent sites and a mix of nonretail uses.

Such locations pose substantial challenges. According to Harold Blank, of Hoyts Cinemas Corporation, "With the hefty land costs and limited space availability, we are facing more vertical theaters" in entertainment complexes, which require auditoriums to be stacked one upon the other, as at the Patio Olmos Mall, in Cordoba, Argentina. The site resulted from the acquisition of two perpendicular ten-meter-wide parcels. At Patio Olmos, three stories of theaters arranged in a T-shaped plan are attached to a shopping center.

Another example is the San Agustin Cinema, located in the center of Santiago, Chile's, premier retail district. Ten screens were finessed into a small basement space filled with columns and sheer walls supporting a 12-story tower and a 400-year-old church above. To better integrate the theater into the retail context, two entrances from a street-level plaza were incorporated into the lobby of the subterranean cinema.

As in the United States, the most significant challenges in developing retail entertainment centers with multiplexes include parking, theater planning, and visibility. These issues are amplified in South America. Available parking is scarce in South American city centers, so while many projects are "going up," with stacked theaters, there also is a need to "go down," with stacked parking levels—at substantial cost.

Commenting on the difference between retail and cinema development in the United States and South America, Blank points out, "The difference is in the retail end of it. You don't see a lot of big anchor stores, just a lot of little shops." In the United States, cinemas are often considered an additional anchor; in South America, however, a cinema is usually the only anchor and is therefore a welcome addition to retail developments.

At present, moviegoing in South America is a much more formal event than in the United States, and can more accurately be compared to an evening at the opera or ballet for Americans. This characteristic affects construction costs because the South American public has higher expectations for materials and finishes in cinemas. For example, the Hoyts Cine 12 at Mercado de Abasto, in Buenos Aires, features high-tech, stainless-steel siding and a warm, wood-paneled interior, rather than the artificial stucco and drywall common to the U.S. market. As in the United States, going to the movies can generate an opportunity for synergy with dining out. At Showcenter, in Buenos Aires, for example, the cinema shares an enclosed plaza with restaurants and other entertainment venues.

In South America, zoning and building codes vary widely from country to country and often from city to city within a country. Many codes are quite old and written in a way that leaves them open to interpretation by local officials, requiring a great deal more negotiating with municipal authorities throughout the planning and design process. Accommodations for disabled patrons are only beginning to be addressed in many countries; however, it is generally accepted that facilities should be made accessible.

Building materials and methods also vary widely from country to country. In Chile, for example, steel is commonly used for structural elements, while in Argentina, poured-in-place concrete is the norm, even in high-rise construction. Labor rates in South America are lower than those in the

The Hoyts Cine 12 anchors the new Mercado de Abasto retail entertainment destination in Buenos Aires, Argentina. *Juan Hitters*

Bold color and high-end finishes generate excitement ▶ and a memorable experience. *Juan Hitters*

Three levels of activity overlook the cinemas' dramatic café. *Juan Hitters*
▼

United States, which substantially reduces the cost differential between expensive and inexpensive materials and systems. Masonry construction and plaster, for example, are typically used in lieu of studs and drywall.

In South America, as in the United States, placing cinema complexes within retail entertainment destinations provides a wide range of experiences for the customer and creates an overall synergy that is financially beneficial for many retailers. Proper attention to detail and placement of the cinema will ensure creation of a suc-

cessful entertainment complex that is seamlessly integrated with retail uses. The added variety makes a real difference in attracting the repeat local shopper and pays off in increased activity and sales. ●

Source: Robert S. Holt, AIA, and Dennis B. Carlberg, AIA, Arrowstreet, Inc., Somerville, Massachusetts.

curiosity and draw strollers into the selling space. More so than at a traditional shopping center, interiors and merchandise need to be visible from pedestrian streets because the theme-based environment and the customers within are themselves part of the merchandising. To encourage repeat visits, merchandise displays should ideally be changed more frequently and should be more interactive than those at traditional retail centers.

People

People are the last and perhaps most important energizing element in a successful retail entertainment destination. People generate activity simply by interacting with one another and with their surroundings, and creative design should ensure that this takes place. The other activity generators in a retail entertainment center draw in patrons and give them a sense of excitement and expectancy, but it is the visitors themselves who create the energy and activity that spell magic.

People watching is a perennially interesting activity—and is often the major reason for return visits to a retail entertainment development. One way to accommodate people watching is by ensuring that restaurant seating is placed so that it is not only visible from the street but intrudes into the street

more apt to become contributing elements in a rich and constantly changing scene.

Notes

1. Efforts to counteract the effects of street closures—by introducing buses, as at Nicollet Mall in Minneapolis, or by allowing limited

◀ The Filmworks, a new 20-screen UCI cinema (including an IMAX screen) designed by RTKL for the United Kingdom–based Richardson Developments, is part of The Printworks, an urban entertainment district that is open 24 hours a day in downtown Manchester, England. *RTKL*

without blocking it. The seating should not be secluded or hidden, as it so often is at a traditional shopping mall.

At a retail entertainment destination, patrons stroll and saunter for enjoyment, rather than rushing frantically about to purchase a targeted item. Customers see excursion or recreational shopping as more of an occasion than targeted shopping, and they are often more dressed up when they go—and

automobile traffic, as at Third Street Promenade in Santa Monica—have had mixed results.

2. The Urban Land Institute and the International Council of Shopping Centers recently published a survey of parking in shopping centers, some of which included cinemas themed restaurants, and other entertainment venues. This joint publication, *Parking Requirements for Shopping Centers*, is available for purchase through ULI's Web site, www.uli.org.

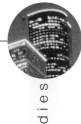

Case Studies

Bayou Place
Houston, Texas

Bayou Place occupies the shell of the former Albert Thomas Convention Center in downtown Houston's theater district. In 1987, when the 127,000-square-foot convention center was abandoned in favor of the newly opened, state-of-the-art George R. Brown Convention Center, it became a functionally obsolete structure—a quintessential white elephant. The Albert Thomas center remained vacant and neglected for almost ten years, while the surrounding neighborhood became increasingly workday oriented.

When the Albert Thomas center first opened in 1967, its location in the theater district supported the fine and the popular arts, as well as nightlife. As modern forms of entertainment brought new needs, outlets, and audiences, the city's cultural critical mass shifted to new suburban venues. The adjacent financial and civic districts filled the vacuum, little by little, until downtown became a grid of tinted-glass high rises—busy by day, but devoid of life at night. Downtown Houston, at least its north end, became known as NoDo, as in "Do Not Go."

By the late 1980s, during the administration of Mayor Kathy Whitmire, the city had realized that only municipal action could stem further decay of the central business district. Houston was determined to maintain the vitality of its symphony, ballet, opera, and theater companies, and to bring back nightlife and weekend activity. In early 1988, the mayor's civic center task force recommended

Bayou Place occupies an abandoned convention center in ▶ the heart of Houston's historic theater district, which is adjacent to the city's financial district. *The Cordish Company*

132 | Developing Retail Entertainment Destinations

Development Team

Developers

The Cordish Company
601 East Pratt Street, Sixth Floor
Baltimore, Maryland 21202
(410) 752-5444

Architects

Gensler
700 Milam Street, Suite 400
Houston, Texas 77002
(713) 228-8050

Contractor

Tribble & Stephens
8580 Katy Freeway, Suite 320
Houston, Texas 77024
(713) 465-8550

that the Albert Thomas center be converted to a "festival market" along the lines of San Francisco's Fisherman's Wharf, Boston's Faneuil Hall, and Dallas's West End Marketplace.

In April 1988, the city sent out a request for proposals (RFP) calling for a developer to enter into a public/private partnership to rehabilitate the old convention center and transform it into an entertainment destination. In return, Houston would grant the developer a long-term lease of the building and partially subsidize its redevelopment.

The winning proposal was an ambitious, $60 million joint venture between George Lucas's Skywalker Development Company and the local Century Development Company. When this partnership failed to meet deadlines, Houston invited the runner-up among the RFP respondents, The Cordish Company, of Baltimore, Maryland, to resubmit its proposal.

When the exterior concrete cladding of the old structure was removed, it became possible to create a light-permeable exterior, which would allow inside activity to be visible from the street.
The Cordish Company

The city agreed to a 25 percent share of the profits, a 60-year lease, and an $8.1 million contribution to the cost of rehabilitation, and promised to provide additional infrastructure.

The $23 million first phase of the project involved gutting 80,000 square feet of the 127,000-square-foot structure, subdividing it, and building it out to meet current codes and to accommodate the physical requirements of the seven entertainment tenants that the project had attracted. Because it had been designed as a convention center, the building was turned in on itself, offering nothing to its surroundings but exposed aggregate-concrete walls. For its new life as a multitenant, multiuse entertainment center, the building had to be turned "inside-out," and individual tenant entrances created along the perimeter. Once the exterior concrete panels were removed, a structural frame was revealed that made possible a light-permeable exterior, which would allow inside activity to be visible from the street. The

columned portico could be used as a promenade and for outdoor dining and entertainment. Inside the building, second levels and mezzanines were constructed to create spaces for public entertainment.

Bayou Place opened on New Year's Eve, 1997, with a full roster of tenants: a combination café and eight-screen multiplex, a performing-arts theater, and five restaurants. Three of the tenants were publicly held companies with a national presence, and the remaining four were local concerns with multiple venues. Today, the half-dozen blocks surrounding Bayou Place are newly revitalized with the kind of day, night, and weekend bustle that the city of Houston desired. Loft-style apartments in the older buildings have become popular, and condominium projects have contributed to a growing residential base. Enron Field, a new downtown ballpark for the Houston Astros, a major-league baseball team, opened for the 2000 season. With the entire downtown swept up in the rediscovery of urban amenities, the revitalizing effects of the convention center project reach far beyond the theater district.

Development

According to its initial agreement with Cordish, the city would remove asbestos under its own contracts; pledge a minimum of $900,000 per year in parking revenues from the two nearby underground parking facilities (provided that the project was 65 percent leased); pledge an annual maximum of $1.2 million in management fees for 55 years; and pledge a six-year property tax abatement—worth an estimated $1.2 million a year—to the project, now officially known as Bayou Place. Cordish's obligations were to pay the city an annual rent of $50,000 plus 25 percent of the profits, and to complete Bayou Place by August 1996. The agreement set no perform-

◀ **The rehabilitation of the Albert Thomas convention center involved adding a second floor to the one-story convention center, to maximize leasable space.**
The Cordish Company

The eight-screen Angelika Film Center, an artplex that primarily shows independent and foreign films, includes an informal café that has become a popular gathering spot. *The Cordish Company*

ance standards for the developer; it guaranteed no revenue beyond rent; and the developer retained all authority to approve tenants.

The agreement was signed during mayor Whitmire's administration, but the administration of the succeeding mayor, Bob Lanier, was critical of the agreement. Though cooperative, the new administration chafed at the terms. When the original deadline for completion became impossible, partially because of the city's failure to complete the asbestos abatement on time, the lease was amended to extend the deadline to year-end 1996. The renegotiated lease reduced the maximum amount of Cordish's annual management fee to $1.02 million for 13 years; reduced the guaranteed number of parking spaces from 1,200 to 300 complimentary and 200 leased; reduced the city's revenue from profits to 22 percent; and included a promise from the city to help the developer obtain an $8 million loan or to grant the developer that amount and eliminate all future management fees. The effect of the reduced management fees was the release of the developer's liens against an annual $7.3 million of the city's hotel occupancy tax and parking revenue.

Another potential delay was averted when the city of Houston and Harris County negotiated to exchange land in order to satisfy an earlier agreement that provided for the Albert Thomas grounds to revert to the county if the center was ever used for a nongovernmental purpose. This ownership issue had been clouding the developer's attempts at securing financing for the project.

In the end, the deadline for project completion was extended to year-end 1997. Bayou Place opened to a New Year's Eve opening party attended by 20,000 paying guests. (Unlike most grand openings, which are considered loss leaders, this one yielded a profit, which the developer retained.) Bayou Place was fully leased at opening and has remained so; cash flow has been positive since the first day.

Design

Bayou Place is located on prime downtown real estate. Its long axis is in an east-west direction, and it backs up to a north-south section of Interstate 45, where Memorial Drive crosses Buffalo Bayou and enters downtown Houston. Designed by CRS of Houston (since absorbed as the Houston office of HOK), the center faces Jones Plaza, the heart of the theater district. Also fronting Jones Plaza, directly opposite the convention center, is the 3,000-seat Jesse Jones Hall, home of the Houston Symphony. The 1,094-seat Alley Theater, also facing the plaza, lies to the north. Also to the north of the convention center is Fish Plaza, and facing Fish Plaza is the Wortham Center, home to the Houston Ballet and the Houston Opera Company, both renowned cultural institutions with international reputations.

Also facing Jones Plaza is the 56-story Bank of America building; behind Jesse Jones Hall, to the east, is the 75-story Chase Tower; and diagonally across from Jones Plaza are the twin 36-story towers of the Pennzoil building.

These three buildings form the northern edge of the financial and civic district, which occupies a twelve-by-four-block area between Houston's city hall, at the western end, and the new George R. Brown Convention Center, at the eastern end.

The westernmost end of the original Albert Thomas Convention Center crosses Bagby, a north-south throughway. That portion of the center is connected to the main building and conveyed with the lease agreement, but had been left largely undeveloped until 2001, when the developer initiated Phase II, which will include an additional 150,000 square feet of restaurant space, entertainment-related retail space, offices, and possibly a hotel.

Tenants

The Skywalker-Century development team had a ready-made anchor tenant— Lucasfilms. The Cordish team, on the other hand, had pledged its own money if financing was not forthcoming, but first had to secure tenants. Both the Skywalker-Century and the Cordish proposals envisioned a complex with futuristic theaters, restaurants, nightclubs, sports bars, and other entertainment venues. Expectations were for large-format theaters, movies in which the viewer helps to change the plot, movies with encircling screens, and movies with gyrating theater seats. Cordish started negotiating with anchor tenants Graham Brothers Entertainment, Iwerks Entertainment, and Showcase Film, and eventually reached agreement with Pace Entertainment. Pace, based in Houston, promised to absorb 50,000 square feet with its Aerial Performing Arts Theater, seating 2,800, and to fill the venue with big-name live musical and comedic entertainment.

Angelika Film Center & Café, an offshoot of its namesake in lower Manhattan, anchors the southeast corner of Bayou Place, and features eight screens showing primarily art films

and high-end commercial titles. There are four additional food vendors: Sake Lounge, at the northeast corner, with its high-tech decor and Japanese-inspired fare; Mingalone's Italian Bar & Grill, on the northern side, facing Fish Plaza; Harlon's Bayou Blues, serving blues with its barbecue; and Slick Willie's Family Pool Hall, one of six Slick Willie's in the Houston area. In 2000, in an addition on the Fish Plaza side, Bayou Place added a 20,000-square-foot Hard Rock Café.

Experience Gained

Developers can manage the risks of RFP-based development by proposing only schemes that make economic sense to them. In other words, the point of the RFP process is for the public agency and the developers to jointly and transparently find the best fit between the public agency's needs and the developer's ability to meet those needs. The point is not necessarily to be the chosen developer. Thus, even after losing a bid, it is important for a developer to continue to monitor the situation to take advantage of changing political, financial, and economic conditions that may place the bid in a more favorable light—for example, if the winning bidder is unable to reach agreement with the agency.

In the case of Bayou Place, Skywalker-Century was awarded the bid on the basis of a concept that appeared to meet the city's desire

▲
An offshoot of its namesake in lower Manhattan, the Angelika Film Center features a sophisticated lobby adorned with hardwood floors, a chandelier, art, and fresh flowers.
The Cordish Company

Harlon's Bayou Blues serves blues with its famous Texas-style barbecue.
The Cordish Company

to catalyze urban development in the faltering theater district: a high-tech multimedia extravaganza that had not yet been attempted anywhere. Cordish's proposal, in contrast, while extending the firm's capabilities, was based on expertise well within the firm's range of experience. When Skywalker Development could not obtain financing within the agreed-upon time frame, Cordish was in place to propose an alternative scheme that had already been accepted as meeting the city's criteria.

When working with prospective local tenants, developers should encourage them to offer unique venues that expand on the themes that have made them successful, but at the same time retain the flavor of the original

schemes for the sake of local patrons. Both Mingalone's Italian Bar & Grill and Harlon's Bayou Blues are offshoots and extensions of successful local dining establishments with good reputations.

Despite the anticipated success of the project, the developer underestimated the need for parking. At the time the lease was negotiated, the surrounding district had a surplus of parking, and even a thorough analysis failed to project the amount of parking that would be necessary to support the entertainment venues that Bayou Place eventually attracted. The problem was only compounded in 1996, when the developer and the city renegotiated the lease agreement and guaranteed parking was reduced from 1,200 to 500 spaces (the guaranteed number included 200 spaces procurable by a lease option). Ultimately, the lack of guaranteed parking resulted in tenant configurations that have failed to maximize the value of the property.

Bayou Place

Site plan. ▶

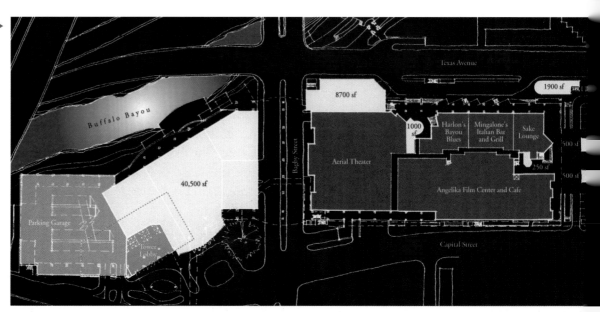

Project Data

Land Use Information

Site area: 2 acres

Gross building area: 160,000 square feet

Theater and cinemas: 123,000 square feet

Restaurants: 37,000 square feet

Gross leasable area (GLA): 130,000 square feet

Parking: 500 spaces (off site)

Floor/area ratio: 1.84

Land Use Plan

Use	Area (acres)	Percentage of site
Buildings	1.8	92
Landscaping, open spaces	.2	8
Total	2.0	1

Retail Tenant Information

Classification	Number of stores	GLA (square feet)
Live-performance theater	1	50,000
Cinema	1	50,000
Restaurants	4	30,000

Annual rents: $22 per square foot

Average annual sales: $3.6 million (restaurants only)

Average length of lease: Ten years

Development Cost Information

Site acquisition costs	$0
Site improvement costs	0
Construction costs	23,000,000
Soft costs	7,000,000
Total development cost	$30,000,000

Development Schedule

Site leased	August 1991
Planning started	August 1991
Sales/leasing started	January 1993
Construction started	November 1994
Phase I completed	December 1997
Phase II completed	March 2002 (projected)

The Block at Orange
Orange, California

The Block at Orange is the first example of a mixed-use entertainment center developed by The Mills Corporation, the developer of the "Mills" brand shopping centers. Nearly three-quarters of The Block's 880,910 square feet are devoted to entertainment and restaurant uses—although, given the concept behind the project, it is sometimes difficult to draw a hard line between entertainment and nonentertainment uses. Located about two and a half miles from Disneyland, in Orange, California, The Block is an open-air center built on the site of an enclosed, traditional mall that shut down in 1994. Designed to look and feel more like a collection of city streets than a shopping center, The Block at Orange includes a 30-theater cineplex, several other entertainment and unique retail anchors, and an expansive restaurant row as well as a food court. The Block opened in November 1998 and had more than 12 million visitors in its first year of operation, encouraging The Mills Corporation to plan other venues around the country.

Located only about two and one-half miles from Disneyland, ▶
The Block at Orange has nearly three-quarters of its more than
800,000 square feet devoted to entertainment and restaurant uses.
Twenty-two "stylons"—huge, vertical signboards, some as tall as 91 feet—
dot the center and surrounding parking lots. This changeable signage is
backlit and provides a spectacular view both day and night.
The Mills Corporation

Development Team

Developer

The Mills Corporation
1300 Wilson Boulevard, Suite 400
Arlington, Virginia 22309
(703) 526-5000

Architect

D'Agostino, Izzo, Quirk
1310 Broadway
Somerville, Massachusetts 02144
(617) 623-3000

Design Consultant

Communication Arts
1112 Pearl Street
Boulder, Colorado 80302
(303) 447-8202

Site Planner

Site Signatures
2120 Freeport Road
New Kensington, Pennsylvania 15068
(724) 339-1899

Lighting Consultant

Frances Krahe & Associates Inc.
580 Broadway, Suite 100
Laguna Beach, California 92651
(949) 376-0744

Site Planning and Design

The Block at Orange occupies an enviable site. Located at the convergence of several freeways (the "Orange Crush"), the 82-acre site sits at the center of a trade area that includes 1.8 million people within ten miles. And, with Disneyland at its doorstep, the project is able to capitalize on the approxi-mately 37 million tourists that visit Orange County each year. In addition, the offices and businesses that have grown up around the site of the former mall provide The Block with a built-in daytime market.

The Block's site planning is somewhat traditional: the mall is located at the center of a sea of surface parking bounded by a ring road. But the innovations are apparent even as visitors approach the parking lot, which is dotted with huge vertical signboards called "stylons" that also appear within the center itself. Designed by Communication Arts, of Boulder, Colorado, the 22 stylons, some of which are 91 feet high, provide mammoth display areas to promote the center and its tenants, pay homage to city residents, or simply function as prime advertising space. Dramatically backlit at night, the stylons serve both as a permanent landmark and symbol of the project, and as temporary and changeable signage, designed to keep the project fresh and new. "We wanted to make an impression on people as soon as they entered our parking lot," notes Jerry Engen, vice president and senior development direc-tor for The Mills Corporation: "The stylons signal that they're in a special place as soon as they get out of their cars."

Like an increasing number of new shop-ping centers, The Block, which consists of nine separate buildings, is open-air. The circulation pattern is racetrack-shaped but resembles a city grid, with major and minor streets and plazas. The two principal "streets" are The Boulevard and The Strip. Each is approximately 1,200 feet long, but they were designed to different specifications to create a different ambience for each.

At 50 feet in width, The Boulevard is the wider of the two streets. The intent of the project architects, D'Agostino, Izzo, Quirk, of Somerville, Massachusetts, was to create a relaxed atmosphere; hence, The Boulevard offers benches; trees with spreading canopies; and old-fashioned, pedestrian-scale lampposts. In deliberate contrast, the high-energy Strip is 30 feet wide, with taller and more vertical trees and streetlights and fewer seating areas. The inspiration for The Strip, according to the project's designers, was Tokyo's high-intensity atmosphere. Several "cross-streets" link The Boulevard and The Strip.

▲ The Strip, at 30 feet in width, is the narrower of The Block's two main "streets" and was inspired by the high-intensity atmosphere of Tokyo. *The Mills Corporation*

◀ The Block at Orange is anchored by a 30-theater AMC cineplex at the center of the site, which acts as the project's "town center." *The Mills Corporation*

The AMC Theatres cineplex occupies center stage, both literally and figuratively. The building terminates The Block's primary cross-axis, and its U-shape creates a large plaza and focal point for the project. "The theater is our town center," says Engen. Two restaurants—Café Tu Tu Tango and Wolfgang Puck Grand Café—complete the "town square," while four other full-service restaurants continue along the main cross-axis to one of the center's six entrances and three valet stations.

Most of the remaining anchor tenants are distributed around the periphery of the project, with the smaller shops grouped toward the interior. A second cross-street is lined with fast-food tenants, The Block's equivalent of the more traditional food court. Four out-parcels are also associated with The Block: two were sold prior to development, two as part of the development.

Signage is used not only to inform but as part of the center's architectural image. *The Mills Corporation*

The Block's exterior facades were designed to serve as a backdrop to a changing choreography of signs, lighting, and special effects. The buildings are conventionally framed, mostly one-level structures, with a stucco finish. The front facades of the various tenant spaces vary—some jut out, and some recede—in order to help define the individual tenants and to reinforce the sense of being on a traditional street. Similarly, rooflines vary in height and profile, and facades are painted in a variety of pastel shades. Steeply pitched metal awnings in bright colors further individualize the facades while ensuring some degree of visual compatibility along the street.

Recognizing that a retail entertainment center's long-term success depends on its ability to stay fresh, The Mills Corporation has chosen to rely on signage, rather than architecture, to define the project. "Architecture gets dated and is expensive to change," notes Engen, "so we increased the signage." In addition to the stylons, The Block includes a variety of other lively—and, most important, changeable—types of signs. Chief among these are billboards. Often disdained by cities as a necessary evil, billboards are used here to introduce a level of visual complexity and excitement typically zoned out of suburban areas. Like their urban counterparts, The Block's billboards seem to grow out of buildings and hang dramatically overhead; they may seem unplanned, but they were deliberately and consciously designed.

As required, The Mills Corporation submitted a comprehensive signage design package to the city of Orange for review and approval. Although the proposed signage exceeded existing code provisions, ultimately, says Engen, the code was rewritten to accommodate it. The billboards are revenue-generating elements, but advertising content is restricted to goods and services available at The Block. The stylons are also revenue-generating features, but corporate policy restricts content to pictures and prohibits text.

Urban imagery provided the inspiration for The Block's lighting. Designed by Frances Krahe & Associates, of Laguna Beach, California, The Block's "street" lighting includes not only old-fashioned pole lighting but takeoffs on more recent, high-mast, "cobra-head" lighting. In addition, vertical light bars, strung from rooftop to rooftop, were designed to create a special identity for the street that leads up to the AMC cineplex.

◄ **Suspended light bars provide dramatic lighting along the cross-street leading up to the cineplex.**
The Mills Corporation

Development Process

The original mall on the site of The Block, called The City, was constructed as an open-air shopping center anchored by JC Penney and the May Company. It was enclosed around 1980; but, by 1994, unable to compete with newer malls, The City closed. The Mills Corporation optioned the property in 1994.

Initially, The Mills Corporation, planning a center not unlike the company's other malls—"City Mills" was the working name—hoped to reuse the original mall structures. But soon, according to Engen, it became apparent that neither the original buildings nor the Mills formula were right. With competition expected from other centers and even from its own Ontario Mills project, then under development, something else was needed. "We didn't want to confuse the market; we wanted to create a new brand," notes Engen.

From the city's perspective, the mall was an 82-acre asset that had ceased to provide needed sales tax revenues, and the city was eager to see a successful new use of the site. Given the track record of The Mills Corporation, the city was open to the developer's plan to create an entertainment-based, open-air center and worked to facilitate its realization. "These kinds of projects require a public/private partnership," notes Engen. The project's environmental review resulted in a mitigated negative declaration, in part because the proposed project essentially replaced the square footage and use that already existed on site. Street widening was required, performed, and paid for by the city.

Developing Retail Entertainment Destinations | **145**

like The Block assumes an opening at about 75 percent occupancy, according to Engen, and takes about three years to achieve stabilized occupancy (95 percent). The Block, according to Engen, is on track to meet these milestones easily.

Tenants

The largest tenant, at 132,000 square feet, is the 6,066-seat, 30-screen AMC cineplex. Twenty-six of the theaters have 100 to 200 seats, and four have 400 to 600 seats; all of the theaters have stadium seating. The lobby of the cineplex is a large rotunda with quotes from films written out in its terrazzo floor and murals of movie stars overhead. According to AC Neilson EDI, Inc., The Block's AMC cineplex was ranked first in the nation in ticket sales for the week of July 16–22, 1999, and consistently remains in the top 50 cinemas in the nation.

Other primary tenants include the following:

- Dave & Buster's: A 60,000-square-foot sports-and-games venue catering to adults. It offers billiards; table shuffleboard; full-swing golf simulators; the Million Dollar Midway (electronic simulators and games); the Turbo Ride Theatre (a motion-based simulator theater) and the Mystery Dinner Theatre; special-events rooms; a grand dining room; and several bars. Overall, Dave and Buster's offers more than 200 interactive amusements. Established in Dallas in 1982, the firm is publicly traded on the New York Stock Exchange and has venues in England and in more than 20 U.S. cities.

- Vans Skate Park: A 46,000-square-foot skateboard and roller-blading facility designed for teens and younger children. The facility includes a 20,000-square-foot skating area, resembling a street course, and a 10-by-80-

View along The Boulevard. At 50 feet in width, The Boulevard is more relaxed than The Strip. Note the urban-inspired streetlights and billboard. Vans Skate Park, catering to teens and younger children, is in the foreground. *The Mills Corporation*

Also, a financial assistance package worth approximately $18 million was worked out between the city and The Mills Corporation, whereby The Mills Corporation shares in the increased sales tax and property tax revenues generated by the project.

The Mills Corporation closed on the property in April 1997 and started construction in May. The project was financed with $56,100,000 in equity from Germany-based Kan Am, an equity partner in many of The Mills Corporation's projects. A construction loan of approximately $138 million, under which the project continues to operate, completed the interim financing. The project was 83 percent leased at its opening in November 1998, with all the anchor positions filled except two. Typically, planning for a project foot ramp. In addition, Vans includes a retail area selling skating equipment, shoes, and related apparel.

- Ron Jon Surf Shop: The 25,500-square-foot Ron Jon Surf Shop is only the third store for Florida-based Ron Jon and is reportedly the largest surf shop on the West Coast. The shop's exterior decor features undulating blue fiberglass waves and large-as-life figures of surfers.

- Hilo Hattie: The well-known Hawaiian retailer's first store on the mainland and the second-largest in its group. The 20,000-square-foot shop, which is decorated on the outside with enormous tropical flowers, offers Hawaiian apparel, home accessories, food, and gifts.

Other major tenants included Borders Books & Music, GameWorks, Virgin megastore, and Off 5th–Saks Fifth Avenue Outlet.

All restaurants at The Block are required to provide outdoor seating. Among the more unusual offerings are the following:

- Café Tu Tu Tango: One of five locations for the Florida-based Tango Group. Designed to represent a Spanish artist's loft, the 340-seat restaurant features local artists painting at stations set up around the dining room.

- Alcatraz Brewing Co.: A 359-seat restaurant with 30 outdoor tables; the restaurant at The Block is the fifth location for this chain.

- Other restaurants include Corner Bakery, Left at Albuquerque, Market Broiler, and Wolfgang Puck Grand Café.

The mix of tenants at The Block appeals to a wide spectrum of market interests. During the day, the restaurants and food court draw on the 50,000 employees who work within a five-mile radius; in the evenings, the AMC cineplex creates demand. Retail tenants remain open until 11 P.M., further reinforcing restaurant sales, and the restaurants reinforce retail sales in turn.

Dave & Buster's attracts adult patrons, while Vans Skate Park appeals to a younger crowd, as does GameWorks. The Block takes the teenage market seriously, says Engen. "We embrace the teen market. We have something for them to do and spend their money on." Neither teen rowdiness nor crowd control in general has been an issue. As at all Mills centers, The Mills Corporation constructed a police substation on site at no charge to the city.

Tourists, defined as visitors who travel more than 50 miles to the mall, account for approximately 5 percent of all visitors to The Block. The Mills Corporation expects this proportion to increase to 10 percent over the next couple of years, as the renovation of the Anaheim Convention Center and road construction around Disneyland are completed. The tourist market is actively courted by The Block's management. Like all the Mills centers, The Block has a tourism director, and the center is actively promoted at conventions and through advertising in tourist publications.

The tenant mix, though successful, is still evolving. The addition of four major tenants and seven smaller shops was announced in April 2000. The four major tenants include Burke Williams Day Spa and Massage Center; MARS Music; Polly Esther's, a 21-and-over, '70s and '80s–themed nightclub; and the Zone, which offers "state-of-the-art" bowling and a microbrewery pub. Notes Engen, "The center is still maturing and evolving, and we are constantly looking for tenants."

Experience Gained

The Block at Orange is a prototype retail entertainment center for The Mills Corporation. The early success of the center derives partly from the strength and uniqueness of the major tenants and partly from the synergistic relationship of tenant types: theaters, restaurants, entertainment venues, and retail. The Block's uniqueness and appeal also lie in its urban design. Although it is located in a suburban environment, with parking on all sides, the interior of the center offers a lively atmosphere that is rare among suburban retail centers. In order to maintain the project's appeal over the longer term, The Block's design focuses on signage—stylons, billboards, and other architectural signage—that can be changed relatively easily to keep up with evolving styles and tastes.

The Block at Orange Tenant Map

Site plan. ▶
The Mills Corporation

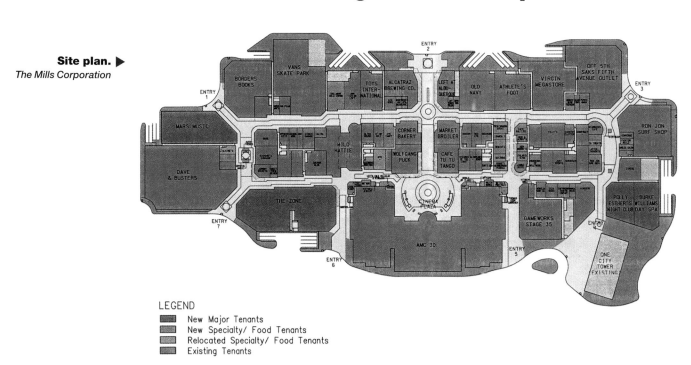

LEGEND
- New Major Tenants
- New Specialty/ Food Tenants
- Relocated Specialty/ Food Tenants
- Existing Tenants

Project Data

Land Use Information

Site area: 82 acres

Gross building area (GBA): 880,910 square feet

Retail gross leasable area (GLA; existing/planned): 774,282/811,909 square feet

Floor/area ratio: .25

Land Use Plan

Use	Acres	Percentage of site
Buildings	20	25
Streets and surface parking	52	63
Landscaping and open space	10	12
Total	82	100

Development Cost Information

Site acquisition cost	$19,700,000
Site improvement costs	15,200,000
Construction costs	110,000,000
Soft costs	52,300,00
Total development cost	197,200,000
Less recoveries	(3,100,000)
Total development cost at completion	$194,100,000

Financial Information

Construction loan	$138,000,000
Equity	56,100,000
Total	$194,100,000

Tenant Information

Classification	Number of stores	GLA (square feet)
General merchandise	5	124,346
Food service	27	99,211
Clothing and accessories	16	73,348
Shoes	5	9,783
Home furnishings and art	3	5,510
Home appliances/music	1	25,01
Hobby/special interest	3	11,414
Gift/specialty	16	25,579
Jewelry	4	3,370
Drugs	3	4,200
Personal services	5	16,668
Cinema	1	112,830
Health club	1	38,000
Other entertainment	5	179,085
Other	3	20,434
Temporary tenants	5	11,441
Vacancies	8	14,039
Total	111	774,273

Percentage of GLA occupied: 98 percent (of constructed space)

Percentage of GLA occupied: 94 percent

GLA not constructed: 37,627 square feet

Annual rents: Approximately $20 to $22 per square foot

Average annual retail sales: Approximately $379 per square foot (specialty stores only)

Average length of lease: Three to ten years

Development Schedule

Site optioned	1994
Planning started	1994
Construction started	May 1997
Sales and leasing started	1997
Project completed	1998

Denver Pavilions
Denver, Colorado

Occupying two full city blocks along the 16th Street Mall in downtown Denver, Denver Pavilions offers a new dimension in retailing and entertainment to residents, in-town workers, and visitors. The project is the first completed by the Los Angeles–based Entertainment Development Group (EDG) and its codeveloper, Northbrook, Illinois–based Arthur Hill & Co. L.L.C. Denver Pavilions is the successful realization of an apparently simple concept: combining retail and entertainment to create a synergistic environment that not only benefits the tenants at Denver Pavilions but creates new traffic for existing tenants along the mall as well.

The design of the three- to four-level, 347,750-square-foot center, which includes four separate buildings, reflects the historic business district in which it is located. Its restrained but open facades, layout, and signage showcase the center's tenants. With a combination of tenants that includes theaters, restaurants, and nightclubs, Denver Pavilions is injecting new life into downtown Denver and extending the hours of vitality beyond the business day.

The most distinctive aspect of the project is the 356-foot-long sign—▶
dubbed the "Great Wall"—that rises 40 feet and spans the Pavilions's
two city blocks. Its 273 perforated metal panels back 27- to 35-foot-high
letters that spell out "Denver Pavilions" and are illuminated with colored
lighting that is programmed to change throughout the evening.
The sign also satisfied the project's public art requirement.
Timothy Hursley/ELS

Development Team

Developer
Denhill Denver LLC, a partnership of Arthur Hill & Co. L.L.C. and Entertainment Development Group (EDG).

Denhill Denver LLC
4333 Park Terrace Drive, Suite 220
Westlake Village, California 91361
(818) 991-2964

Arthur Hill & Co. L.L.C.
5 Revere Drive, Suite 300
Northbrook, Illinois 60062
(847) 498-4848

EDG
4333 Park Terrace Drive, Suite 220
Westlake Village, California 91361
(818) 991-2964

Architect
ELS
2040 Addison Street
Berkeley, California 94704
(510) 549-2929

Site Planner
Martin & Martin
4251 Kipling Street
Wheat Ridge, Colorado 80034
(303) 431-6100

Consultant
Gorsuch & Kirgis LLC
1515 Arapahoe Street, Suite 1000
Denver, Colorado 80202
(303) 376-5000

Other Development Partners
Roche Finanz GmbH
Kaiser Joseph Strasse 255
79098 Freiburg, Germany
49-761-388050

Hensel Phelps Construction Co.
420 Sixth Avenue
P.O. Box O
Greeley, Colorado 80632-0717
(970) 352-6565

The Site
Denver Pavilions occupies two city blocks on the southeastern end of the 16th Street Mall between Tremont and Welton Streets, formerly the site of two surface parking lots. Previous development proposals had been thwarted, including one to develop a downtown regional mall on the site. The recent departure of several venerable department stores had brought the upper end of the 16th Street Mall somewhat into decline relative to the Lower Downtown, or LoDo, section of Denver.

Entertainment Development Group (EDG) president Bill Denton proposed building the project in Denver because of the city's exceptional demographics and commitment to its downtown. The city has more than 4,000 downtown residents, an additional 65,000 residents in the surrounding central-city area, and 120,000 downtown workers. As the only major downtown within 500 miles, Denver also enjoys significant loyalty from its suburban population. And, not least important, the city has been active in locating attractions downtown, including the new Coors Field, the Pepsi Center, and the historic Elitch Gardens Amusement Park.

Denton had come to Denver for the specific purpose of redeveloping the historic Union Station, a project that quickly proved to be infeasible. Besides the fact that the site was too small and was owned by a half-dozen railroad companies, the site would have had to be expanded onto land owned by the U.S. Postal Service. Still convinced that Denver was an ideal city for an entertainment and retail project, however, Denton quickly turned his attention to the 16th Street Mall.

Built between two downtown bus terminals, the 16th Street Mall was developed as a transportation corridor, shuttling 45,000 passengers per day, free of charge, along its route. As the urban spine of the city, it had the critical mass necessary to support the proposed type of development. The parking situation—8,000 spaces from nearby office buildings available each evening within a block and a half of the site—also made the project attractive. In addition, the site had only two landowners, making land assembly a somewhat less formidable task.

Development Process

Development of Denver Pavilions required coordination among the developer, the architect, the tenants, the city, the contractor, and the lenders. Denton likened the development process to constructing a house of cards: the loss of any one player would have meant the loss of the project.

Assembling the land was one of the first difficulties. Partly because they had hoped to develop the land themselves, the current landowners had been reluctant to sell in the past. Once they were persuaded of the value that Denver Pavilions would add to their remaining land, however, the owners agreed to a complex arrangement in which they would keep a portion of the existing lot, and the land that they retained would be used to develop future office, hotel, or residential space. Denver Pavilions retained perpetual easement rights behind the Pavilions for service alleys; in exchange, the sellers would share in the parking-garage revenue and would be entitled to develop office, hotel, or residential space.

Creating the necessary partnerships and pulling together equity were additional hurdles. Denton worked for two years to form Denver Pavilions LLP, which was incor-

▲ The 347,750-square-foot Denver Pavilions occupies two city blocks along Denver's 16th Street Mall. Featuring high-energy tenants, a flagship cinema, and destination restaurants and nightclubs, the project is extending downtown Denver's hours of vitality.
Timothy Hursley/ELS

◄ The facades of the four buildings are elegant and restrained in design and materials. Visual excitement comes from creative lighting and signage and from the large display windows that face the street.
Timothy Hursley/ELS

porated in 1996. The partnership consisted of the German firm Roche Finanz, the Denver Urban Redevelopment Authority (DURA), Hensel Phelps (a contractor), and Denhill LLC, which was composed of EDG (75 percent) and Arthur Hill & Co. (25 percent). The partnership represented $18,850,000 in equity, plus $24,395,000 in tax-increment financing (TIF).

In 1986, DURA had sold more than $60 million in TIF bonds, which had been placed in escrow and were to be repaid with sales and property taxes. But time was running out for use of the funds. A profit participant in the project and one of the first partners Denton acquired, DURA had long been seeking appropriate projects to revive this area of downtown. Even with an equity partner in place, however, the lenders still required 70 percent of the space to be preleased.

Thus, time became a critical factor in the development of Denver Pavilions. In addition to DURA's need to use (or lose) the TIF money, the lenders' preleasing requirement placed a great burden on the construction schedule and created a Catch-22 situation for the developer. The "billboard" tenants that EDG was seeking—tenants that place an emphasis on entertainment through exciting signage and interactive retailing—typically would not sign leases more than two years in advance of completion, but construction could not even begin without leases from those tenants. It was imperative to lobby the tenants to commit to leasing and thereby secure debt financing from the lenders.

EDG's philosophy for creating a tenant mix was straightforward yet difficult to achieve. To give people a reason to visit the project, the tenants had to be unique to the region; but the project also required tenants that would inject an element of entertainment into their marketing and merchandising philosophy. One of the most important components of the project, according to Denton, was the flagship theater. Talks that had begun in 1994 with AMC Theaters eventually fell apart. Fortunately, EDG was able to quickly secure a lease with Denver-based United Artists for a 15-screen, 80,000-square-foot multiplex. The next step was to secure the billboard tenants. Finally, the project needed to include destination restaurants and nightclubs.

It was important that the project be high-end, but not too upscale. Because the project serves several market segments—suburbanites, downtown workers, downtown residents, and tourists—prices could not exclude any of these groups. At the same time, the center's tenant mix, particularly its nightclubs and restaurants, had to appeal to a sophisticated customer.

Although Denver had not been on the company's short list of potential sites, Denton began in September 1995 to lobby Nike to locate the last NikeTown store in North America in Denver Pavilions. In addition to favorable downtown demographics, he touted the city's strong sports orientation: area residents show a high level of participation in outdoor activities, and Denver is home to professional football, baseball, basketball, and hockey teams. Nike's existing relationships with the Denver Broncos and the University of Colorado in Boulder were also strong selling points. At the same time, EDG undertook negotiations with several other high-powered retailers, including Virgin Records megastore and Hard Rock Café. Also important to the tenant mix were restaurants such as the Corner Bakery, Maggiano's, and Wolfgang Puck Café. While intrigued by the synergistic concept espoused by Denton, each of the major national firms was reluctant to be the first to sign on, and each waited for another to commit. Denton eventually secured letters of intent from the companies, who nonetheless were not willing to sign leases four years before occupation. Between December 1995 and August 1996, the theater and billboard tenants executed leases.

With a major regional mall and several existing or planned specialty centers within a few miles of Denver Pavilions, competition for many of the other tenants was stiff. Some had radius clauses that prevented them from locating in Denver Pavilions. Finally, with commitments in hand for the required 70 percent of space, EDG was able to persuade the lenders of the project's viability. The construction loan closed, and construction began in February 1997.

Design

Denver Pavilions was envisioned as an integral part of downtown Denver, and it reflects the scale and pattern of the downtown grid. The Pavilions comprises four distinct three- to four-story buildings linked by open streets, courtyards, and bridges. The complex faces the 16th Street Mall, and this public space extends into the Pavilions via two midblock passages and Glenarm Place, redesigned as a pedestrian-friendly street.

The open-air, multibuilding design by ELS Architects was inspired by other thriving urban shopping districts such as San Francisco's Union Square and Chicago's Michigan Avenue. The network of pedestrian walkways within the project not only provides multiple entries from the mall but significantly increases the amount of retail frontage for the Pavilions's 55 tenants. Large, open stairways sweep down to the ground from the second floor, creating a street presence for second-floor tenants.

The architecture of Denver Pavilions takes its cue from nearby landmark buildings. The forms and details vary from building to building, giving the impression of a complex that, like its downtown neighbors, developed over time. The facades are elegant and

▲
The forms and details vary from building to building, giving the impression of a complex that, like its downtown neighbors, developed over time. *Timothy Hursley/ELS*

restrained in both design and materials. Visual excitement comes from creative lighting and signage and from the large display windows that face the street.

Project and tenant signs were coordinated to incorporate tenant brand imaging into the architectural design. The most distinctive aspect of the project is the 356-foot-long landmark sign dubbed the "Great Wall," which rises 40 feet and spans the Pavilions's two city blocks. Costing $1.5 million, the wall is constructed of 273 perforated metal panels with 27- to 35-foot-high letters that spell out "Denver Pavilions." Programmed to change colored lighting throughout the evening, the curving sign creates a memorable visual image for the project. The sign also satisfied DURA's public art requirement for the project.

Retail shops and restaurants fill the first and second levels of the development. Each of the high-profile tenants in the project—Barnes & Noble, Hard Rock Café, Maggiano's,

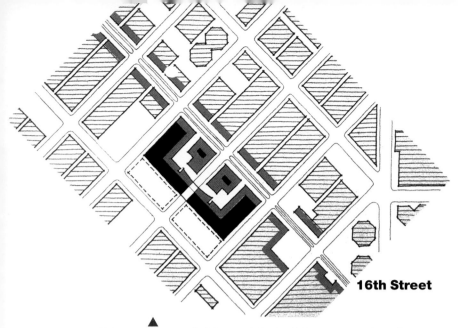

Retail frontage along 16th Street.
ELS/Elbasani & Logan Architects

16th Street

NikeTown, Virgin Megastore—has frontage along the 16th Street Mall. The Wolfgang Puck Café forms a bridge over Glenarm Place that links the two blocks of the complex.

The third level is reserved exclusively for nightclubs and other destination tenants, such as the 18,000-square-foot, 450-seat Café Odyssey, whose elaborate design and high-tech features transport diners to another world in one of three areas depicting Atlantis, Machu Picchu, and the Serengeti Plain. Part of the third and all of the fourth level are reserved for a United Artists cinema. Acoustical insulation for the 15-screen cinema was established through a "floating floor" of three-inch reinforced concrete, separated from a six-and-a-half-inch floor slab by a series of two-inch isolation pads.

Two underground parking garages provide more than 800 on-site parking spaces. The Pavilions also relies on another 8,000 spaces within a block and a half of the project that become available to shoppers and cinema patrons after office workers have left for the day. This ample supply of close-in parking space was vital to the feasibility of the project.

Construction

After the closing with the lenders, the project was on a tight, 20-month schedule to open, which required a fast-track design and construction process. The schedule was compli-

cated by design reviews by the city, DURA, and some of the tenants. To expedite the construction process, steel was ordered on the basis of design drawings, a practice that could conceivably have put the project severely over budget.

As a partner in the project, the city worked to expedite approvals while maintaining proper due diligence. The contractor, Hensel Phelps, an equity partner, also took great pains to bring the project in on schedule, using technology to expedite construction practices. Excavation of both blocks took place simultaneously, a significant feat of organization that had dump trucks leaving the site every 45 seconds. After quickly relocating utilities, the contractor began construction of the underground parking garages. Special probes set into the concrete measured time and temperature so that work crews could be alerted when deck forms had cured, eliminating the need to send samples off site for analysis. Using video surveillance technology, the company closely scrutinized on-site practices, searching for ways to improve productivity.

Because of the large number of spectators who began to gather, the developer and contractor opened the site to the public and even set up special bleachers with clear lines of sight. The public gesture was received favorably and created so much local media coverage that the Associated Press ran a wire story that appeared in newspapers all over the country. Construction was completed on schedule in November 1998, in time for the holiday shopping season.

Management

As part of the 16th Street Mall, Denver Pavilions is a paying member of the downtown business improvement district (BID). Denver Pavilions receives a number of services through the BID, such as police, landscaping, maintenance, and sanitation; the project provides its own additional security. Management is not substantively different from that at a typical regional mall, but it tends to be more intense because of the open nature of the development. The project's visibility requires a highly proactive management style to maintain the property's appearance and sustain good relations among tenants.

Most of the tenant leases are based on typical regional mall leases and include remodeling and renovation clauses. However, leases for some of the stronger tenants were drawn from their own base leases and included some unorthodox conditions.

Experience Gained

Denver Pavilions is achieving sales in excess of $450 per square foot, and the multiplex cinema boasts the highest weekly gross sales on a per-screen basis of 40 cinemas in the metro area. Denver Pavilions has also contributed to the success of other businesses along the 16th Street Mall. Traffic counts in the area near Denver Pavilions have increased nearly 50 percent since it opened, and nearby stores and restaurants are reporting increased sales.

Nevertheless, it is difficult to be first with an unproven concept. Strong partners with an earnest belief in the project are essential. Likewise, the cooperation and commitment of local officials is indispensable in complex and expensive projects.

The urban entertainment concept will not work in every downtown. A city's in-town and suburban residents must already display a strong disposition to visit downtown, and the downtown population needs to be strong, or at least on the upswing. Adequate parking is essential to the viability of downtown enter-

tainment projects. While it may be tempting to locate these projects near existing downtown attractions, care must be taken that they do not compete for parking.

Working with strong, high-quality tenants can be difficult. Many take justifiable pride in doing things their way. Nevertheless, a balance must be struck between the needs of individual tenants and the goals of the overall project.

Denver Pavilions Site

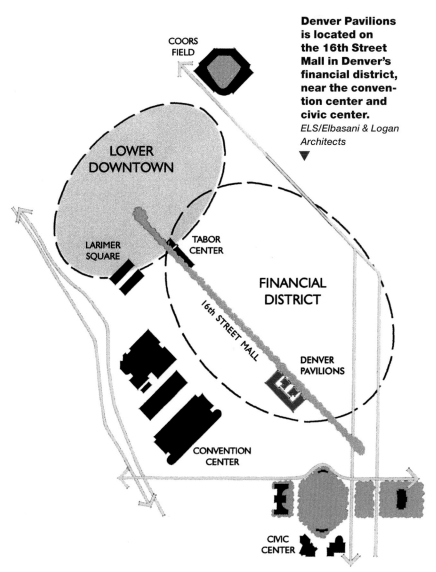

Denver Pavilions is located on the 16th Street Mall in Denver's financial district, near the convention center and civic center.
ELS/Elbasani & Logan Architects

Project Data

Land Use Information

Site area: 3.21 acres

Gross building area (GBA)

Use	Gross square feet
Retail	206,838
Entertainment	114,545
Restaurant	77,076
Common areas	31,950
Parking	312,063
Total (excluding common open-air space)	710,522

Gross leasable area (GLA): 347,750 square feet

Floor/area ratio: 5.08 (GBA); 2.48 (GLA)

Land Use Plan

Use	Acres	Percentage of site
Buildings	2.72	85
Landscaping/open space	.49	15
Total	3.21	100

Tenant Information

Classification	Number of stores	GLA (square feet)
Food service	6	68,167
Clothing and accessories	19	92,165
Shoes	1	1,501
Home appliances/music	1	5,000
Hobby/special interest	4	29,766
Gift/specialty	14	21,765
Jewelry	2	1,058
Personal services	1	4,146
Cinema	1	79,419
Other entertainment	2	20,549
Other	4	4,214
Total	55	327,750

Percentage of GLA occupied: 87 percent

Annual rents: Approximately $19 to $80 per square foot

Average annual retail sales: Approximately $450 per square foot, excluding theater

Typical lease provisions: Base rent, percentage rent, pro-rata pass-throughs, common-area maintenance charges, taxes, insurance

Development Cost Information

Land cost	$18,000,000
Construction costs	45,028,000
Owner construction	171,000
Tenant improvements	20,264,000
Architectural services	4,255,000
Engineering services	365,000
Material testing and inspection	207,000
Bank consultant	134,000
Design analysis	17,000
Construction management	1,024,000
Travel and entertainment	216,000
Development fee	2,020,000
Syndication fee	1,000,000
Legal services	1,959,000
Government fees and insurance	866,000
Leasing commissions	1,412,000
Promotions and advertising	208,000
Taxes	409,000
Title	167,000
Predevelopment expenses	489,000
Miscellaneous consultants	25,000
Utility relocations	642,000
Utility relocation credit	−575,000
Lender fee	865,000
Investment banker equity	613,000
Investment banker letter of credit	250,000
Preferred equity return	2,315,000
$10M letter of credit (bank)	343,000
$2M letter of credit (Denver Urban Development Authority)	273,000
Carrying costs	1,996,000
Hensel Phelps interest costs	107,000
Capital equipment	193,000
.75 percent on $10M letter of credit	150,000
1 percent on $8M letter of credit for Hensel Phelps	100,000
Bank administrative fee	84,000
Interest rate protection	79,000
Contingency	573,000
Total	$106,244,000

Financing Information

Financing source	Amount
Denver Urban Renewal Authority	$24,395,000
Denver Pavilions LP equity	18,850,000
Construction loan (one-third Canadian Imperial Bank of Commerce; one-third Bank One Colorado; one-third Société Génerale)	63,000,000
Total	$106,245,000

Public financing: 23 percent

Denver Urban Renewal Authority: $24,395,000 tax-increment financing (sales and real estate taxes) nonrecourse to development or developer

Debt financing: 59 percent

Equity financing: 18 percent

Annual Operating Expenses for 1999

Taxes	$820,000
Insurance	51,000
Services	397,000
Maintenance	90,000
Janitorial	240,000
Utilities	108,000
Legal services	60,000
Management	300,000
Miscellaneous	237,000
Total	$2,303,000

Development Schedule

Site purchased	February 1997
Planning started	November 1994
Construction started	February 1997
Leasing started	March 1995
Project completed	November 1998

Desert Passage
Las Vegas, Nevada

Desert Passage, which surrounds the Aladdin Resort and Casino, in Las Vegas, is perhaps the most elaborate and innovative entertainment shopping center in a city that is coming to be known more for shopping than gambling. Billing itself as a "shopping adventure," this latest addition to the Las Vegas retail scene conjures up the sights, sounds, and even the scents of ancient spice routes, from India to Morocco and the Arabian Sea. The main attraction is the architecture—the anchor, in shopping-center terms—supplemented by live entertainment and special effects with similar themes. Costumed dancers, acrobats, and musicians roam the "streets" of Desert Passage, entertaining visitors and drawing them further into the center. Pedicabs, like those one might find in the streets of Bombay or Fez, make the rounds, and customer service representatives, decked out in period garb, stroll the halls, almost begging to tell their story. Even the security guards are smartly outfitted in colonial berets and rope epaulets.

The merchandising is also keyed into the theme: selected retailers feature goods from the regions being celebrated, and storefronts are designed to contribute to the exotic ambience. According to Lee H. Wagman, President of TrizecHahn Development Corporation, Desert Passage is "the story of a

Desert Passage conjures up the sights, sounds, and even the scents of ▶ ancient spice routes, from India to Morocco and the Arabian Sea.
Gregg Photographic

Development Team

Developer

TrizecHahn Development Corporation
6834 Hollywood Boulevard, Suite 500
Hollywood, California 90028
(323) 993-7723
and
4350 La Jolla Village Drive, Suite 700
San Diego, California 92122
(858) 546-3474

Architect

RTKL
333 South Hope Street
Los Angeles, California 90071
(213) 633-6101

Theme Contractor

KHS&S Contractors
3480 Cavaretta Court
Las Vegas, Nevada 89103
(702) 597-3200

Desert Passage was developed through a partnership between the Sommer Trust, which owns the Aladdin Resort and Casino, and TrizecHahn Development Corporation. The Sommer Trust contributed the land, valued at approximately $30 million, and TrizecHahn contributed approximately $60 million in project equity. The remainder of the $284 million in development costs was provided through a market-rate loan funded by Fleet Bank.

Opened in August 2000, Desert Passage hosted 300,000 visitors its first weekend and had welcomed 1 million visitors by its 12th day of operations. Though subject to the daily ups and downs of convention flow, in its first three months the project averaged approximately 55,000 visitors per day—a rate that, if maintained, will yield more than 20 million visitors in the first year of operations.

Site Planning and Design

Desert Passage is physically integrated into the Aladdin Resort and Casino complex: the hotel is above, and vehicle circulation is below. In plan, Desert Passage looks like a stylized "A," with the Theatre for the Performing Arts and the casino enclosed by the letter's strokes. The two primary pedestrian entries that flank the casino—Morocco Gate and India Gate—are oriented to Las Vegas Boulevard ("the Strip"). Visitors arriving by automobile park in a 6,000-car garage at the opposite end of the "A."

In keeping with the "journey" metaphor, the floor plan is divided into seven districts—each with its own theme, each corresponding to a port of call along the spice route. This arrangement made it possible to create distinct "places" along the route and to assign

journey," and this story has been the guiding focus of design and development throughout the project. From the authentic custom tile-work to the elaborate, storybook tenant-criteria package, an unusual effort has been made to integrate the retailing into the project's theme.

The 500,000-square-foot Desert Passage is part of the new, billion-dollar Aladdin Resort and Casino complex, which in 2000 replaced the older Aladdin Hotel and Casino on the 30-acre site. The rebuilt complex includes a 39-story, 2,600-room hotel, a 100,000-square-foot casino, a 35,000-square-foot luxury gaming salon by London Clubs International, and the 7,000-seat Theatre for the Performing Arts, a venue for live theater and concert performances.

each district its own architectural and merchandising identity. Starting at the 90-foot-high Morocco Gate, for example, the storefronts—inspired by the fabled cities of Marrakech, Rabat, and Fez—reflect the characteristic earth tones and hand-painted tile-work of North Africa. As visitors continue along the route, walking under a painted *trompe l'oeil* "sky," they arrive at the Fragrance Market, a courtyardlike fork in the road where, in keeping with the theme, health, beauty, and fragrance retailers have been clustered. "We've merchandised the retailers much like a traditional department store model," notes Paul Beirnes, Desert Passage director of marketing. The clustering allows for comparison shopping, and, along with the architectural theme, creates a stronger identity for the retailers.

From the "outdoor" Fragrance Market, visitors proceed through the Treasure House, a large hall with a decorative ceiling, and emerge into the Lost City. Patterned after ancient rock cities such as Jordan's Petra, the Lost City features an eight-story-high "mountain" under an 11-story "sky." Buildings and towers line the rock wall, opening onto a large public square with a tiled fountain. Several of the center's restaurants, along with a food court, are located here, complete with "outdoor" seating in the square, and tables set up on balconies overlooking the square.

The next stop along the journey is the Sultan's Palace, a domed space designed by fashion designer Todd Oldham and architect David Rockwell, which also serves as the entry from the parking garage. Evoking the palace of an imagined sultan who surrounded himself with treasures from around the world, the Sultan's Palace district is brimming with home decor retailers. Occupying the most visible storefront in the district is a Z-

Gallerie shop, which, in its opening months, has become the number-one performer in that retailer's lineup.

Next is the Medina, selling artisan wares, and the Merchants' Harbor. Patterned after a North African port town, Merchants' Harbor offers the clubs and restaurants that one might expect in a port of call. Hovering over the port is a 155-foot-long model of a 1920s steamer. Further reinforcing the theme—and serving as a tourist attraction in its own right—is a "thunder squall" that develops periodically, darkening the "sky" and raining briefly into a "tidepool" below.

Another station in the tourist's pilgrimage is the Dome of the Spirits, a beautifully painted space lit with blue glass pendants reminiscent of the mosques of Istanbul. Beyond the Dome of the Spirits are the larger Rotunda and the adjacent Hall of Lamps. The Rotunda, with its 65-foot-high dome, serves as a lobby for the Theatre for the Performing Arts, and frames the walk to the hotel and casino. Trading on a location very near to the casino, the Hall of Lamps features art, designer fashions, and high-end jewelry.

Although the architecture of Desert Passage does not literally reproduce that of historic structures, substantial time and resources were invested in capturing authentic detailing for the various destinations of the "journey." Materials, design motifs, and

▲
In the Lost City, buildings and towers are built into an eight-story-high "mountain," under an 11-story "sky."
Gregg Photographic

A 155-foot-long model of a 1920s steamer overlooks Merchants' Harbor. A "thunder squall" develops periodically over this seaport district, and rain falls from the "sky" into a "tide-pool" basin.
Gregg Photographic

The designers of ▶ Desert Passage researched design motifs, colors, and materials of North Africa, Spain, and India to provide a sense of the architectural detailing one might find in each destination along the Desert Passage "journey."
Gregg Photographic

even construction methods were meticulously researched and documented by the designers and fabricators, both for the core and shell work and for tenant improvements. Much of the ironwork, tile, lighting, and plaster castings were custom fabricated for the project. Some 700 material samples were produced for approvals, including over 100 different plaster textures and finishes. As a final step, painted finishes were "aged" to reflect study findings on the effect of oil lamps and natural elements on various materials.

Some of the research and development for the project were conducted in the field—in Morocco and other locations. The Moroccan government was consulted, and relationships were forged with Moroccan artisans and vendors. Some of the finishes at Desert Passage, including light fixtures, tiled benches, and leatherwork, were fabricated by

skilled artisans in Morocco. Other finishes, particularly ironwork, are antiques found overseas or within the United States.

Marketing and Leasing

Tenant leasing for Desert Passage focused on several objectives: (1) using restaurants as anchor tenants—in particular, signing renowned, one-of-a-kind restaurants; (2) signing tenants whose merchandise supports the Desert Passage theme; (3) signing unique tenants of any type; and (4) working with all tenants to ensure that their shops were consistent with the Desert Passage design concept.

Of the more than 100 shops and restaurants that opened their doors on the center's opening day, 52 were new to Las Vegas. Restaurants include Anasazi, of Santa Fe; Bice and Blue Note Jazz Club, both of New York; and the famous Commander's Palace, of New Orleans. Among the most theme-oriented retailers are African Odyssey and A Thousand and One Boxes. All together, Desert Passage was approximately 93 percent leased (or committed) on opening day. "The challenge of Desert Passage leasing," notes Paul Beirnes, "was not just to find the right tenants, but to place the tenants where most appropriate thematically."

Tenants were asked to stretch beyond their standard corporate look and develop their store—or at least their storefront—in a manner that would reinforce the design elements of the district they were to be located in. Like actors in a movie, the retailers were given their "motivation." Each prospective tenant received a handsomely produced "district brochure," a pamphlet designed along the lines of a travel guide, which described, through words and pictures, the district story line and the appropriate architectural response. The India Gate brochure, for example, frames the overall design goals this way: "In this historic retail street, where the desire is to preserve the existing architecture, the Tenant's interaction with the building yields a unique expression of their identity while remaining respectful of the neighborhood." Or, as stated in the accompanying *Desert Passage Technical Guidebook*, "The requirements for store design are as follows: (1) Store images must be creatively adapted, (2) A total store design must be developed, and (3) The customer experience must be enhanced."

In practice, some tenants have risen to the occasion more readily and successfully than others. In some shops, signage has been rendered in mosaic or other appropriate materials, and storefronts are adapted to the regional aesthetic. In several cases, the Desert Passage themes have even been incorporated into the interior design of the shop. A few tenants, on the other hand, were less willing to forgo their corporate design parameters, and are less clearly attuned to the Desert Passage concept.

▲ Well-known restaurants are employed as anchor tenants; restaurants include Bice (above); Commander's Palace, of New Orleans; Anasazi, of Santa Fe; and Blue Note Jazz Club, of New York. *TrizecHahn*

Management and Operations

The marketing and management arm of TrizecHahn Development Corporation has developed a finely tuned technique known as the Daily Sales Program to track visitors and sales at Desert Passage, and a Daily Sales Tool Box to intervene at an early stage where appropriate. Laser counters, located at each entry and at other locations within the center, tabulate both the number of visitors at each point and the direction of flow. TrizecHahn has also developed a program in which each tenant keys in its sales totals each day, to be tabulated by the center's management staff. In return, each tenant gets a daily report of (1) visitors to the center, (2) total sales within the tenant's retailing classification, and (3) the tenant's rank within that retailing classification.

The Daily Sales Program helps both tenants and management. In addition to learning where they stand in relation to their competition, tenants get a sense of whether the sales they are capturing are adequate in relation to visitor attendance. For management, the numbers are a versatile tool for planning as well as for reacting to difficulties. The numbers can be correlated with convention dates, for example, to see what

◀ Tenants were encouraged to develop their storefront designs in concert with the project's overall design themes, using appropriate materials and details. *TrizecHahn* merchandise appeals to various groups of visitors and demographic profiles. As Wagman puts it, "How we pitch those 70,000 [daily visitors] varies, based on the insights obtained from the Daily Sales Program." Alberta Davidson, senior vice president for corporate marketing, notes that "the Daily Sales Program helps management to nurture stores, and conversely to identify deficiencies."

The numbers get translated into action by means of the Daily Sales Tool Box—a helping hand for management when particular districts, retail sectors, or overall sales are in need of support. For example, should the numbers indicate that visitors are bypassing a particular district, live entertainers can be used to draw visitors to that area. Or, in a second example, a coupon program can be brought out to influence shopping patterns. One recent program provided $25 in restaurant coupons as a reward for $250 in store purchases.

Site plan.
TrizecHahn
▼

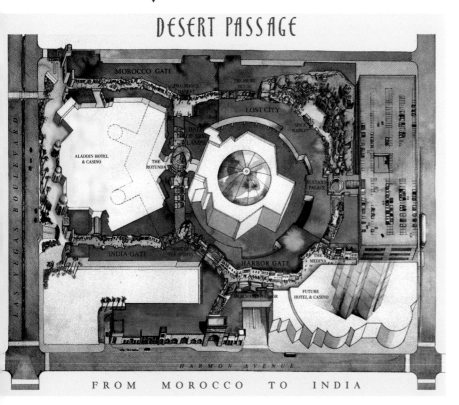

Conclusion

Desert Passage has advanced the entertainment shopping center format in several areas:

■ Design: Desert Passage represents a further exploration of the potential of a theme-based environment and architecture. The designers have used architecture to differentiate the spaces within the center into several thematic and merchandising districts, increasing overall appeal to consumers as well as creating defined identities for the places and retailers within. The use of live entertainers supports the theme and varies the experience for visitors.

■ Merchandising: Desert Passage also represents a closer marrying of the retailers to the entertainment concept, as evidenced by the selection of theme-appropriate tenants, the clustering of tenants into theme-related districts, and the focus on tenant storefront design. As Wagman notes, "The tenants are an essential part of the story. Like an existing city, each shop must fit within its building and context."

■ Management: The almost real-time monitoring of visitors and sales through the project's Daily Sales Program enlarges management's ability to understand and control activity in the center, leading to optimal results both for owner and tenants. "Shopping centers are no longer a formula business," notes Wagman—and in that environment, information is a fundamental key to success.

Project Data

Land Use Information

Classification	Number of stores	GLA (square feet)
General merchandise	10	52,560
Food service	22	181,151
Clothing and accessories	42	127,110
Shoes	5	7,595
Home furnishings	15	39,835
Gift/specialty	22	49,957
Jewelry	13	19,054
Health and beauty	10	15,761
Total	139	493,223

Percentage leased or committed: 93 percent

Percentage of GLA occupied: 83–85 percent

Annual rents (approximate; per square foot): $70.55

Average annual retail sales (approximate; per square foot): Exceeding $780 pro forma

Average length of lease: Eight to ten years

Development Cost Information

Development Costs

Site acquisition	$30,000,000
Excavation and grading	0 (received finished pads)
Sewer, water, and drainage	0 (received finished pads)
Subtotal, development costs	$30,000,000

Construction Costs

Retail	$134,700,000
Other (parking, paving, curbs, sidewalks, and landscaping)	44,400,000
Subtotal, construction costs	$179,100,000

Soft Costs

Architecture and engineering services	$11,100,000
Project management	4,700,000
Marketing	3,400,000
Legal and accounting services	1,900,000
Taxes and insurance	1,400,000
Subtotal, soft costs	$22,500,000

Other

Financing	$9,900,000
Leasing	34,400,000
Development fee	8,600,000
Subtotal, other costs	$52,900,000
Total development costs	$284,500,000

Development Schedule

Site purchased	Not applicable
Planning started	May 1996
Construction started	August 1998
Sales/leasing started	December 1997
Project completed	August 2000

Case Studies

Easton Town Center
Columbus, Ohio

With a central town square that serves as the focal point of the community for shopping, dining, entertainment, and socializing, Easton Town Center is a revisitation of the classic American downtown. The design and construction of the 725,000-square-foot complex reflect the application of modern retail and leisure-time concepts to a traditional urban street setting. Traditional building materials include red brick and white-painted trim; nostalgic exterior fixtures, such as cast-iron lampposts, help define the project's character. To create the appropriate scale and increase the sense of intimacy, ceiling heights in enclosed areas were lowered to 13.5 feet. Pedestrian-friendly in the more traditional, town-planning sense, the development's grid of real streets, curbside parallel parking with meters, wide sidewalks, and numerous crosswalks and pathways accommodate cars and people alike.

The 13 buildings are not mere facades but real, three-dimensional edifices, organized into eight city blocks. Service areas are fully designed and integrated into each building; there is no unsightly "back of the house." Year-round, a mix of indoor and outdoor activities is offered: winter, for example, brings holiday

**The retail shops are primarily street oriented, although ▶
there is also an abundance of enclosed spaces, giving
variety to the leisure-time destination experience.**
Walter Larrimore

Development Team

Developers

Steiner + Associates, Inc.
4016 Townsfair Way, Suite 201
Columbus, Ohio 43219
(614) 414-7300

The Georgetown Company
667 Madison Avenue
New York, New York 10021
(212) 755-2323

The Limited, Inc.
3 Limited Parkway
Columbus, Ohio 43216
(614) 479-7980

Architects

Development Design Group, Inc.
7 St. Paul Street
Baltimore, Maryland 21202
(410) 962-0505

Meacham & Apel Architects, Inc.
6161 Riverside Drive, Suite A
Dublin, Ohio 43017
(614) 764-0407

Planner

Cooper Robertson & Partners
311 West 43rd Street, 13th Floor
New York, New York 10036
(212) 247-1717

but increase activity at the second-floor level and add a business component to the traffic through Easton.

Easton Town Center, which opened in July 1999, has succeeded primarily because it is a real neighborhood center. The development meets more than the simple market demand for brand-name retail and theme-based entertainment on the outskirts of Columbus; it provides a safe urban setting that fulfills the community's need for social interaction while providing a mix of uses, including retail, entertainment, restaurant, and office space. Free summer concerts on Thursdays and a Saturday morning farmers' market are just a few of the events enjoyed by the community. Garage parking is free of charge; revenue from street meters—in addition to the revenue from any tickets for parking violations—is donated to charities.

Easton Town Center was carefully planned and merchandised from the beginning. To ensure that the project's architecture and design would accommodate both the needs of modern retailers and the demands of modern consumers, merchandising informed the entire planning process, and tenant mix was given the highest priority. A clear vision of Easton Town Center's essence—its tenant mix, merchandising, and spirit—shaped the design, development, and construction stages, and continues to make its presence felt in current operations. As a result, in Easton Town Center's first year, more than 9 million people visited the project, and the heavy customer traffic reportedly produced extraordinary first-year sales of more than $400 per square foot. Several of the retail stores and restaurants are the most productive in their chain; many of these tenants are producing well in excess of $600 per square foot, making them the highest-grossing stores in the greater Columbus market. These sales levels

festivities to the town square, which, in the spring, accommodates children playing in the interactive "pop" fountain. Offices above street-level storefronts not only benefit the companies that locate in Easton Town Center

have helped to create a project income stream that is producing yields in excess of 12 percent (unleveraged) on project costs of about $120 million.

Development

The story of Easton Town Center parallels the story of The Limited, Inc., a multiline retail chain headquartered in Columbus, Ohio. Both Easton and The Limited originated with the vision of Leslie Wexner, the founder, chairman, and chief executive officer of The Limited. In the early 1980s, building on its 18 years of constant growth, The Limited started to operate as a venture capitalist, creating new businesses and purchasing existing specialty retailers. In this climate, Wexner formed a real estate development unit within The Limited; one of the unit's early projects was the 1,200-acre country-club community of New Albany, just a few miles east of Easton.

Envisioning a business park for The Limited's national headquarters and operations center, along with a multiuse development of retail, office, residential, hotel, and entertainment venues, Wexner began, in 1986, to purchase farmland centered around Morse Road, in the northeast quadrant of Columbus. Within the city limits and just within the I-270 beltway, the land that Wexner eventually named Easton was a large infill parcel surrounded by low-density development that had been encouraged by city legislation offering a ten-year, 100 percent abatement of property taxes for new development. With each purchase of a parcel, Wexner's development team had to win zoning approval for the conversion from agricultural to commercial use. By the time Wexner announced the start of construction, in early 1996, the fully assembled

A nighttime view of the town center illustrates how a sophisticated lighting scheme can add drama and elegance, creating an enticing environment that draws customers to shop and be entertained in the evening.
Walter Larrimore

Victoria's Secret catalogue distribution center and The Limited, Inc. The widening of nearby I-270 from six to 12 lanes had begun in anticipation of increased traffic.

A 35-acre town center had been an integral part of the plan since Easton's inception as a master-planned community. By 1996, enough of the desired balance of residential, office, and retail space had been achieved to justify planning the town center, and the development partners began to look for outside expertise to help create a special environment for Easton. They found it in CocoWalk, a pioneering, $38 million, 145,000-square-foot, three-story retail and entertainment complex in Coconut Grove, Florida, that had opened in November 1991, attracting 35 tenants within its first six months of operation.

Constructa, CocoWalk's developer, had stepped in to rescue a faltering project, transforming it into a tremendous financial and critical success. Yaromir Steiner, who was both Constructa's president and the project manager for CocoWalk, was invited to recreate CocoWalk's magic in Easton. Steiner resigned from Constructa, formed his own development company, Steiner + Associates, and moved his entire operations to Columbus. Steiner + Associates shares an equity position in Easton Town Center with The Georgetown Company; The Limited, Inc.; and various private investors, one of whom is Arnold Schwarzenegger. Steiner + Associates acts as Easton Town Center's management company, allowing The Limited, Inc., to continue its gradual sell-off of noncore assets.

Site Planning and Design

To create a site plan for Easton, Wexner brought in Cooper Robertson & Partners; Steiner + Associates had a prior relationship with Development Design Group. Together, Cooper Robertson & Partners and Development Design Group reviewed the best of past town-

parcels formed a contiguous 1,200 acres, an area twice the size of the local Ohio State University campus.

Meanwhile, the recession of the early 1990s led to drastic corporate restructuring at The Limited, Inc. As a publicly traded company focused on maximizing shareholder value, The Limited responded by spinning off its various store brands as stand-alone businesses and by shedding noncore activities. One of the noncore businesses was Easton, of which The Limited sold 50 percent to The Georgetown Company, of New York, which became a partner in the development.

Easton and its environs continued to develop during the startup phase of Easton Town Center. By year-end 1995, 4 million square feet of office space had been constructed, providing a local and regional presence for Chase Manhattan Mortgage Corporation, Price Waterhouse, and M/I Schottenstein Homes, along with the world headquarters for the

center designs—including Country Club Plaza, in Kansas City, Missouri; and Reston Town Center, in Reston, Virginia—to extract useful ideas, then develop and improve upon them.

The development and design team used a storyboard process to identify specific elements that would naturally be present in a small town: a post office, a library, a high school, a movie theater, and so forth. The "library" is the Barnes & Noble superstore, the "high school" houses Life Time Fitness, and the "old" movie theater building now houses a Pottery Barn store. The result creates the impression that Easton Town Center has evolved over a number of years. For instance, the project's main atrium, in Easton Station, is reminiscent of a train station. But instead of simply applying a train station theme, the team designed Easton Station to look like the plaza in front of an abandoned train station that had been retrofitted with a glass roof.

This "back story" lends a layer of authenticity to the experience of spending leisure time in a familiar world.

Although metered, on-street parking is available, most of the parking is provided free in two multilevel parking garages tucked into the corners of the 33.8-acre parcel. Parking is easy to find, but the surface lots are tucked between buildings and are not generally visible from the street. Tax-increment financing was procured to offset the costs of public infrastructure, but otherwise the developers financed the project.

In addition to Easton Town Center, Easton includes Easton Market, a 900,000-square-foot retail center just west of the town center; Easton Commons, a 700-unit apartment complex just south of the town center; 5 million square feet of office space; and three hotels: the 310-room Columbus Hilton and Towers, a 120-room Residence Inn by Marriott, and a 120-room Extended Stay America. Currently under construction is the Town Center Fashion District, a 48-acre expansion of the town center that will be anchored by a 170,000-square-foot Nordstrom store.

◄ **To underscore the "back story" that Easton Town Center is an urban village that has evolved organically over time, the architecture is a deliberate mix of both traditional and contemporary styles and materials, giving the impression that older buildings have undergone modern-day renovations.**
Walter Larrimore

Easton Station, the enclosed portion of the town center, is styled after a Victorian-era train station that has been renovated for modern-day use, thus combining the familiarity and comfort of traditional architecture with a contemporary retail purpose.
Walter Larrimore
▼

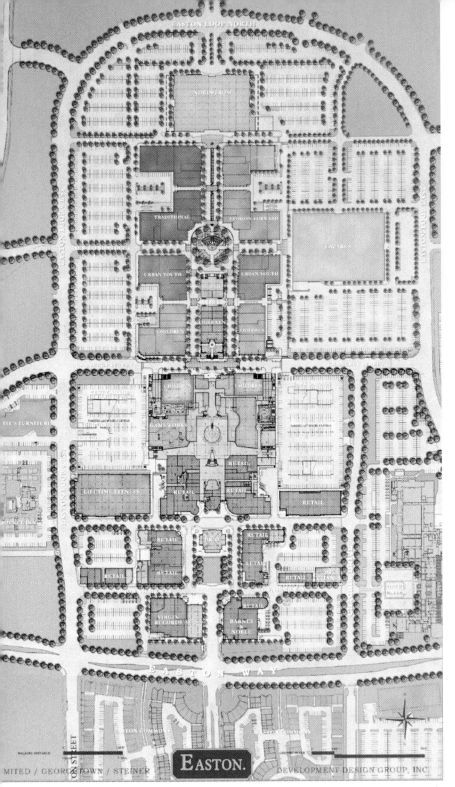

The ring road that surrounds the town center is a public thoroughfare, but the street grid within consists of private streets, allowing management to divert traffic and close off streets to accommodate various events. The upper half of this site plan shows the 48-acre second phase, to be called the Town Center Fashion District. The second phase will effectively double the size of Easton Town Center.

Development Design Group, Inc.

Tenants

Easton Town Center is designed to offer patrons a variety of ways to spend their leisure time. As a lifestyle center, it has no true anchors. The mostly two-story buildings are laid out around a town square and along urban streets. The development team wanted not just a "Main Street," but a Columbus Main Street. They sought out local restaurateurs to develop new concepts based on local preferences; two notable examples are the Ocean Club and Brio Tuscan Grille, serving seafood and Italian fare, respectively. Local fast-food providers include Panera Bread and C.V. Wrappers.

Large-format, sit-down restaurants include PF Chang's China Bistro, Cheesecake Factory, Fado's Irish Pub, and Hama Sushi. Planet Hollywood and All-Star Café are located adjacent to the 30-screen multiplex, a partnership of Planet Hollywood and AMC Theatres. Together, the two companies created a nostalgic theme using authentic props from movie sets, including cars, boats, airplanes, and wardrobe items from famous movies. Planet Hollywood also introduced a new ice-cream shop, Cool Planet, adjacent to the movie theater. Planet Hollywood itself departs from its usual concept by being more a restaurant where stars would dine than a restaurant about movie stars. Other national restaurant chains include Johnny Rockets and two Starbucks coffee shops.

Life Time Fitness, a Minneapolis-based health club, leased an entire 95,000-square-foot, two-story building to house its facilities—which, in addition to the expected aerobics studios, sauna, and fitness equipment include two swimming pools, two basketball courts, squash courts, climbing walls, and a child-care facility. Other lifestyle venues include Pottery Barn, Williams-Sonoma, Smith & Hawken, and Restoration Hardware.

A partnership of AMC Theatres and Planet Hollywood produced a prototype with a Planet Hollywood at ground level and a 30-screen cineplex emptying out on the second level.
Walter Larrimore

Some of the fashion venues include Banana Republic, Eddie Bauer, J. Crew, Baby Gap, Gap Kids, Gap, Ann Taylor, Talbots, and the first-ever World Foot Locker—and, of course, The Limited, Inc.'s, lineup of specialty clothing stores: Limited, Too; Victoria's Secret; Abercrombie & Fitch; abercrombie; and Bath and Body Works.

Entertainment venues include Virgin Records megastore; Jeepers, an indoor amusement park for children; a 35,000-square-foot GameWorks; the Shark Club, a billiards and bowling venue; Columbus's first-ever all-night jazz club, Round Midnight; and the Funny Bone Comedy Club. A local entrepreneur has opened a nightclub with a South Beach theme, and a local theater group performs daily at the Shadowbox Cabaret.

Experience Gained

- Time was well spent in planning and designing public spaces that were large enough to handle crowds during events but not so large that they seemed empty at other times.

- Bringing new retail and entertainment names (30 percent of the tenants) to the Columbus market contributed to the project's success.

- More than 20 local or regional businesses were actively recruited to add to the tenant mix.

- Not enough attention was paid to the planning and design of peripheral retail locations.

- Easton Town Center's success has proven that leisure-time destination concepts that worked in southeastern Florida can be transported to a smaller market, a colder climate, and a suburban location without a large tourist base.

Project Data

Land Use Information

	Current	Planned expansion
Site area (acres)	33.8	48.0
Gross building area (square feet)		
Office	83,178	
Retail (includes theaters, health and fitness center)	672,230	349,145
Department stores	0	407,000
Total gross building area	724,730	839,323
Office net rentable area (square feet)	48,000	77,000
Retail gross leasable area (GLA; includes theaters, health and fitness center)	599,865	314,230
Parking spaces	3,800	2,695
Floor/area ratio	.43	

Office Tenant Information

Percentage of net rentable area occupied: 85 percent

Number of tenants: 15

Average area occupied by tenants: 3,500 square feet

Annual rents: $16–$20 per square foot

Average length of lease: Five to ten years

Retail Tenant Information

Tenant classification	Number of stores	GLA (square feet)
General merchandise	3	7,750
Food service	18	75,576
Clothing and accessories	20	106,297
Shoes	3	21,165
Home furnishings	4	28,081
Home appliances/music	1	22,376
Hobby/special interest	2	6,675
Gift/specialty	6	45,607
Personal services	1	1,107
Recreation/community	8	282,821
Financial services	1	1,044
Health and beauty	5	11,366
Total	72	599,865

Annual rent: $24–$32 per square foot

Average annual sales: $444 per square foot

Average length of lease: Five to ten years

Land Use Plan

Use	Current (acres)	Percentage of site	Planned expansion (acres)	Percentage of site
Buildings	12	36	13	26
Streets, surface parking, sidewalks	12	36	27	58
Landscaping, open spaces	3	9	5	11
Parking garages	6	17	2	5
Planned building			0.5	2
Total	34		48	

Development Cost Information

Site acquisition costs	$16,000,000
Site improvement costs	9,000,000
Construction costs	78,000,000
Soft costs	32,000,000
Total development cost	$135,000,000

Development Schedule

Site purchased	1996
Planning started	October 1996
Sales/leasing started	January 1997
Construction started	June 1998
Phase I completed	June 1999
Phase II completed	August 2001

Glorietta Mall at the Ayala Center
Makati, Manila, Republic of the Philippines

Located in Makati, the heart of metropolitan Manila's business district, Glorietta Mall at the Ayala Center is the Philippines's premier urban entertainment and retail destination. In the 1970s, Glorietta Mall was a suburban strip shopping center that attracted customers with its ample parking and imported merchandise. As the Ayala Company developed the land surrounding the mall into a high-density urban environment, the original outdoor mall was enclosed and expanded into Glorietta Mall—the centerpiece of the Ayala Center.

The mall's retail mix attracts both high-end and value-conscious shoppers. The movie theaters, new food court, restaurants, parks, cultural programs, and special events draw on a diverse base of customers from the surrounding hotels, offices, and residential areas. Glorietta Mall's festive atmosphere, combined with the urban environment of the Ayala Center, makes it Manila's most popular destination for daily outings and nightlife.

**The new serviced apartment buildings—the first in the ▶
Philippines—articulate the entrance to Glorietta Mall.**
Ayala Land, Inc.

Development Team

Planning and Development

Ayala Land, Inc.
Tower One
Ayala Triangle, Ayala Avenue
Makati, Manila
Philippines

Operations and Management

Ayala Land Commercial Centers Group
Fifth Level
Glorietta 4, Ayala Center
Makati, Manila
Philippines

The Site

The rapid and unplanned growth of metropolitan Manila has resulted in poor air quality, extreme traffic congestion, and cramped conditions. In stark contrast is the Ayala Center, in Makati, a carefully planned urban oasis within sprawling metropolitan Manila. Once an outlying area of Manila that was largely covered by rice fields, Makati has grown into a high-density, mixed-use commercial district; it is the address of choice in the Philippines for domestic and multinational corporations, embassies, luxury hotels, and banks.

The Ayala Center, the heart of Makati, offers mixed-use commercial development that includes four hotels, four supermarkets, four high-rise apartment buildings, two malls (Glorietta and Greenbelt), the Philippines's first serviced apartments, a public park, and more than 5,000 parking spaces. Total combined development (gross floor area) at the Ayala Center covers 2,777,474 square feet,

with 1,038,278 square feet of gross leasable area (GLA). Within the Ayala Center, Glorietta Mall is the primary attraction for entertainment, shopping, and nightlife.

The Ayala Company was the impetus for Makati's dramatic transformation from an agrarian suburb to a high-quality urban district unique in the Philippines. Most of the recent land development has been carried out by Ayala Land, Inc., the development arm the Ayala Company created in 1988. The decision to maintain ownership—offering tenants long-term land leases instead of selling them parcels—has afforded the company considerable control of land use decisions, allowing Ayala Land to develop according to its own vision. Pert Rodriguez, assistant vice president of Ayala Land, points out, "We have been very successful in creating a quality environment to live, work, and play because we are extremely careful to balance new development with the capacity of the existing infrastructure."

History

The design of the original shopping center built by the Ayala Company in the 1970s was similar to that of early American suburban strip malls. It was not enclosed, and its two wings (Glorietta I and II) converged at a central area, where there was an outdoor bandstand called the Glorietta. (*Glorietta* is the Spanish word used to describe the public meeting place in Philippine towns that were designed during the Spanish colonial era.) The original mall, which housed a collection of competing merchants who sold goods imported from Hong Kong, lacked a unified theme. Moreover, because the Ayala Company had little retail experience, it leased the land to retailers and allowed them to design and build in whatever way they saw fit; the result was poor circulation and a lack of cohesion.

As the leases on the stores in Glorietta I and II ended, Ayala Land took the opportunity to redevelop the shops and improve the tenant mix and design. Hellmuth, Obata + Kassabaum (HOK) was commissioned in 1988 to create a redevelopment plan for the Makati Commercial District, the earlier name of the Ayala Center. The HOK plan, which added two more wings and placed anchor stores at the ends of the axes, was based on a cruciform design. In response to the increasing density of new commercial development, the plan also called for parking structures—the first of their kind in the Philippines. Although the plan provided a good vision for the Makati Commercial District, it lacked details.

By 1990, the Makati Commercial District had changed dramatically, from a rural suburb of Manila to a high-density, mixed-use district. A 1990 plan by The Architects' Collaborative (TAC) followed up on the HOK plan, increasing the floor/area ratio of the surrounding office and residential land uses. In addition, TAC's plan recommended enclosing the mall, adding air conditioning, and turning the outdoor bandstand into the mall's main activity center. Until this point, the wings of the cruciform had not been connected, and the shops still faced outside.

Building a major addition and transforming the original strip center into an enclosed mall while simultaneously maintaining operations was an ambitious undertaking that required careful coordination. Construction was constrained by the existing structures, utilities had to be repeatedly relocated, staging-area space was scarce, and "unknowns" constantly appeared as the project progressed. Ayala Land minimized the impact of the renovation by screening ongoing construction, working at night to reduce noise, and

The 44,000-square-foot activity center called the Glorietta is the centerpoint of the mall's radiating cruciform design. Before the mall was enclosed, the Glorietta was the site of an outdoor bandstand.
Ayala Land, Inc.

phasing the work. The company also had to be extremely sensitive to its tenants, who were temporarily relocated during construction. In a testament to its successful management of the process, Ayala Land did not lose a single tenant throughout the entire construction phase.

Planning and Design

Now complete, Glorietta Mall's cruciform design radiates from the 43,000-square-foot activity center called the Glorietta. The Glorietta has a domed glass atrium with a fountain at the center that shoots a plume of water to the height of the atrium's 190-foot ceiling. The Glorietta's open floor plan, designed for maximum flexibility, is used for new product launches, cultural exhibits, and entertainment; it also serves as a resting place and a children's playground.

The rest of the mall is divided into four quarters—Glorietta I, II, III, and IV—and the quarters and the land uses just outside the mall are further grouped into quads. For example, Quad I includes the Glorietta I portion of Glorietta Mall, the adjacent Park Square I shopping center, and the Hotel Nikko Manila Garden.

Glorietta I and Glorietta II were both part of the original outdoor strip mall, but they underwent a spectacular transformation when the mall was enclosed and renovated. Glorietta I, with two levels of retail space, a gross floor area (GFA) of 214,538 square feet, and a GLA of 137,482 square feet, appeals to a broad spectrum of both value-conscious and midrange consumers. Many of the tenants are local merchants selling shoes, bags, leather goods, textiles, and books. Glorietta I's original 55,696-square-foot, four-screen multiplex theatre—the first in the Philippines—was maintained after renovations. Glorietta II, with three levels, a GFA of 129,204 square feet, and a GLA of 78,529 square feet, caters

primarily to children and teens. Oversized toys in the hallway create a playful atmosphere, and a new store called Kids@Work provides a shop-and-play service that allows parents to leave their children supervised in a stimulating environment.

Glorietta III, completed in 1993, consists of 285,628 square feet of all-new construction on three levels and targets a young and upwardly mobile crowd. It is part of the Quad III complex, which includes the Shangri-La Hotel Manila and 6750 Ayala Avenue, an office high rise with ground-floor retail. Quad III's trendy clubs and restaurants—Zoo and Giraffe—combined with those at Glorietta III—Hard Rock Café, TGI Friday's, Streetlife, and a microbrewery—make it Manila's premier place for nightlife, balancing the mall's many daytime attractions. Glorietta III was also the first mall to attract high-end international retailers such as Louis Vuitton, Armani, and Prada.

Construction of Glorietta IV was finished in 1999, completing the mall's cruciform layout. Glorietta IV focuses on family entertainment and has 1,053,500 square feet of space (400,653 square feet GLA) that includes a new food court, seven movie theaters, a serviced apartment building, and the Timezone family amusement center. Tenants include California Pizza Kitchen, Calvin Klein, Escada, Marks & Spencer, Tower Records, and Warner Bros. Studio Store.

The serviced apartment building, the first in the Philippines, caters to executives in need of temporary residences close to their business in Makati. The two high-rise apartment towers have 306 units, a business center, conference rooms, and a fitness club. A joint venture of Ayala Land and Rodamco N.V., a Netherlands-based invest-

ment company, the project is managed by Oakwood Asia Pacific, a U.S. company based in Singapore.

Ayala Land overcame the challenges of renovating the obsolete strip mall and combining it with new construction to create a virtually seamless enclosed mall. Only the most careful observer would notice from the interior that it was not all-new construction. The high level of interior finishes throughout the mall, including marble floors, creates an upscale atmosphere, and the mall's graphics and directories, designed by RTKL in 1996, give the mall a unified theme and make it easier to navigate the hub-and-spoke floor plan.

Renovating the exterior was equally challenging. Dave Blass, project architect for Ayala Land, points out that the project has some inherent shortcomings: "The exterior evolved incrementally and does not yet have a unified theme. Other factors beyond our control, such as Manila's pollution and harsh weather extremes, make the exterior difficult to maintain." Improving the exterior facade is a priority for Ayala Land, and the company has persuaded some tenants to abandon their older facades in favor of newer finishes. With its bright neon lights and large logos marking the entrances to the restaurants and clubs, the exterior design of Glorietta III creates a well-defined space and an exciting atmosphere.

Transportation

Transportation and pedestrian links are a major part of the Ayala Center's development strategy. Private automobile ownership is not as common in the Philippines as in the United States, so it was critical to ensure easy access to the mall via mass transit. A major bus and jeepney (an ornately decorated vehicle smaller than a bus) terminal is located near the entrance of Glorietta Mall, providing easy access for customers, mall employees, and workers in Makati. Because of Manila's notorious traffic, many commuters adjust their shopping schedules around their commute, generating a substantial amount of business after working hours. Ayala Land recently completed a network of elevated covered pedestrian walkways and underground street crossings to protect pedestrians from the monsoon rains and tropical sun, as well as to improve access to the mall from the adjacent offices and hotels. The walkways have already been successful in encouraging pedestrians to walk rather than take short trips by vehicle.

Ayala Land is also a partner with MRT Holdings, Inc., a consortium that won the bid to construct and operate the new Metro Rail Transit System (MRT-3). With a station located at the Ayala Center, the MRT-3 will provide an efficient transit alternative to the congested bus and jeepney thoroughfares, and will greatly improve access to Glorietta Mall and bolster its prominence as a super-regional center.

More than 5,000 covered, surface, and underground parking spaces, shared with adjacent offices and hotels, are located at the mall. The above-grade parking structures include retail on the ground level.

▲
The carpeting; plush, stadium-style seating; and digital sound of the new theaters offer a higher level of quality than is typically found in theaters in the Philippines.
Ayala Land, Inc.

Entertainment

Entertainment, particularly activities for people of all income and age levels, is a key to the Ayala Center's success. By keeping up on the latest entertainment and retail development trends from around the globe and combining them with its own ideas, Ayala Land has created an entertainment and retail experience well suited to the Filipino market.

Going to the movies has always been a popular Filipino pastime and an ideal way to escape the tropical heat. Ayala Land capitalized on this, making theaters an integral part of its development strategy by locating 15 of them throughout the Ayala Center. The company introduced the Philippines's first multiplex cinema at Glorietta I and recently opened seven state-of-the-art theaters in Glorietta IV; the new theaters' carpeting; plush, stadium-style seating; and digital

sound offer a higher quality and level of finish than are typically found in the Philippines. The ArtFilm program, which reserves one theater solely for noncommercial retrospectives and classic films, attracts a diverse clientele, ranging from students to more mature and sophisticated moviegoers.

Guaranteed seating is another unique feature at Glorietta Mall. (Traditionally, theaters in the Philippines oversell seats, leaving people standing in the aisles.) Ayala Land has also started to offer advanced screenings of selected feature films, charging more than twice the normal price. Although this approach has been successful as a means of promoting new films and advertising by word of mouth, movie prices are generally kept affordable to ensure that large crowds from all income levels are drawn to the mall.

Strategically located adjacent to the theaters is the Timezone entertainment center, a joint venture of Ayala Land and Leisure and Allied Industries, an Australian amusement-center operator. Timezone has the latest in interactive high-tech games, which appeal both to kids and to a more mature market. The energetic atmosphere is enhanced by the latest music and sports videos, projected onto giant walls. The affordably priced games capture impulse spending from shoppers or moviegoers with a little extra time.

No other place in the Philippines offers the variety and quality of restaurants and nightlife found at the Ayala Center. The selection of dining venues is well balanced, supporting both daytime and evening itineraries. The new food court in Glorietta IV, called Food Choices at Glorietta, caters to busy shoppers, students, and the office lunch crowd. In addition to Food Choices, a diverse mix of international and local restaurant chains are located throughout the mall.

The restaurants were clustered together to create a central destination for nightlife as well as to make it easier to control access and security from within the mall. While California Pizza Kitchen, Chili's, Häagen-Dazs, Hard Rock Café, TGI Friday's, Starbucks, Streetlife, and the microbrewery are open throughout the day and evening, the atmosphere at night is markedly different.

Streetlife, a grouping of restaurants with an outdoor urban theme—including streetlights, brick walks, and outdoor café seating—serves a busy lunch crowd during the day; during the evening, the restaurants offer dinner and drinks, and the area takes on a lively atmosphere. Many of the theme and signature restaurants play a more significant role in nightlife in the Philippines than they do in the United States. TGI Friday's, Häagen-Dazs, and Starbucks, for example, are all packed, late-night hangouts. Hard Rock Café regularly hosts live concerts with famous musicians; in addition to being a popular bar, it is also a hot dance spot. Numerous other trendy clubs and restaurants, such as Giraffe, Tony Roma's Ribs, and Zoo, are located just outside the mall.

The Ayala Center is a major destination for nonshoppers as well. Just outside the mall is Greenbelt Park, with landscaped grounds and mature trees reserved in perpetuity by the Ayala Company for use as a public park. The park has an open-air church, which draws many worshipers to the Ayala Center. The Ayala Company also built the History Museum of the Philippines at the Ayala Center. These gifts to the public are located on some of the highest-priced land in the country and demonstrate the Ayala Company's commitment to the community. Other, smaller parks with sculptures and

rich landscaping are located just outside the mall, creating an attractive transition to the mall's entrances.

As pollution increases in Manila and green space becomes increasingly scarce, a trip to the Ayala Center has, for many residents, replaced traditional family outings to the park. No other place in Manila offers the excitement, options, safe and clean environment, and relaxing atmosphere that the Ayala Center does.

Marketing and Management

The Ayala Company's Commercial Centers Group manages operations and marketing for the mall. Its services include construction and property management; cinema, family entertainment, and food court operations and leasing; advertising and promotional campaigns; and maintenance.

Promotional events are held continuously in the mall. Midnight Madness, during which all of the shops offer big discounts, is held three times a year. Another major event is Bank of the Philippines (BPI) Appliance Madness, when the major appliance stores sell their products at a large discount, and all items purchased with a BPI credit card are interest free. The popular chocolate festival allows customers to turn in their receipts for Toblerone candy.

In addition to many promotional events, the Commercial Centers Group organizes entertainment, including a millennium party that was televised around the world through a partnership between a local television channel, ABC, and the British Broadcasting Corporation. The mall's annual Christmas show, which features Warner Brothers characters, is very popular and draws an audience from outside the normal capture area. For Valentine's Day, the mall sponsors Moonlight Serenade, a program that brings some of the top performers in the Philippines to the mall.

The Ayala Center was Tower Records's first choice when it entered the Philippine market.
Ayala Land, Inc.

averaging 500,000 visitors a day. Fifteen to 30 percent of the market enters the mall after office hours. Although many Filipino office workers do not have high salaries, it is traditional for single adults to continue to live with their parents, so many have high disposable incomes.

The Ayala Center is considered the prime location for luxury retailers: because no other area in the Philippines has an equivalent concentration of persons with high incomes living and working nearby, most foreign companies—such as California Pizza Kitchen, Hard Rock Café, Starbucks, TGI Friday's, Tower Records, Louis Vuitton, Prada, and Warner Bros.—make the Ayala Center their first location when entering the Philippine market.

Experience Gained

Innovation and high-quality development are the keys to keeping ahead of the competition. The Ayala Company was the first in the Philippines to build a fully planned and integrated shopping center, the first to introduce theme-based entertainment, and the first to build multiplex theaters. Through long-term planning and careful coordination of the development of the surrounding area, the Ayala Company was able to create the demographics needed for success as a super-regional center and entertainment destination. The result has been a good mix of office and residential uses that support the activities of the mall, keeping it vibrant and active throughout the day and night.

The surrounding office and residential uses, which include a concentration of residents with relatively high disposable incomes, create a solid customer base, allowing the Ayala Center to position itself as "the" location for high-end retailers and businesses that probably could not operate successfully anywhere else in the Philippine market. Nevertheless, providing shopping,

To keep the public informed, the Ayala Center offers "Ayala on Air," a daily three-minute radio program that showcases events at the mall.

The management emphasizes safety and service. The presence of large numbers of armed guards throughout the Ayala Center may seem intimidating at first, but most customers find it reassuring. The guards are trained not only to provide security but also to assist customers and to provide information about the mall. Recognizing that the center's long-term viability is tied to the tenants' success, the management also provides customer-service training for staff at some of the smaller stores.

The Ayala Center's location in the heart of the business district, which has 1 million workers, draws a high volume of foot traffic, entertainment, and services for *all* income groups is critical. Compared with those in the United States, incomes in the Philippines are less evenly distributed. The Ayala Company has responded to market needs by offering many activities that are free or affordable and by ensuring that the mall includes stores targeted to value-conscious shoppers.

For long-term success, it is important to balance development with infrastructure capacity. Ayala Land has avoided increasing traffic congestion by refraining from overbuilding. It has also taken a proactive approach to improving the existing infrastructure and allowing for future growth—for example, by integrating a new light-rail transit system into the Ayala Center and by building pedestrian walkways.

Renovating the original strip mall instead of starting all-new construction was challenging. However, renovating allowed the center to grow incrementally and to develop at an appropriate scale. A downside of incremental growth is the noticeable lack of a unified exterior theme and finish for the mall.

Glorietta Mall at Ayala Center represents the transformation of a mall over time, in keeping with the growth of the surrounding area. Mixing entertainment and retail is a key component of the Ayala Company's strategy and one that it plans to intensify in the future as the mall continues to evolve.

Ayala Center

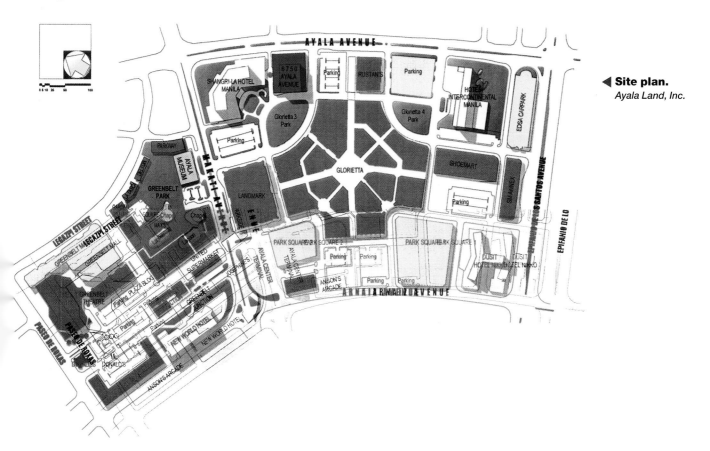

◄ **Site plan.**
Ayala Land, Inc.

Project Data

Land Use Information

Use	Lot area (square feet)	Gross floor area (square feet)	Gross leasable area (square feet)	Parking spaces
Quad I				
Glorietta I	113,305	0	0	
Retail	0	214,538	137,482	
Cinema	0	55,696	45,161	
Kowloon House	14,577	26,735	26,735	
Park Square I	167,636	140,793	90,289	1,225
Hotel Nikko Manila Garden	134,117	696,149	62,726	92
Parking lot	63,124	514,517	0	254
Total	492,759	1,648,428	362,393	1,571
Quad II				
Glorietta II	60,469	129,204	78,529	843
Makati Supermarket	41,893	83,667	80,808	
Anson's Arcade	17,415	69,660	69,660	
Ayala Center Terminal	82,463	0	0	
Goldcrest	20,027	39,216	34,873	
Park Square II	36,163	33,529	28,735	
Parking lots	89,623	0	0	209
Total	348,053	355,276	292,605	1,052
Quad III				
Glorietta III	87,537	285,628	196,123	
Landmark Department Store	102,329	577,297	577,297	
Northmall	50,450	166,313	166,313	
6750 Ayala Avenue	51,159	387,591	23,510	532
Glorietta III Park	48,827	0	0	
Shangri-La Hotel Manila	180,589	860,645	75,035	484
Parking lots	92,278	755,424*	0	488
Total	613,169	2,277,474	1,038,278	1,504

Note: *Not included in gross floor area.

Use	Lot area (square feet)	Gross floor area (square feet)	Gross leasable area (square feet)	Parking spaces
Quad IV				
Glorietta IV	121,142	1,053,500	400,653	
Shoemart Makati	63,124	370,553	370,553	
Shoemart Makati Annex	35,959	228,223	228,223	
Rustin's Department Store	44,742	222,815	222,815	6
Glorietta IV Park	50,536	538	538	518
Hotel Intercontinental Manila	167,367	374,573	37,303	37
Parking lots	98,019	0	0	445
Total	580,889	2,250,201	1,260,083	1,081
Other				
Additional	108,984	139,428	0	
Right-of-way	617,426	0	0	
Total	726,410	139,428	0	
Grand total	2,761,280	7,426,231	2,953,359	5,108

Development Schedule

Original mall built	1970s
Planning for renovations started	1988
Renovations finished (Glorietta I and II)	1990
Phase III finished (Glorietta III)	1993
Phase IV finished (Glorietta IV)	1999
Serviced apartments finished	2000

Metreon
San Francisco, California

Metreon is the newest attraction in San Francisco's Yerba Buena Center, an 87-acre master-planned district of cultural facilities and gardens. Although the San Francisco Museum of Modern Art and the Yerba Buena Center for the Arts are its neighbors, Metreon offers a different sort of attraction: theme-based amusements, games, shopping, restaurants, and cinemas. The 417,000-square-foot retail entertainment center includes attractions based on Maurice Sendak's children's book *Where the Wild Things Are* and on David Macaulay's book *The Way Things Work,* as well as a games arcade based on the work of the French comic-book author and graphic artist Jean Giraud, who is known as Moebius. In addition to these paid-admission attractions, Metreon has several unusual retail tenants, including Sony Style, microsoftSF, and a PlayStation combination store and video "bar." Adding to the mix are a 16-theater cineplex (including a SONY•IMAX theater), several restaurants, and a food court—Taste of San Francisco—that is worthy of a trip in its own right.

The newest attraction in San Francisco's 87-acre Yerba Buena Center, ▶ Metreon is a four-level, 417,000-square-foot retail entertainment center featuring amusements, games, shopping, restaurants, cinemas, and a 600-seat SONY•IMAX theater.
©Sony Development, Inc., 1999/Timothy Hursley

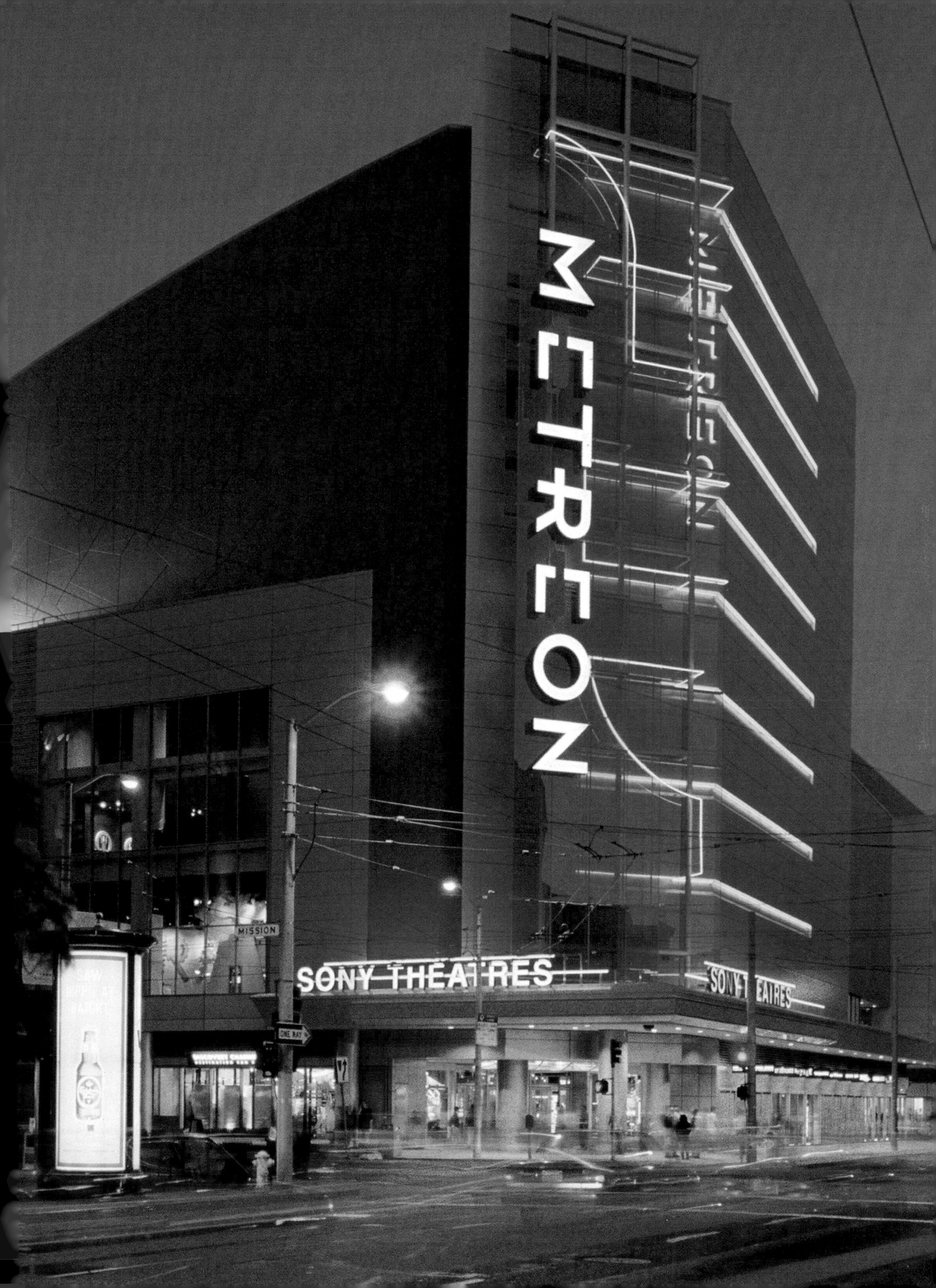
METREON
SONY THEATRES
MISSION
ONE WAY
SONY THEATRES

Development Team

Owner and Developer

Yerba Buena Entertainment Center L.L.C., a partnership of
Yerba Buena Retail Partners and Sony Development, Inc.
Yerba Buena Retail Partners is a partnership of Millennium Partners
and WDG Ventures.

Millennium Partners
1995 Broadway, Third Floor
New York, New York 10023
(212) 595-1600

WDG Ventures
107 Stevenson Street, Fifth Floor
San Francisco, California 94105
(415) 896-2300

Sony Development, Inc.
3001 North San Fernando Boulevard
Burbank, California 91504
(818) 295-2313

Other Development Team Member

San Francisco Redevelopment Agency
770 Golden Gate Avenue
San Francisco, California 94102
(415) 749-2400

Architects

Simon Martin–Vegue Winkelstein Moris
501 Second Street, Suite 701
San Francisco, California 94107
(415) 546-0400

Gary E. Handel & Associates
1995 Broadway, Third Floor
New York, New York 10023
(212) 595-4112

Though the offerings are varied, appealing to an unusual number of market segments, Metreon's design unifies the disparate elements into a cohesive entertainment destination. The four-level project, open since June 16, 1999, has brought a new, evening-oriented dimension to the life of the Yerba Buena Gardens neighborhood, reinforcing the status of the ambitious redevelopment project as the nucleus of the emerging South of Market Street (SoMa) district.

History

Metreon is located on Fourth Street, at the west end of Yerba Buena Gardens. The 550-foot-long structure, which occupies the entire Fourth Street frontage from Mission Street to Howard Street, is built over the subterranean ballroom of the Marriott Hotel, which is located across Mission Street from Metreon. Though the below-grade ballroom was completed in the late 1980s, the above-grade portion of the site remained undeveloped until 1992, when the city of San Francisco issued a request for proposals (RFP) for a mixed-use retail and entertainment project to be built over the ballroom. The RFP spelled out the city's intentions for the project: (1) to create a mix of entertainment uses that would complement the area's cultural activities and enliven the neighborhood day and night; and (2) to establish a reliable, long-term revenue stream that would be used to operate and maintain the public facilities in Yerba Buena Gardens.[1]

A joint venture of Millennium Partners and WDG Ventures was selected as project developer in 1993 on the basis of Millennium's Lincoln Square Project, a highly successful mixed-use project in New York; the firm's established tenant and financing relationships; and the depth of WDG's local San Francisco experience. The original concept for the project included several large national retailers:

Barnes & Noble, Reebok, a music tenant, and a Sony Theaters Cineplex. According to Mike Swinney, president of Sony Development, Inc., Sony was beginning to explore the potential for expanding its presence in the emerging entertainment-center field. The Metreon concept therefore began to evolve from the "big-box-plus-theater" model to one in which Sony Development, Inc., would serve as the master tenant and orchestrator of an integrated entertainment center. Planning and design continued from 1993 until 1997, while the developer carried on simultaneous negotiations with Marriott—whose approval was required for anything built above the ballroom—as well as with city officials, lenders, and Sony Development, Inc. "All issues affected everyone, and everyone had to agree," notes Mark Farrar, of Millennium Partners. The project that emerged retained the cineplex as an anchor, but jettisoned the other large national tenants in favor of more unusual stores—some highlighting the Sony brand—and more purely entertainment-oriented attractions.

More than with most retail or entertainment centers, the design and construction of Metreon was a difficult and complicated task. The core-and-shell architects, Simon Martin–Vegue Winkelstein Moris (SMWM) and Gary E. Handel Associates, had to contend with the existing below-grade ballroom as well as with the highly charged design context of the Yerba Buena project site. In addition, notes Linda Sobuta, project architect for SMWM, once the concept for the project changed, substantial adjustments to the design had to be made to accommodate the more open, atriumlike space envisioned by Sony Development, Inc. Sony itself designed much of the interior common areas and led the design effort for the Where The Wild Things

▲
Reflecting the Sony product line, the exterior finishes of the building are metallic, refined, and controlled.
©Sony Development, Inc., 1999/Timothy Hursley

Are and The Way Things Work attractions. Several other architects and designers participated in designing these two features, as well as the cineplex and other tenant spaces.

Construction of the complex project took approximately two years. To facilitate Metreon's opening, the city established an interdepartmental committee that met with the contractor, architect, and owner every week while the project was being completed. In all, notes Millennium's Farrar, more than 20 different permits and certificates of occupancy had to be signed in the closing days of construction in an inspection process that continued nearly uninterrupted for eight weeks.

Design

The architecture of Metreon is sleek and modern, in keeping with the aspirations of its major sponsor, Sony. Like much of the Sony product line, the exterior finishes of the four-story Metreon structure are metallic, refined, and controlled. The bulk of the exterior is modulated by glass panels, balconies, and stairs, as well as by the articulated volumes of various project components. The shaped box of the SONY•IMAX theater, with its 80-foot-high screen, dominates and anchors the street side of the project, while the open, glassy facade responds to the esplanade and view on the Yerba Buena Gardens side.

Storefronts occupy the ground level on both the street and garden sides, making for pleasant window-shopping—but, bowing to the "mall" model of operations, there are few direct entrances into tenant spaces. Instead, three entrances and passageways open into Metreon from the street and two additional entries lead from the gardens. The entrances converge on the 60-foot-high Metreon Gateway, the main circulation space. Within the Gateway are two information counters where attendants sell cards that are used for admission to the themed attractions. Also located in the Gateway and elsewhere throughout the project are self-service ATM-like kiosks, dressed in high-tech, stainless-steel-and-wood cases, which dispense or replenish cards.

By design, tenant spaces tend to merge with the common areas and with each other. In a departure from the design of a more traditional retail center, there are few full-height demising walls: tenant spaces are defined more by their finishes and displays than by shop fronts and signage. In some cases, visitors can walk directly from shop to shop without going through a common corridor at all.

The first floor is occupied by shops—Sony Style, PlayStation, a flagship Discovery Channel Store, and the Metreon Marketplace—as well as by Taste of San Francisco, which offers, in addition to a number of other restaurants, smaller versions of four trendy local restaurants. The second floor includes theme-based attractions (The Way Things Work and Airtight Garage), the microsoftSF store, a 3-D holographic imaging experience, and another restaurant. Sony Theatres Metreon and the SONY•IMAX theater occupy the whole of the third floor, and the fourth floor is the home of Where The Wild Things Are and its associated restaurant, In the Night Kitchen.

Connecting the floors is a sunlit, multistory atrium that looks out over the gardens, providing dramatic views of San Francisco. At the second and fourth levels are terraces that allow for outdoor dining and viewing. The terraces have proven to be highly popular, and they are rented out for use after hours and on special occasions.

No parking is provided in the Metreon building. The project relies instead on public transit and on a recently constructed public parking garage across the street. Along with a shopping guide, all Metreon visitors receive a transportation guide that lists all the transit options for getting to Metreon, which are considerable. Access has not been an issue, notes Kari Novatney, Metreon's vice president and general manager, because of the highly publicized transit options and the mix of local residents and workers, conventioneers, and tourists. Surveys sponsored by Metreon indicate that only about one-third of Metreon visitors arrive by car. Another

third arrive by transit, and the remaining third walk from nearby hotels, the convention center, offices, and residences.

Ownership and Leasing

The city of San Francisco retains ownership of the land under Metreon and, through the San Francisco Redevelopment Agency, leases the site to the project owner and developer, officially listed as Yerba Buena Entertainment Center L.L.C. Yerba Buena Entertainment Center is a partnership of Yerba Buena Retail Partners (a partnership of Millennium Partners and WDG Ventures, Inc.) and Sony Development, Inc. The lease runs through 2046, and the developer has the option to extend the lease for two 18-year periods. The lease includes the following provisions:

- Holding rent: Through this provision, a minimal rent was paid to the city during the development period.

- Minimum rent: On completion of construction, the initial base rate was set at $1.75 per square foot of gross leasable area (GLA) per year, with a $500,000 annual minimum. Minimum rent will be increased 15 percent every five years.

- Percentage rent: After the developer receives a preferred return of 14 percent of the cost of development, the redevelopment agency will receive 30 percent of net operating income, in addition to base (minimum) rent and other fees.

- Index rent: The total of minimum and percentage rent will be adjusted periodically based on the consumer price index, to a maximum of 5 percent per year.

- Gardens, maintenance, operation, and security obligation: Metreon tenants will be assessed a fee for gardens, maintenance, operation, and security (GMOS), based on each tenant's occupied square footage, plus a share of the GMOS fee accruing to vacant square footage. The GMOS obligation will be adjusted annually based on the consumer price index, with a cap of 5 percent per year.

The center includes interactive children's attractions, including one based on Maurice Sendak's *Where the Wild Things Are.*
©Sony Development, Inc., 1999/Timothy Hursley

■ Sales proceeds: The redevelopment agency will receive 10 percent of the net proceeds from the sale or refinancing of the project as prepaid land rent.

Project developer and owner Yerba Buena Entertainment Center L.L.C., in turn, entered into a master lease for the entire building with Sony Development, Inc. Sony owns and operates various venues, including Airtight Garage, microsoftSF, PlayStation, Sony Style, The Way Things Work, and Where The Wild Things Are. Sony Development, Inc., also participates in a joint venture for Montage, one of Metreon's restaurants, and leases space to third-party tenants, including the remaining restaurants, the Metreon Marketplace, the Discovery Channel Store, and the theaters (Loews Cineplex Entertainment, which is partially owned by Sony).

Marketing and Tenants

In the months since Metreon's June 1999 opening, attendance has far surpassed projections. Some 2.5 million visitors were counted in the first few months, leading to projections of 8 to 10 million patrons in Metreon's first year of operation. Peak weekends have brought as many as 40,000 visitors, though the more typical numbers are 20,000 to 25,000 for weekend days and 15,000 for weekdays. Of these totals, approximately 65 percent of visitors come from the nine-county San Francisco Bay area, and 35 percent are nonlocal (tourists, conventioneers, etc.).

The varied offerings at Metreon have attracted diverse market segments and have had varying levels of initial success. "The known quantities—theaters, restaurants, Sony Style, PlayStation—have done better right out of the box," says Novatney. The Sony Style store, one of only two Sony stores, showcases Sony's consumer electronics—everything from Walkman cassette players to compact disc players to flat-screen TVs. But in contrast to an electronics or department store, Sony Style displays the wares on finely designed pedestals and shelves and illuminates them to highlight their design as much as their performance. Mike Swinney notes that Sony Style "took the showroom idea and made it into a lifestyle concept"; as a result, according to Swinney, the store "promotes the brand and makes money."

The restaurants and Taste of San Francisco are also surpassing expectations. Unlike the food court in a typical mall, Taste of San Francisco has no national or regional fast-food outlets. Instead, it offers mini-versions of four of San Francisco's small, trendy restaurants—Buckhorn, Firewood Café, Longlife Noodle Company, and Sanraku. The food court and freestanding restaurants do well during both the day and evening, buoyed by lunch-time office workers, convention-center visitors, and evening theater patrons. In The Night Kitchen, the restaurant associated with Where The Wild Things Are, is among the highest-grossing restaurants in Metreon. "The restaurant is for kids," notes Swinney, "but the high quality of the food is for parents."

Response to the theme-based attractions has been varied. The most successful by far has been Airtight Garage, Sony's answer to Dreamworks's GameWorks. Within an environment of futuristic imagery designed by Moebius, Airtight Garage offers several Sony-designed games (HyperBowl, Quaternia, and Badlands), as well as Malvina's, a cantina based on a Moebius character. Says Swinney, "HyperBowl has been running at 70 percent

occupancy, and no game on the planet does that." Airtight Garage devotees include adolescents and, on weekend evenings, an older, over-21 crowd.

Where The Wild Things Are, in contrast, is designed for younger children. The attraction consists of a walk-through (and "play-through") environment modeled on the characters and scenery from the children's book, with kinetic figures, noises, and activities. Though successful, given the age group, patronage has marked peaks and valleys that fluctuate with school days, weekends, and vacations.

The third paid-admission attraction, The Way Things Work, has been the least successful, though its associated shop has been doing well. In the initial configuration, visitors would go through a series of pre-event holding rooms, then view a 12-minute, three-screen, 3-D video based on David Macaulay's popular book. Sony recently retooled the attraction, working with San Francisco's Exploratorium on changes intended to make the experience more interactive. Sony also recently collaborated with the San Francisco school district on developing a learning guide and a program to bring school classes in to view the exhibit.

The theater component of Metreon consists of 15 theaters ranging from 106 to 589 seats, plus a 600-seat SONY•IMAX theater, the largest of its type on the West Coast. The box office is located conveniently on the first floor, while the theaters themselves are located on the third floor. The theaters are grouped around a large concession area and lobby that are fronted by a glass wall overlooking the gardens and the city. Along with Metreon's Taste of San Francisco and the restaurants, Sony Theatres

Metreon has proven extremely popular, and the cineplex has ranked among the top five highest-grossing theater complexes in the country since its opening.

Metreon's management schedules events and activities to keep Metreon's name before the public and to encourage patronage. Regular programming includes a disc jockey at Airtight Garage on Wednesday nights, and a Friday-night music series. Metreon also programs holiday events, such as a haunted house for Halloween and "Nutcracker" tea parties, as well as special events like a celebration in honor of Martin Luther King Jr. "There is a need to continually come up with good, solid programming to get people to come back week after week," notes Novatney. Adds Marlene Saritzky, director of communications and marketing for Metreon, "We want to create traditions at Metreon, to make it a gathering place."

Experience Gained

The success of Metreon is due in part to the uniqueness and strength of the tenants and to the broad market they attract. The combination of one-of-a-kind retail, theme-based attractions, unique food outlets (in lieu of fast-food chains), and the cinemas and IMAX has generated a strong complementary patron base, ranging from daytime workers to evening and weekend visitors, convention attendees, and tourists.

To achieve the project's market position, the developer and master tenant of Metreon have ventured considerably beyond the norm, both architecturally and programmatically. In a departure from the arrangement in a traditional mall, the individual tenant spaces open onto each other, and the design of each tenant space contributes to the overall character of the project.

Metreon's developer and master tenant partnership has provided benefits to both parties. Through its design and marketing expertise, Sony Development, Inc., has given a unique cast and market edge to the developer's project, while at the same time providing a showcase for Sony's products and image. Metreon's public/private partnership has also been successful. The city's substantial investment in the creation of Yerba Buena Gardens and in the surrounding cultural uses has provided a stable environment for the development of a private sector retail center in San Francisco's SoMa district. In return, Metreon creates a substantial draw to the district, enlivening it day and night and providing a stable revenue stream pledged to the continuing maintenance of the public gardens.

Note:

1. Robert Wetmore and Helen L. Sause, "A Public/Private Deal," *Urban Land* (January 1995).

Metreon Building

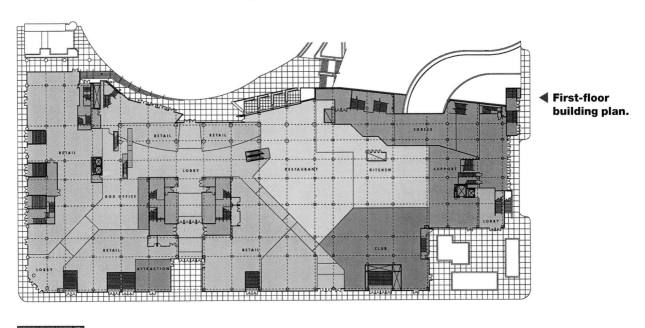

◀ First-floor building plan.

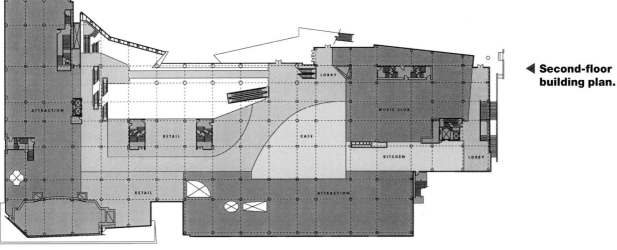

◀ Second-floor building plan.

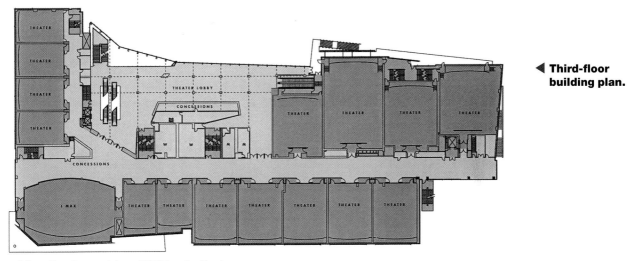

◀ Third-floor building plan.

©Sony Development, Inc., 1999/Timothy Hursley

Metreon Building

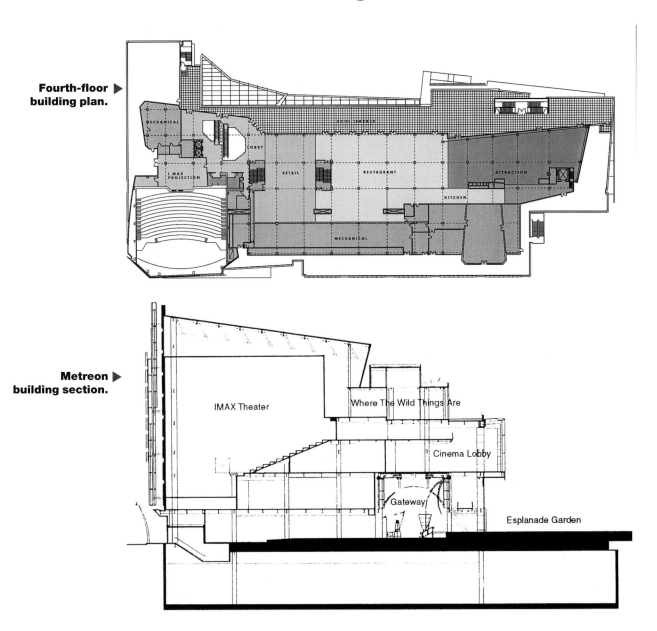

Fourth-floor building plan. ▶

MECHANICAL · LOBBY · MULTI-CINEMA · I MAX PROJECTION · RETAIL · RESTAURANT · KITCHEN · ATTRACTION · MECHANICAL

Metreon building section. ▶

IMAX Theater · Where The Wild Things Are · Cinema Lobby · Gateway · Esplanade Garden

©Sony Development, Inc., 1999/Timothy Hursley

Project Data

Land Use Information

Site area: 2.75 acres

Gross building area	Gross square feet
Retail	45,850
Entertainment	184,475
Restaurant	46,150
Public park	6,823
Support	133,925
Total	417,223

Gross leasable area (GLA): 276,475 square feet

Floor/area ratio: 4.10

Land Use Plan

Use	Acres	Percentage of site
Buildings	2.34	85
Open space and landscaping	.41	15
Total	2.75	100

Tenant Information

Classification	Number of stores	GLA (square feet)
Food service	9	46,150
Gift/specialty	9	45,850
Cinema	16	144,505
Other entertainment	3	39,970
Total	37	276,475

Master lease

Term: 20 years with two ten-year options

Rent: $7,000,000 base rent, plus percentage rent

Development Cost Information[1]

Direct construction costs	$75,000,000
Indirect construction costs	20,000,000
Financing and interest costs	5,000,000
Total	$100,000,000

Financing Information[2]

Sakura Bank (construction and minipermanent loan)	$70,000,000
Yerba Buena Entertainment Center	$30,000,000

Development Schedule

Site leased	May 1997
Planning started	June 1995
Construction started	May 1997
Project completed	June 1999

Notes:

1. Core and shell only, not including tenant improvements.
2. Core and shell only, not including tenant improvements.

Old Pasadena
Pasadena, California

In barely more than three generations, Old Pasadena has gone from fashionable town center to skid row and back. Once the booming center of a growing resort city, Old Pasadena declined during the years of the Great Depression and the period of postwar retail flight, and was on the verge of wholesale redevelopment before the value of its heritage—both spiritual and economic—was fully realized. Chastened by the damage already done to the district's historic character, Pasadena's government and citizens mounted a vigorous program to save Old Pasadena's remaining historic structures and revive its economic life. Today, after 20 years of public and private sector investment and nurturing, the 20-square-block district is once again vibrant and healthy, and its historic patrimony secure.

The current Mediterranean Revival and art deco streetscape of ▶
Old Pasadena dates to 1929, when Colorado Boulevard was
widened and building sections 14 feet deep were removed from
the structures on either side. *Steve Fader*

The current success of Old Pasadena, obvious from the crowds of tourists and local residents strolling by, can be measured on a variety of scales:

- Over 100 historic buildings in the district—totaling approximately 1.5 million square feet—have been renovated.

- Between 20,000 and 30,000 people visit Old Pasadena on a typical weekend.

- The private sector has invested between $400 and $500 million in Old Pasadena.

- Between 1983 and 2000, sales volumes increased from $10 million to $200 million, and tax-increment revenues from $100,000 to $1.9 million.[1]

Early History

Founded in 1873 by settlers from the Midwest, Pasadena began to grow in earnest when the transcontinental railroad was completed in the 1880s. Colorado Boulevard, which was first paved in 1893, became the town's main street. By the 1920s, however, the boulevard was already considered too narrow and "old fashioned" (that is, Victorian); based on the 1925 Bennett Plan for Pasadena, Colorado Boulevard was widened in 1929. Building sections 14 feet deep were removed from the structures on either side of Colorado, and new facades were built—this time in the Mediterranean and art deco styles then gaining currency. At approximately the same time, inspired by the City Beautiful movement, city government built a new civic center just to the east of the historic core.

The depression of the 1930s brought an abrupt end to Old Pasadena's boom and left the district's period architecture frozen in time. When retail expansion finally resumed in the years after the Second World War, retailers in search of larger floor plates and more up-to-date surroundings started moving eastward along Colorado Boulevard. In 1947, Bullocks

Pasadena opened on South Lake Avenue, two miles east of Old Pasadena, ushering in postwar Pasadena's newest shopping district and sealing Old Pasadena's fate.

Old Pasadena continued to decline through the 1950s and 1960s, until many considered razing and redevelopment to be the only appropriate response—a sentiment echoed in the 1971 Pasadena Central District Improvement Plan, which recommended that the small lots of Old Pasadena be assembled for large new corporate office buildings with surface parking. Demolitions began to occur in the 1970s, and large-scale construction, such as the Parsons Engineering Building, took a toll on the district's historic architecture.

At the same time, in an effort to recapture its lost retail base and revitalize Colorado Boulevard, the city pursued what was then a progressive idea: building a downtown regional mall. Through its redevelopment agency, the city acquired (partially through eminent domain) 14.9 acres of land in the civic center district, fronting on Colorado Boulevard and just east of Old Pasadena, for a project that came to be known as Plaza Pasadena. As part of this effort, the city demolished 35 structures (some considered to be historic); relocated 122 businesses and households; constructed public improvements, including parking; and sold the air rights at a highly subsidized rate. To finance the redevelopment agency's expenditures, $58 million in tax-increment bonds were sold.

In all respects except its location, the 600,000-square-foot Plaza Pasadena, which opened in 1980, was a suburban mall. With three department stores as anchors, the mall was almost completely inward-looking, leaving a two-block-long retail "dead zone" along Colorado Boulevard. Although built with the best intentions, the mall was perhaps

the worst intervention possible from an urbanistic point of view. In addition to severing the pedestrian and retail continuity of Colorado Boulevard, the mall closed off Garfield Avenue, a key north-south street that had been part of the 1925 Bennett Plan. Formerly, the vista down Garfield Avenue terminated at the historic Central Library at one end of the street and at the Pasadena Civic Auditorium at the other. With the completion of Plaza Pasadena, the grand axis was replaced by a glass wall representing the axial view that had been lost. And in place of the beaux-arts, art deco, and Mediterranean-style structures that preceded it, the new mall presented a mostly blank brick wall to the street.

Revitalization Efforts

Somewhat ironically, the building of Plaza Pasadena was to some extent responsible for saving Old Pasadena. The public outcry over the eminent domain proceedings, the loss of historic structures, and the amount of public

subsidy involved in redevelopment—both in Plaza Pasadena and in other projects—resulted in the abolition of the redevelopment agency and the creation, in 1978, of the Save Old Pasadena plan. Financed by a grant from the National Endowment for the Arts, the city of Pasadena, Pasadena Heritage, and the Junior League, the plan took the position that historic preservation could be a catalyst for revitalization—which was not, at the time, a widely accepted idea. The plan called for the establishment of a small-business loan program to aid rehabilitation, and was followed up in 1979 by the creation of an urban conservation overlay zone (to deter further demolitions) and the adoption of formal design guidelines for Old Pasadena.

In the early 1980s, the city took several actions to facilitate rehabilitation of the district's historic structures and build confidence in Old Pasadena's future. In 1983 Old

situation, between 1985 and 1987 the city developed three parking garages with a total of approximately 2,300 spaces, strategically sited to support retail and pedestrian activity throughout the district. Commenting on the critical relationship between parking and retail, Marsha Rood, former development administrator for the city of Pasadena, notes, "Without the garages, the district just wouldn't have happened."

To maintain and strengthen street-level pedestrian activity, the parking garages were developed with retail and restaurants on the ground floor. The city took particular care to maintain a diversity of uses that might otherwise get priced out of the market—for example, reserving space in the garages for neighborhood services such as grocery stores.

The first garage was financed with industrial development revenue bonds, and the second and third with certificates of participation. Debt service was paid from the net operating income of the parking operations; retail and restaurant rents; tax-increment funds; fees from zoning-credit contracts; and, in the initial years of the bonds, general fund revenues. The city was taking a risk on Old Pasadena, but the effort was considered critical to enticing businesses back to the district. With the garages in place, the city adopted a parking entitlement program, whereby businesses could satisfy their zoning-based parking requirements by contracting, for a nominal fee, for parking entitlements in the public garages.

With the federal tax-credit program in full swing and the parking garages underway, the momentum and impact of building renovations grew, and developers and prominent retailers began to take notice. By the early to mid-1980s, "you could see that things were happening," recalls Marilyn Buchanan, a long-time property owner and developer in Old Pasadena, "though [the area] was still pretty

Pasadena was listed in the National Register of Historic Places, which made it eligible for federal tax benefits for historic rehabilitation. The city also sold state-authorized Marks Historic Bonds to facilitate the rehabilitation of three key office buildings, and adopted an ordinance establishing the Old Pasadena Redevelopment Project.

One of the key public actions, and one of the critical elements in Old Pasadena's turnaround, was the development of public parking garages. As was typical of the era in which Old Pasadena was originally developed, the district had virtually no off-street parking, other than surface lots where historic structures had been torn down. To remedy this

derelict." One of the first major projects was the 1,800-seat United Artists Cineplex, which opened in 1986. Constructed on a vacant Colorado Boulevard parcel across the street from one of the new public parking garages, the cineplex provided a much-needed nighttime anchor for the district.

The most significant component of Old Pasadena's renaissance was the One Colorado project, which covered a full square block and ultimately included the renovation of 17 historic structures and the construction of one new building. More than a decade in the making, the 275,000-square-foot project, which opened in 1991–92, was controversial from its first conception to its last building permit. The most significant issue was how to treat the multiplicity of small 1920s structures and rear alleys within the context of a large, unified retail project. The original developer's proposal—to gut everything except the street facades and establish a single, mall-like building behind them—was met by considerable resistance from the recently born Pasadena Heritage and the city at large.

Ultimately, under a new developer, the Stitzel Company, of San Francisco, the design was revised, and the supposed liability created by the historic building-and-alley system was transformed into an asset and identity for the project. The historic shells of the buildings were retained, including most of the demising walls between the buildings; instead of an interior, mall-style circulation system, the designers used the five historic alleys to create an outdoor circulation system and plaza, as well as an additional layer of retail entrances and opportunities facing the interior of the block. With some 102 conditions attached by the city—which covered everything from the setback of the project's marquee to providing public art and preserving or recreating the original cobblestone alley swales—the project was permitted in 1990.

Holly Street Village is a 374-unit apartment building within walking distance of the center of Old Pasadena. The project, which has retail on the ground floor, was also designed to accommodate a future station of the planned light-rail system.
Steve Fader

The $70 million completed project has 31 shops and restaurants, including such national retailers as Banana Republic, Crate & Barrel, J. Crew, Gap, Victoria's Secret, and a Rizzoli bookstore, as well as a 2,000-seat, eight-screen AMC cineplex in a newly built structure, and six office tenants. The major tenants have frontages and entries from Colorado Boulevard, and, in some cases, from the side streets and alleys. Midblock alley breaks between the street-fronting buildings visually open up the project to the interior, and alley storefronts, lighting, and site art invite strollers within. A valet stand is located at the primary alley entry on Colorado Boulevard, beneath the project marquee. As in a more standard mall, management, marketing, and maintenance for One Colorado are handled via a central management office, and deliveries are centralized through docks built into the new building.

The continued success of the retail revival in Old Pasadena in the 1990s spawned non-retail growth as well. Since 1994, nearly 500 new housing units have been built in and adjacent to Old Pasadena. The largest project is Holly Street Village, with 374 apartments in a mid-rise, Mediterranean-style building. Twenty percent of the units are reserved for very low-income households, and the remainder are market-rate units. The 1994 project includes retail at the ground level, 16 live/work loft units in the adjacent renovated former Hall of Justice, and accommodation for a future station of the planned light-rail system.

To strengthen Old Pasadena's existing identity and to help spread its rejuvenation to the interiors of the midblock alleys and to the district's outermost edges, the city embarked in 1995 on the Old Pasadena Streetscapes and Alley Walkways Project. Funded by $5 million in parking-meter revenues and a supplemental donor program, the project resulted in the addition of street trees, benches, and trash receptacles; the creation of a signage program; improvements to the alleys; and the installation of three different types of custom-fabricated, pedestrian-scale streetlights based on those in use in the district during the 1920s. The signage program, which included directional signs and directories, took its inspiration from the "reclining S" in the signage of Pasadena's historic train station.

One of the project's major goals was to improve the condition and usability of Old Pasadena's alleys. Twenty-six alleys—most named for prominent local businessmen—criss-cross the district. Except for those of One Colorado, most of the alleys were used primarily for services (such as trash collection) and were in poor condition. The Streetscapes Project provided new paving for the alleys, with the name of each alley cast in bronze letters and set into the paving. Alley "street signs" were installed, as well as bronze markers describing the derivation of the name for each alley. In addition, standards

FRASER ALLEY

NAMED FOR DR. J. CARVASSO FRASER,
PHYSICIAN FOR THE RAYMOND HOTEL IN THE
1890s. THE RAYMOND HOTEL, PERHAPS THE
FINEST OF PASADENA'S EARLY GRAND RESORT
HOTELS, WAS LOCATED ON SOUTH RAYMOND
AVENUE ON RAYMOND HILL, TWO MILES
SOUTH OF COLORADO BOULEVARD. IN 1900,
DR. FRASER SERVED AS PRESIDENT OF THE
FIRST NATIONAL BANK OF PASADENA. THE
ORIGINAL VICTORIAN BANK BUILDING,
LOCATED AT THE NORTHWEST CORNER OF
COLORADO BOULEVARD AND FAIR OAKS
AVENUE, WAS DESTROYED BY FIRE IN 1929.

THIS HISTORICAL MARKER WAS DONATED BY:
DANIEL S. KATZ

CAFÉ XPRESS   CHAMBER OF C

The Old Pasadena Streetscapes and Alley Walkways Project provided the district with light fixtures, landscaping, signage, benches, and other street furniture based on historic designs. In addition, the $5 million program, funded largely through parking-meter revenues, provided for the alleys to be repaved and for the creation of historic markers and signage for the alleys. *Steve Fader*

for private, owner-supplied, wall-mounted lighting were developed, along with standards for consolidating trash collection. The recently completed improvements appear to be encouraging pedestrian use of the alleys, as well as encouraging more businesses to open up to the alleys.

Current Efforts

By the late 1990s, with the success of Old Pasadena in hand, the city turned back to the task of remedying an earlier problem of its own creation—namely, the adjacent Plaza Pasadena. Since the mall was completed in 1980, Old Pasadena's contributions to tax revenues had steadily increased, but Plaza Pasadena's contributions had declined as the center struggled to remain competitive. Overall, according to calculations prepared by

Marsha Rood, while the city's $28.8 million investment in Old Pasadena netted approximately $400–$500 million in private investment (a 14:1 ratio), the city's $58 million investment in Plaza Pasadena netted only $40 million in private investment, or $2 of private investment for every $3 in public investment. In addition, the deadened streetscape along Colorado Boulevard had hindered the regeneration of the civic center area and the playhouse district just to the east of it.

To address these and other issues, the city formed the Civic Center Task Force in 1997. The task force formulated several objectives for the Plaza Pasadena site:

- To restore the city street grid, in particular the Garfield Avenue view corridor
- To restore retail activity to Colorado Boulevard
- To provide for pedestrian circulation and gathering spaces
- To provide a mix of uses, including housing as well as retail.

The TrizecHahn Development Corporation, whose precursor, The Hahn Company, had an ownership interest in Plaza Pasadena, participated in the Civic Center Task Force deliberations, and was philosophically attuned to its urbanistic objectives. TrizecHahn took on the assignment, and began the process of assembling the site, developing the design, negotiating with lenders, and securing city entitlements and support. Ultimately, the city provided $26 million in financing for the $130 million Paseo Colorado project, in the form of certificates of participation backed by the lease on the center's parking structure.

The Paseo Colorado concept, which entailed the demolition of everything above the subterranean parking structure except the Macy's department store, is referred to in the project's literature as an "urban village." Based on a design by Ehrenkrantz, Eckstut, & Kuhn Architects, the project is divided into several "neighborhoods," responding both to its urban context and to its mixed-use program requirements. Now under construction, Paseo Colorado will offer 565,000 square feet of commercial space, including a fully remodeled Macy's, a 14-screen cinema, "high-profile" sit-down restaurants, a health club, a day spa, a full-service Gelsen's supermarket, and adaptable space for office use or two-level retail. The project will also contain 400 rental apartments and live-work lofts above the retail, developed by Post Properties.

Inspired by its neighbor, Old Pasadena, Paseo Colorado will have both streetfront retail on Colorado Boulevard and interior-block walkways lined with more intimately scaled shops and restaurants. Perpendicular to Colorado, Garfield Avenue will be opened up once again, this time as Garfield Promenade, a 77-foot-wide pedestrian walkway. Flanked by formal plantings and period light fixtures, the Promenade will restore the intent of the 1925 Bennett Plan and reveal the previously hidden vista of the civic auditorium. A grand stairway will lead from Garfield Promenade

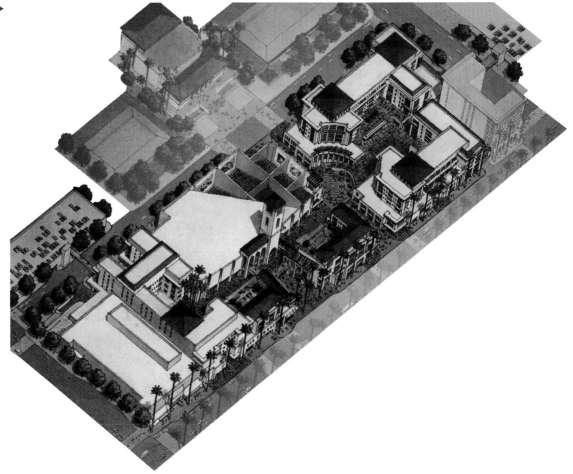

Paseo Colorado, ▶ a mixed-use "urban village" now under construction, will include 565,000 square feet of commercial space, including a 14-screen cinema, restaurants, a health club, a day spa, a supermarket, and a remodeled Macy's. The project will also contain 400 apartments and live/work lofts.
TrizecHahn

to the Fountain Court, a second-level plaza with outdoor dining and shops. A linear midblock walkway called the Paseo will connect Garfield Promenade and Fountain Court on the west to Euclid Court and Macy's on the east.

The developers and designers of Paseo Colorado have gone to considerable lengths to recreate not only the more intimate scale of the old city pattern but the textures and materials of Old Pasadena. This concern for appropriate materials has been conveyed to prospective tenants through two very detailed tenant-criteria publications. The first, entitled *Athens of the West: Pasadena Style,* is a handsome, coffee-table-style book, with full-color images on glossy paper, detailing the Pasadena heritage, the design objectives for each of Paseo Colorado's "neighborhoods," and development standards for storefronts, signage, and similar elements. The book also profiles local and national artisans and artists and provides appropriate examples of their work. The second publication, a paperback entitled *Craftsman's Journal,* provides additional technical criteria and a list of contacts. The introduction to *Craftsman's Journal*

describes TrizecHahn's philosophy and objectives: "The creative contributions of individual tenants are critical to Paseo Colorado's success in creating an environment where the visitor feels a tangible sense of place. . . . Each merchant will be required to creatively alter or adapt their predetermined design concepts to meet the specific existing conditions."

▲
Inspired by its neighbor, Old Pasadena, Paseo Colorado will have both streetfront retail and interior-block walkways, with a fine-grained mix of materials and finishes.
TrizecHahn

Managing Success

The Old Pasadena Business and Professional Association was formed in 1989 to provide a management structure for the increasingly successful Old Pasadena district. Representing mostly Colorado Boulevard interests, the association was financed through a surcharge to the Pasadena business license fee collected by the city. The parking-meter program, initiated in 1993, considerably expanded the geographic definition of Old Pasadena and enlarged its stakeholder base. As a result, a new management entity was formed, the Old Pasadena Management District, and was shifted to a property-based financing system to establish a stronger and more stable financial footing. The current budget for the district is $1.2 million, approximately half of which is derived from property tax assessments and half from the parking-meter program.

The scope of the Old Pasadena Management District's mandate has five elements, summarized by the following keywords: *clean, safe, marketing/promotion, management,* and *development.* One of the principal issues for the district is "managing success"—that is, maintaining the unique characteristics, both physical and entrepreneurial, that have made Old Pasadena a singular destination. To this end, the city has offered a seminar called The Art of Small Business Survival, which included workshops aimed at assisting small businesses in their efforts to strengthen their marketing, customer service, financial, organizational, and business skills. Though the district has attracted several national and regional retailers, small business is considered the key to the uniqueness of Old Pasadena. Marsha Rood notes that visitors "may come for the nationals, but they come back for the independents."

Conclusion

- Old Pasadena has been most successful when it has drawn on its unique assets: its historic buildings and its fine-grained street and alley system. Projects that have been built around these assets, such as One Colorado, have been considerably more successful than large-scale, monolithic redevelopment efforts. The newest major project in the area, Paseo Colorado, now under construction, promises to extend the example of Old Pasadena's pedestrian-scale development to new mixed-use construction.

- Public intervention, in the form of parking facilities development, played a highly significant role in reversing the downward slide of Old Pasadena. The parking improvements satisfied one of the district's key retailing deficiencies and at the same time demonstrated the city's commitment to improving the district.

- Ongoing street and alley improvements, loan programs, business assistance programs, and management district activities have further improved and stabilized Old Pasadena, and reinforced the city's partnership role in maintaining the Old Pasadena heritage.

Note:

1. Based on information provided by Marsha V. Rood, AICP, former development administrator for the city of Pasadena.

Old Pasadena

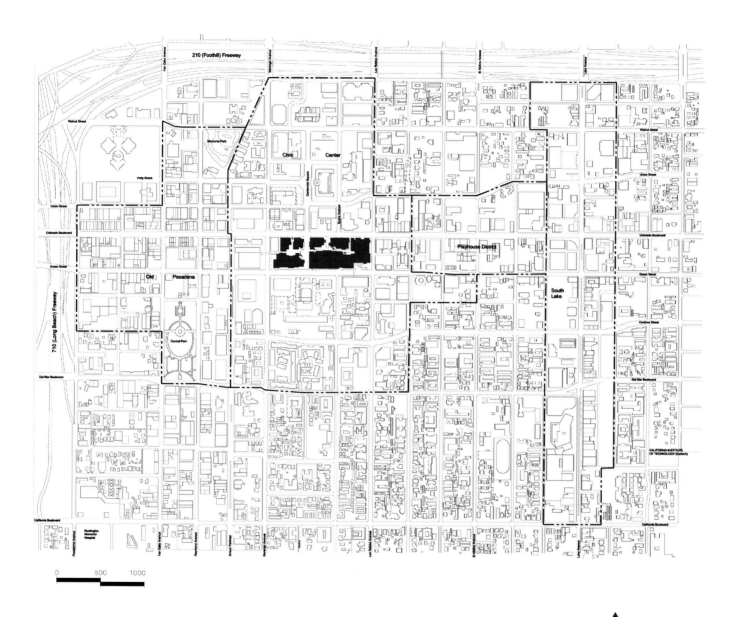

▲
**Old Pasadena, with
Paseo Colorado
(under constuction)
shown in red.**

Pacific Place
Seattle, Washington

Located at the corner of Sixth Avenue and Pine Street, Pacific Place is a five-level, 335,000-square-foot shopping, dining, and entertainment complex that is at the heart of the revival of downtown Seattle's retail district and part of an estimated $2 billion construction boom.

The picture was totally different in the mid-1990s, when Seattle's critical mass of urban retail stores was rapidly declining. The Frederick & Nelson (F&N) department store closed in 1992, followed two years later by its neighbor, I. Magnin. Although national retailers were attracted by the region's growing economy, they were skittish about the future of Seattle's urban core and opted to locate outside of downtown. Jeff Rhodes, a veteran shopping-center developer who helped create Boston's Copley Place and Chicago's Water Tower Place, had moved to Seattle to retire, but he was troubled by the desolation creeping across his adopted city's downtown.

In 1993 Rhodes started working with Seattle business and political leaders on a plan to transform three downtown blocks, including the vacant ten-story F&N department store, into a new retail center. He brought in development partners Ken Himmel and Tom Klutznick, with whom he had worked on the

The five story, 335,000-square-foot Pacific Place ▶
retail entertainment center is part of an estimated $2 billion
construction boom and retail revival in downtown Seattle.
Pine Street Development, L.L.C.

Development Team

Developer

Pine Street Development, L.L.C.
520 Pike Tower, # 2200
Seattle, Washington 98101
(206) 340-9897

Architects

NBBJ
111 South Jackson Street
Seattle, Washington 98104
(206) 223-5555

Elkus Manfredi Architects Ltd.
530 Atlantic Avenue
Boston, Massachusetts 02210
(617) 426-1300

Structural Engineer

Skilling Ward Magnusson & Barkshire
1301 Fifth Avenue, Suite 3100
Seattle, Washington 98101-2699
(206) 292-1200

General Contractor

Lease/Sellen
107 Spring Street
Seattle, Washington 98101
(206) 622-0500

Development Process

Pine Street Associates's retail resuscitation plan called for buying the old F&N store and trading it to Nordstrom in exchange for its smaller store on Fifth Avenue, between Pine and Pike Streets, and for the adjacent ten-story Seaboard Building, which Nordstrom used for office space. The plan was to knock down a parking garage and other buildings and turn the block into a shopping center with underground parking. The larger building would allow Nordstrom to partly consolidate some of its many office users into one central downtown space. When Nordstrom moved out, Pine Street Associates would take possession of the old store, create retail space on the lower floors and offices on the upper ones, then renovate the Seaboard Building.

Norm Rice, then Seattle's mayor, and city business leaders championed the plan as a way to stem downtown's downward spiral. In the *Seattle Post-Intelligencer* (May 3, 1996), Rice described the Pacific Place plan as "the biggest revitalization effort in downtown Seattle since we rebuilt from the Great Fire" (in 1889). But the plan drew considerable opposition, primarily because it required the city's participation. Pine Street, which had been closed to vehicle traffic between Fourth and Fifth Avenues to make way for an urban pedestrian park, would have to be reopened. The developers—and most downtown businesses—contended that the closure had cut off access to several affluent urban neighborhoods and ultimately sent the message that access to downtown was difficult. Nordstrom said that it could not justify investing $100 million in a downtown that was hampered by the closure of a critical thoroughfare.

The developer teamed up with the Downtown Seattle Association to mount a carefully orchestrated campaign to pitch the reopening of the street as an important

Boston and Chicago projects. To manage the development, he also brought in Matt Griffin, who had developed a number of Seattle's premier office and retail developments. In 1994, they formed Pine Street Associates, which later became Pine Street Development (PSD).

opportunity to improve downtown. Together they corralled the support of almost every downtown retailer, including shopkeepers at Seattle's enshrined Pike Place Market. The street reopening, which had been the subject of debate for several years, was approved by public vote, garnering a significant 62 percent of votes cast.

The parking garage was another critical piece of the plan. Almost every study of downtown retail conducted in the early 1990s cited the lack of affordable, convenient, short-term parking as a main deterrent to shopping downtown. The Pacific Place plan called for the city to chip in by purchasing the center's underground garage from the developers. Opponents insisted that the price of $73 million was too high because it exceeded the cost to the developers of building the structure. Moreover, although cities routinely encourage urban revitalization projects by directly subsidizing the cost of developing auxiliary parking, in Seattle this type of public/private cooperation is stymied by the state's strict constitutional ban against gifts of public money to private business. As a result, cities in Washington state have had to devise alternative ways to help developers. After a barrage of negative press, audits by city and state departments, and legal battles, the garage deal was deemed appropriate by the state attorney general's office. The *Seattle Times* ultimately recanted its harsh criticism and endorsed the agreement.

In May 1996, Pine Street Associates acquired the F&N building and conveyed it to Nordstrom in exchange for rights to the old Nordstrom store and the Seaboard Building. Nordstrom immediately started renovating the F&N building into a new, 380,000-square-foot flagship store topped by 320,000

▲
The soaring, crescent-shaped atrium lined with shops and restaurants is designed to resemble a European-style plaza. *Pine Street Development, L.L.C.*

square feet of office space. The building reopened in August 1998. In January 1997, the developers started construction on the six-level underground garage at Pacific Place to serve the shopping center and the entire retail core, including Nordstrom's new store. When Pacific Place opened in October 1998, downtown Seattle's retail epicenter shifted from Fifth Avenue and Pike Street to Sixth Avenue and Pine Street.

Although the specialty shopping center contains no department store anchors, Nordstrom—just a skywalk away—essentially serves that function. Moreover, Nordstrom's commitment to invest more than $100 million in its hometown sent a strong message to the finance and retail communities, who knew that developers frequently offer Nordstrom large incentives to locate at their centers.

The final stages of the three-block makeover are now nearly complete. PSD, headed by Matt Griffin, completed redevelopment in late 1999 of Nordstrom's former store into a mixed-use building with multilevel retail shops and offices above. PSD will next redevelop the adjacent Seaboard Building into new office space with high-end condominium units, scheduled to be completed in March 2001.

Financing

Venture capital came from the original partners—Rhodes, Griffin, Himmel, and Klutznick—and the founding investors, a group of prominent local families and businesspeople (including the heads of Costco, McCaw Cellular, and Starbucks) who eventually contributed more than $10 million. Says managing partner Matt Griffin, "I don't think any of these local investors would have taken the financial risk if it weren't our hometown. We all knew downtown was in trouble." When the founding investors were first approached, the project had no tenants and no equity partner. The developers did not yet have a deal with Nordstrom, and Pine Street had not been reopened. "So this investment was an act of faith," notes Griffin. Some of the same families that invested in the three-block project were involved a generation ago in bringing the world's fair to Seattle.

The local investors were later joined in the equity financing by the Multi-Employer Property Trust (MEPT), a pooled equity real estate fund that invests in both commercial and multifamily residential projects in communities where participating pension plans are located. Kennedy Associates Real Estate Counsel, Inc., a full-service investment firm based in Seattle, is MEPT's investment adviser. Eighty percent of the equity capital in Pine Street Development was provided by MEPT and 20 percent by Pine Street Associates and the founding investors. Three of the original partners—Rhodes, Himmel, and Klutznick—sold their interest to Pine Street Associates in October 1998.

Construction financing was more difficult to come by. By late 1996, the developers had secured a commitment from the city for the garage-development plan as well as a commitment from Seafirst Bank for the construction financing, subject to finding financial partners—but they could not find partners. Lease commitments for around 50 percent of the project did not satisfy the lenders, who required the project to be at least 60 percent leased. Although Nordstrom had committed to building its new flagship store downtown, potential tenants were still skittish about downtown's physical deterioration—the graffiti, the boarded-up storefronts, and the prevalence of street people.

By the end of 1996, the developers' option to purchase the ground on the Pacific Place block was due to expire. If construction did not get started, the project would not be ready for Christmas 1998. MEPT eventually provided a subordinate loan (which replaced part of the construction loan) to make up for the missing leasing, allowing the developers to proceed with construction financing. In April 1997 the developers secured construction financing from Seafirst Bank, as agent, with Washington Mutual Bank and MEPT. Between January and July of 1998, Pacific Place went from being 50 percent to 85 percent leased. The tremendous pace of development downtown—the new symphony hall, the eventual expansion of the convention center, and a new Nordstrom Store—assuaged retailers' fears. They realized that if they wanted a spot at Pacific Place, they needed to move quickly.

Early in the project, under the Section 108 program of the U.S. Department of Housing and Urban Development (HUD), Pine Street Associates obtained a loan to address urban blight. The city backed the

HUD guarantee, which the developers then backed with a letter of credit. The developers used the loan to purchase the vacated F&N department store, which had been languishing for a number of years.

In the end, the costs associated with the HUD loan—creating the documents, securing letters of credit, and paying interest rates—made the loan just as expensive as the construction financing. In retrospect, the loan probably did not warrant the costly effort and heightened public scrutiny that it attracted. (Some local housing advocates, who mistakenly believed that the Section 108 program was designated for housing development, argued that the money should have been used to build low-income housing instead.) On the other hand, the city's endorsement of the loan sent the message that the city supported the project, which was especially important in the early stages.

The city's main contribution was its agreement in late 1995 to purchase the garage from Pine Street Development after completion and a successful startup. The city took an entrepreneurial approach to help reverse the slide of downtown Seattle and to address an important public issue: the lack of affordable, short-term parking for shoppers. Although the garage costs were $50 million, the city agreed to pay the developers $73 million for the completed garage, for which it would issue bonds to be paid off with the garage cash flow within 30 years. It was because of the anticipated cash flow that the city agreed to pay the higher amount; it also created a number of requirements designed to increase cash flow.

As part of the deal, the developers agreed to build at least 300,000 square feet of retail space above the garage and to secure a commitment from a department store of at least 200,000 square feet to occupy the F&N building. Also, the city would not take over

▲
Pacific Place is highly permeable, with more than a dozen entry points from the surrounding streets into the building. Pedestrians are invited to take shortcuts through the building and to use the ground-floor lobby as an extension of the sidewalk.
Pine Street Development, L.L.C.

the garage until 150,000 square feet at the center had been occupied, the theaters were up and running, and a six-month shakedown period had worked out all the bugs in the fully operating garage. As an additional protection, the developer further agreed that if the garage was not generating sufficient money to cover the city's debt service payments after 20 years, the city would have the option of "putting it back" to the developer for up to $50 million.

The city took over the garage in November 1998. Both the developer and the city agreed that as an incentive to bring people downtown, it was important to keep parking rates low—and, as long as the cash flow covers its debt-service payments, the city will keep them that way. The parking rates at Pacific Place are comparable to meter parking and are the lowest in the retail core.

Planning and Design

To make circulation faster and easier, the six-level, 1,200-space underground garage—the largest in downtown Seattle—has a double-helix configuration: with distinct travel systems and double sets of entrances and exits, the two interlocking ramps function almost like two separate garages. In addition to valet parking, the garage uses a "pay-on-foot," self-park system whereby shoppers pay at the concourse level before returning to their cars. This system, which was put in place because of concern about potential congestion when moviegoers leave the theaters, not only accelerates traffic flow out of the garage but has the added advantage of bringing additional traffic to concourse tenants.

To achieve the most efficient and user-friendly design, NBBJ, who designed Pacific Place along with Elkus Manfredi Architects, first created a mockup of the garage. This exercise showed that it is easier for drivers to maneuver when support columns are placed in front of rather than to the side of vehicles, so that they do not block vehicle doors. Removing the columns from their standard positions also improved visibility and minimized concerns about someone hiding in a corner or behind a column. As many stalls as possible were made full size. Ceilings, walls, and structural beams were painted white to brighten the space. High-quality design elements—such as bright lighting, coffered ceilings with cove lighting, and handsome stainless-steel doors—were used to create the look of a hotel drop-off rather than a basement. The elegant, curved, wood-and-glass cashiers' stations are designed to look like the concierge's desk at a hotel.

Each atrium level is connected by standard escalators. An express, up-only escalator whisks diners and moviegoers directly to the fourth floor. Sight lines were critical, especially of the shops as viewed from the escalators. The architects used a model scope—a minuscule camera mounted on a penlike structure—to simulate the visual experience of a shopper from specific vantage points throughout the interior. Some columns were moved to free up sight lines.

Although Pacific Place occupies one of the largest blocks in downtown Seattle, it was designed to look like a collection of smaller buildings that were built over time. Many of the tenants, such as Pottery Barn, Starbucks, and Tiffany & Co., feature signature storefront designs and separate street entrances. The exterior design of the center was made deliberately simple to better showcase the individual storefronts. Although tenants were encouraged to express themselves with different finishes and colors, they worked within a standardized modular panel system that established a cohesive framework for the development.

In contrast to the fortress style of many suburban shopping malls, Pacific Place is highly permeable, with more than a dozen entry points that lead from the surrounding streets into the building. Pedestrians are invited to take shortcuts through the building and to use the ground-floor lobby as an extension of the sidewalk. Pacific Place was designed to create the sense of energy and openness of a bustling retail street. "We've managed to bring a taste of Michigan Avenue to downtown Seattle," says developer Matt Griffin. "But what sets Pacific Place apart from Chicago is that here all the shops are under one roof."

Shops and restaurants are built around an interior thoroughfare. Materials such as textured, colored concrete flooring for sidewalks and terra cotta–like panels for the walls, as well as ornamental streetlights, create a city streetscape. The soaring, crescent-shaped atrium lined with shops and restaurants is designed to resemble a European-style plaza. Natural light from an enormous skylight fills the atrium throughout the day, creating a welcoming year-round oasis. In this rainy climate, where people crave light during the long winter months, the plaza is a favorite place to linger over espresso and Italian pastries from Il Fornaio, which has a café in the center of the atrium.

On the fourth floor, restaurants and sidewalk cafés are aligned along a pedestrian promenade complete with sidewalks and street furniture. Details such as awnings and flower boxes add to the outdoor ambience. Several of the restaurants provide decks for outdoor dining, where patrons can enjoy views of the downtown skyline. City planners were pleased with the several ground-floor sidewalk cafés, as well as with the canopies framing store windows and with the multiple entrances, features that combine to add interest and help mitigate the "blank-wall syndrome."

A steel-and-glass skywalk over Sixth Avenue connects the third level of Pacific Place with the fourth level of Nordstrom's new flagship store. The historic landmark status of the former F&N department store placed constraints on the skywalk design. For example, to protect the older, terra cotta face of the F&N building, a drawbridge design was selected that places all the weight on Pacific Place. Although the city generally discourages skywalks, which can block views and take people off the streets, the developers

showed that the skywalk would not block water views. The developers reasoned that the bridge was essential for moving shoppers between Nordstrom and Pacific Place—and that without it, they would have had to build a much smaller shopping center, which would have reduced the number of people on the street more than would a bridge.

Tenants

Seattle's retail boom is tied closely to the host of entertainment, cultural, and tourist facilities that have recently appeared downtown, including three new or improved live-performance theaters, a new symphony hall, and multiplex cinemas, not to mention the new Safeco Field baseball stadium. The convention center expansion, which will nearly double the existing space, will open in 2001. These facilities have attracted a multitude of entertainment-oriented stores and restaurants to the downtown, among them FAO Schwarz, a Warner Bros. Studio Store, and a Wolfgang Puck eatery. The Meridian entertainment and retail complex opened in 1996 with a 16-screen cinema, a GameWorks video arcade, a Levis store, NikeTown, and Planet Hollywood.

Although Pacific Place offers a variety of entertainment features, including a broad mix of restaurants and a state-of-the art multiplex cinema, the developer emphasizes that

▲
On the fourth floor, restaurants such as Gordon Biersch Brewery and Desert Fire Southwestern Grill are aligned along a pedestrian promenade complete with sidewalks and street furniture.
Pine Street Development, L.L.C.

creating a lively environment for shopping and dining, where people come to mingle and enjoy the urban experience.

Three restaurants are located on the fourth floor as well as at the entrance to the two-level movie theaters. The 11-screen General Cinema Theaters complex features stadium seating for 3,100 people and state-of-the-art sound and projection systems. The cinema works with the fourth-floor restaurants to draw visitors to the top floors, always a big challenge in vertical retail developments. Because the theaters were too large to fit on half a floor, they were stacked on the fourth and fifth floors.

In keeping with the developers' vision of the project as a place for everyone, the restaurants offer a broad range of prices and menus. Hometown coffee king Starbucks selected the center for its new restaurant concept, Café Starbucks, a European-style café and coffee bar. Desert Fire, offering Southwest cuisine, is a family-priced restaurant. More elegant dining is featured at Stars Bar & Dining, which caters to the after-symphony crowd. Il Fornaio has three restaurant formats and a bakery at Pacific Place. Most restaurants keep extended hours for late-night diners attending the symphony or a movie. Likewise, some retailers stay open late to complement the restaurant and cinema hours.

the primary entertainment is the actual experience of visiting the center, whether it is lingering over a latte in the sunlit central piazza or checking out the J. Peterman Co., store, famous for its quirky catalogue. A recent intercept survey reported that some 45 percent of visitors come to Pacific Place to walk on the indoor pedestrian promenade, check out the shops, or just sit at a café and people watch, with no specific destination in mind. This figure supports the developers' goal of

Pacific Place benefits from Seattle's robust tourist industry. Just a short walk from the Washington State Convention and Trade Center, the shopping center attracts travelers and convention-goers from around the world—a strong inducement for the 45 stores and restaurants that chose to locate at Pacific Place, of which about one-third were new to the Pacific Northwest. Although it was anticipated that as much as 40 percent of visi-

Pacific Place

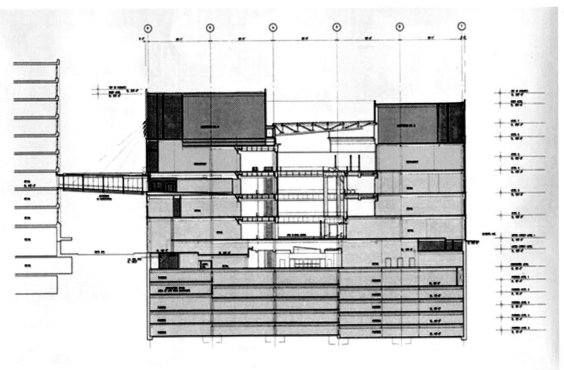

◀ **Building plan.**
*Pine Street
Development, L.L.C.*

tors would be tourists, the developer felt equally committed to serving the local market. Fueled in part by the technology boom, "Seattle is a much wealthier community than it used to be. And Seattle people deserve great stores without having to get on an airplane," says Griffin. High-end retailers like Cartier, Tiffany & Co., and MaxMara (Italian clothiers for women) recognized this unfilled niche when they chose Pacific Place as the location of their first stores in the Northwest.

Experience Gained

Many factors influence an investor's decision to support a project that appears risky. Were Seattle not their hometown, the group of local investors probably would have been reluctant to get involved before Nordstrom had committed and before the project had an equity partner and tenants. According to the developer, the investment was an act of hope.

Griffin emphasizes the importance, especially during trying times, of teaming up with partners and investors who fervently believe in the project. In hindsight, the developers would probably not have applied for the HUD loan, whose associated costs made it just as expensive as construction financing, and whose benefits probably did not warrant the costly effort and the heightened public scrutiny that the loan attracted.

The center's exterior design, which looks like a collection of smaller buildings and allows tenants such as Pottery Barn and Tiffany & Co. to have separate street entrances and individual storefront designs, was a significant draw. Recognizing that many retailers were seeking venues outside malls to strengthen their identity, the developers of Pacific Place selected a design that would offer tenants a greater street presence.

Project Data

Land Use Information

Site area: 2 acres

Building coverage: 100 percent

Gross building area	Gross square feet
Office	2,700
Retail	223,000
Entertainment (cinema)	65,000
Restaurant	48,000
Parking	500,000
Common areas	160,000
Total	998,700

Gross leasable area (GLA): 335,000 square feet

Parking: 1,200 spaces

Floor/area ratio: 4

Office Tenant Information

Percentage of net rentable area occupied: 100 percent

Number of tenants: One (property management office)

Tenant size: 2,700 square feet

Annual rent: Approximately $25 per square foot

Retail Tenant Information

Classification	Number of stores	GLA (square feet)
General merchandise	11	58,000
Food service	6	48,000
Clothing and accessories	19	87,000
Shoes	1	1,900
Home furnishings	3	35,000
Hobby/special interest	2	6,000
Jewelry	2	10,000
Cinema	1	65,000
Financial services	1	5,900
Total	46	316,800

Percentage of GLA occupied: 97 percent

Annual rents: Approximately $25 to $90 per square foot

Average annual retail sales: Approximately $500 per square foot (excludes cinema and Barnes & Noble)

Average length of lease: Seven to ten years

Typical lease provisions: Base plus percentage rent; tenant allowance provided

Development Cost Information

Site Acquisition Costs $18,000,000

Construction Costs

Demolition	$1,180,000
Excavation and grading	7,225,000
Sewer, water, and drainage	230,000
Paving, curbs, and sidewalks	200,000
Landscaping and irrigation	15,000
Fees and general conditions	1,130,000
Retail buildings and garage	122,000,000
Subtotal, construction costs	$131,980,000

Soft Costs

Architectural and engineering services	$10,000,000
Project management	5,300,000
Marketing	3,000,000
Legal and accounting services	3,000,000
Taxes and insurance	600,000
Title fees	90,000
Construction interest and fees	8,800,000
Other	2,230,000
Subtotal, soft costs	33,020,000
Total development cost	$183,000,000

Financing Information

Financing source	Amount
Seafirst Bank, as agent (construction financing)	$106,000,000
Multi-Employer Property Trust (construction financing)	21,000,000
Equity and other	56,000,000
Total	$183,000,000

Publicly financed: 0 percent

Debt financed (private): 70 percent

Equity financed (private): 30 percent

Development Schedule

Site optioned	1994
Site purchased	January 1997
Planning started	1994
Construction started	January 1997
Sales and leasing started	Fall 1994
Project completed	October 1998

Case Studies

Sony Center
am Potsdamer Platz
Berlin, Germany

In the 1920s, Berlin's Potsdamer Platz stood at the center of a city that was arguably the cultural capital of Europe. With its outstanding architecture and vibrant social and intellectual life—not to mention its throngs of traffic—Potsdamer Platz was the dynamic hub of the city. But by 1945, most of Potsdamer Platz had been reduced to rubble. In the years following the Second World War, the square was remarkable only for the fact that it served as the meeting point of the Soviet, British, and American sectors of occupied Berlin. With the onset of the Cold War, the fate of Potsdamer Platz seemed sealed: the Berlin Wall, constructed in 1961, ran right through the middle of what had once been Potsdamer Platz, and on either side was a heavily fortified wasteland. The glory days of the 1920s were a distant memory.

In November 1989, however, as the world watched in amazement, the Berlin Wall fell, and the city entered another period of transformation. With the city government eager to rebuild, the Berlin Senate Department of Town Planning and Environmental Protection held a competition in 1991 to select a plan for the entire Potsdamer Platz area—a competition that was won by the firm of Hilmer and Sattler. Although the Hilmer and Sattler plan specified the dimensions of sites, the layout of streets, and the height and massing of buildings, it did

**In the 1920s, Postsdamer Platz was the ▶
intellectual and social hub of Berlin.**

Development Team

Owner

Sony, with its partners Tishman Speyer Properties and Kajima Corporation, operating as BE-ST Bellevuestrasse Development GmbH & Co. First Real Estate KG.

Sony Berlin GmbH
Kemperplatz 1
10785 Berlin, Germany
(49 30) 2575 5700

Kajima (Deutschland) GmbH
Niedenau 61-63
6035 Frankfurt am Main, Germany
(49 69) 740-372

Developer

Tishman Speyer Properties
Quartier 205 Friedrichstadtpassagen
Friedrichstrasse 67
10117 Berlin, Germany
49-30-2094-5400

Architect

Murphy/Jahn, Inc.
35 East Wacker Drive
Chicago, Illinois 60601
(312) 427-7300

Potsdamer Platz as a location for shopping, entertainment, and culture, but to recreate the sense of excitement that had once permeated the square. With the hope that a firm with Sony's reputation and international standing would create a development of the highest quality, the Berlin Senate gave Sony an opportunity to purchase the property that would become the Sony Center; Sony signed the purchase contract in June of 1991. Apart from the broad planning framework set out in the Hilmer and Sattler plan, the contract also included several specific obligations: first, Sony was required to preserve what was formerly the Grand Hotel Esplanade as an historic structure; second, the contract stipulated that Sony would have to build a permanent home for the Filmhaus, an important organization within the German film industry, and offer the organization a long-term rent subsidy.

Sony then held a competition of its own, inviting seven renowned architectural firms to take part. Helmut Jahn's bold design was unanimously selected as the winner in August 1992. Although some members of the Berlin government were unenthusiastic about Jahn's decidedly modern design, Sony was insistent, and the government eventually agreed. In 1994 Sony formed a joint venture with Tishman Speyer Properties and the Kajima Corporation to make good on its plans for the Potsdamer Platz site. Within the joint venture, Tishman Speyer was given responsibility for developing, managing, and leasing the project, while Kajima served as an equity partner and technical advisor.

The site of the Sony Center represents one of the largest inner-city redevelopment sites in all of Europe. Immediately to the north is the peaceful Tiergarten park, and just beyond that the famous Brandenburg Gate and the Reichstag (the German parliament), recently relocated from its former home in Bonn. To

not address the uses that would be permitted or the architectural forms that the new buildings would take. The initial plan became the basis for subsequent competitions that were used to select both the guiding architectural principles and the detailed designs for each building site.

A central goal of Hilmer and Sattler's plan was not only to restore the preeminence of

Potsdamer Platz was largely destroyed during World War II; after the Berlin Wall went up in 1961, the area became a no-man's-land.

Today, Potsdamer Platz is undergoing a radical transformation. In addition to the Sony Center, a variety of projects are bringing offices, hotels, residences, shops, and entertainment facilities to the once-desolate square.

▼

the west of the site is the Berlin Kulturforum, home of the Berlin Philharmonic Orchestra, the Chamber Music Concert Hall, and the Mies van der Rohe–designed Neue Nationalgalerie.

At Potsdamer Platz itself are a number of different building sites, all of which are being redeveloped in spectacular fashion. As in other parts of Berlin, massive amounts of public money are being invested to build or upgrade infrastructure. In and around Potsdamer Platz, the Berlin government; the German government; and Deutsche Bahn AG, the German railway, have collectively invested more than DM 4 billion in infrastructure improvements.

Planning, Design, and Construction

The Sony Center is a genuine mixed-use project, with eight buildings providing space for office, retail, entertainment, and residential uses. Ranging in height from eight to 26 stories and offering approximately 132,500 square meters of space, these buildings are arranged around an exciting public space called the Forum, which is capped by a dramatic roof. Each building maintains a distinct identity, but the project also presents a coherent overall vision. The Sony Center is connected with the subway and regional railroad station next door, and an underground garage provides 980 parking spaces for

tenants and visitors. Because of the way that the pieces of the project are tied together, phasing the development of the Sony Center was not even considered as an option, even though this approach reduced the margin for error during construction.

Tishman Speyer had to work with a number of different government agencies in the course of the planning process. For example, the Berlin state government had approval authority for the master plan, the Tiergarten district issued building permits and made decisions on day-to-day matters, and the city government was involved throughout the process. The plans for the Sony Center also

had to be submitted for public review and comment for a period of three months; this process resulted in a number of changes, including a reconfiguration of the site's open space and the relocation of the cinemas to below grade.

The construction of the Sony Center presented tremendous difficulties for the development team. First, because the site had been heavily bombed during World War II, a major soil cleanup was required, and initial excavations had to be done with extreme care (in case of unexploded shells). Second, Berlin's water table is only about two meters below the surface, which required the construction of deep slurry walls on the perimeter of the foundation, as well as the injection of a gel blanket 22 meters below the surface to prevent water from seeping into the site.

Strict environmental and historic regulations created a third set of obstacles. Germany is known for the vigor of its environmental legislation, and regulators were watching the construction of the Sony Center closely. Among the requirements for historic preservation was a stipulation that no columns penetrate the historic rooms at the Grand Hotel Esplanade. To support the construction of apartments above the Esplanade, the development team had to create a bridge of massive roof trusses weighing 520 tons; attached by steel rods, seven floors of apartments hang from these trusses.

In another feat of engineering, the development team moved the historic 1,300-ton Kaisersaal (Emperor's Hall), a luxurious room where the German kaiser used to hold functions, by lifting it on air cushions and delicately moving it 75 meters to its new home beside the other historic rooms of the Grand Hotel Esplanade. Despite all these challenges, Tishman Speyer was still able to use a variety of value-engineering techniques to save almost DM 300 million on construction costs. Needless to say, coordinating all this activity was a management task of enormous proportions. And, despite the fact that the city of Berlin was highly supportive of the Sony Center, innumerable special permits were required to bring the project to completion.

The concerns of the development team did not end at the edge of the site. Tishman Speyer worked closely with the city of Berlin to build an underground arterial road running north-south next to the Sony Center site, which offers the additional bonus of providing access to the loading docks at the Sony Center. The developers also worked with Deutsche Bahn AG on the reconstruction of the neighboring Potsdamer Platz subway and rail station, including the creation of a below-grade connection to the Sony Center site.

Building the Sony Center was not cheap. Total development costs for the project are expected to be roughly DM 1.5 billion. Nineteen banks were involved in putting together the DM 975 million debt package—the largest real estate financing scheme in

Government regulations stipulated that the historic Grand Hotel Esplanade could not be structurally altered. This requirement led to the creation of an innovative bridge of trusses, from which seven levels of residences are suspended. ▼

German history. Dresdener Bank and Westdeutsche Immobilien Bank were the lead managers.

Architecturally, the Sony Center is stunning. Helmut Jahn's design makes extensive use of steel and glass to create a series of buildings that are highly transparent but that still show a great deal of character and attention to detail. One of Jahn's goals was to combine traditional notions of urbanism and public space with a vision for the technologically oriented city of the future. The design of the Sony Center works as a coherent whole, yet is also porous enough to connect closely with the surrounding area.

Because diversity and an interaction between public and private spaces are often viewed as essential to the creation of great urban places, a mixture of uses was a central part of the vision for the Sony Center. While some local residents find the Sony Center's architecture too modern for their taste and for Berlin, the design has generally been very well received and clearly stakes out Berlin's position as one of Europe's leading centers of contemporary architecture.

Operations and Management

The Forum, the elliptical public space at the center of the project, is where all the users of the Sony Center come together and interact. With an area of 4,000 square meters, a fountain at its center, and skylights into the theaters below, the Forum provides the setting for many kinds of events and represents a type of public space rarely found in construction projects today. Many of the offices and residences at the Sony Center look out onto the Forum, creating a sense of both enclosure and interaction.

The Forum, a 4,000-square-meter public space, is the centerpiece of the Sony Center. Capped by its signature roof, the Forum is enclosed by the buildings of the Sony Center and is bustling at all hours of the day.

▲

A marvel of engineering, the Forum roof is already a landmark on the Berlin skyline. Weighing 920 tons, the roof sits on a gigantic ring beam and offers protection from the elements while creating an endless play of light and shadow in the space below.

High above the Forum is one of the signature components of the Sony Center. Immediately recognizable on the Berlin skyline, the Forum roof is a marvel of engineering developed by Helmut Jahn and Ove Arup and Partners. Made of 5,250 square meters of Teflon-coated fabric and 3,500 square meters of laminated glass, the roof follows the shape of a hyperbolic cone and is more than 100 meters across at its widest diameter. Peaking 75 meters above the space below, the Forum roof creates the single largest covered outdoor area in all of Berlin—offering protection from the elements, yet, because it does not completely seal off the space below, permitting the circulation of air. Because it is constructed of alternating transparent and opaque materials in a folded-over design, during the day the roof allows a never-ending variety of light and shadow to fall on the space below; at night, it is lit up in vivid color.

Although they do not dominate the project, the residential uses at the Sony Center are an important part of the overall concept. The 67 rental apartments and 134 condominiums have been built to the highest quality, and are selling for the highest prices in the Berlin market. The design of the units is unique, and the materials used, such as solid wood and natural stone, are luxurious. Custom fittings, separate climate controls for individual rooms, concierge service, and valet parking all create a special atmosphere.

Despite its cutting-edge design, the Forum takes advantage of the European tradition of outdoor cafés and restaurants, offering tenants and visitors a number of places where they can relax, eat, and watch the people go by. Indeed, in addition to the sense of excitement generated by its architecture, much of the center's vitality comes from the people who are coming and going, or lingering over a meal. Retail uses at the Sony Center are focused on the Forum, and Tishman Speyer has concentrated its leasing efforts on retailers and restaurants that would add to this lively atmosphere. The Sony Style store, for example, a high-tech, four-story environment offering an innovative range of products, stands at the nexus of shopping, lifestyle, and entertainment. Other retailers at Sony Center include WebFreeTV.com and Volkswagen AG, both of which have developed stimulating retail entertainment environments.

Although the Sony Center opened in June of 2000, not all the retail space had been leased, in part because Tishman Speyer was holding out for the sort of tenant that would fit in with the Sony Center concept. Given the attractiveness of this project, Tishman Speyer does not expect these retail vacancies to last very long.

Entertainment uses, a key part of the Sony Center concept, have contributed to the project's success. The Deutsche Mediathek and the Filmhaus occupy one of the buildings at the Sony Center. The Mediathek is devoted to the study of radio and television,

while the Filmhaus offers space to a variety of users, such as the German Film and Television Academy. Among the exhibitions that the Filmhaus offers to the public is the Marlene Dietrich Collection, a film museum that celebrates the career of the famous actress from Berlin. Also within the Filmhaus is the Arsenal Repertory Cinema. As noted earlier, the development team was required to provide space for these uses, but they also make significant contributions to the overall plan.

Any good mixed-use project draws outside visitors to the site, and the Sony Center succeeds in doing so through a host of other entertainment options. Apart from the Filmhaus building, 17,000 square meters of space is devoted to entertainment uses, including an eight-screen CineStar multiplex offering the latest releases, and an innovative CineStar 3-D IMAX cinema.

Through the Music Box, an exciting new facility that explores the theme of music in all its glorious variations, Sony itself has contributed to the entertainment uses at the center. Using cutting-edge technology, the Music Box offers patrons a variety of interactive and informative activities. At the Beatles Yellow Submarine Adventure, for example,

guests can ride in a simulated-motion submarine. Another feature gives patrons a chance, by standing in front of a series of screens, to try their hand at conducting the Berlin Philharmonic Orchestra. Visitors can view a harp that makes music with jets of running water instead of strings, and can visit a recording studio where a virtual Beethoven is brought back to life.

Center. Other major tenants include Sanofi-Synthelabo and Sony Music. These and other tenants have been drawn to the Sony Center because of its location, high-quality architecture and construction, and prestige.

In 1990, expectations for the Berlin real estate market were uniformly optimistic; forecasts held that office absorption would top 1 million square meters per year at ever-increasing rents. Reality turned out quite differently. Even in the late 1990s, vacancy rates were approaching 10 percent, with more than 1.5 million square meters of space on the market. It is therefore all the more remarkable that the office space at Sony Center was fully leased before opening day, well ahead of schedule and despite a premium price tag.

The Sony Center has succeeded in emphasizing technology and the future without abandoning the past. Built around 1910, the Grand Hotel Esplanade, with its beautiful sandstone facades and luxurious, neobaroque interior, was once one of the centers of Berlin social life. The building barely survived World War II, however, and only a few of its public rooms remained. As noted earlier, the Berlin city government required the developers of the Sony Center to protect and restore these historic spaces.

One of the rooms, the Breakfast Hall, was broken down into 500 pieces, moved, and reconstructed on site. The Kaisersaal, on the other hand, had to be moved en masse. In their new homes on the site, the rooms have since been painstakingly restored, and now serve as restaurants that are also available for private functions. Two of the interior walls of the Breakfast Hall were left in their original location when the rest of the room was moved, and are on view to the

The offices at the Sony Center offer tenants one of the most prestigious addresses in the city, along with state-of-the-art telecommunications infrastructure and security systems. Space is available in four buildings, with a total floor area of 68,000 square meters. One of these buildings is a 103-meter (26-story) tower with a semicircular glass facade offering stunning views of the city. The entire building has been leased to the German railway company.

Not surprisingly, the European headquarters of Sony are to be found at the Sony

public through a specially designed series of protective glass panels on the Sony Center's outer facade; the effect creates an intriguing blend of old and new.

The Sony Center has been a tremendous financial success. The office space in the project was completely preleased, and all the uses have generated premium rents. Nevertheless, this level of success was by no means assured. Despite its history, Potsdamer Platz was not obviously the best location in the market. In fact, the Sony Center and the other projects at Potsdamer Platz have faced fierce competition with other, more established locations within Berlin, such as the Kurfurstendam area in the former West Berlin and Friedrichstrasse in the former East Berlin. In view of the market situation, Tishman Speyer undertook a major marketing effort more than five years before the opening of the project. One portion of this effort was the InfoBox, an innovative center where visitors to Potsdamer Platz could learn about the area and the development projects underway. It attracted more than 2 million visitors a year. Good marketing, outstanding architecture, a high-caliber mix of tenants and uses, and a high-profile location are the elements that made the Sony Center as successful as it is.

Experience Gained

Finding the right combination of location, accessibility, and target market was essential to the success of the Sony Center. The architecture was also central: the design of the center distinguishes it from the competition and helps to make it a compelling destination for businesses and consumers. Creating a special urban place through architecture is well worth the investment.

▲
Thousands of people came to celebrate the gala opening of the Sony Center in June 2000.

The time has come for mixed-use projects, as consumers show increasing interest in attractive and compelling urban places. Nevertheless, developers and planners need to think carefully about how the pieces of a mixed-used project fit together. Not all uses are compatible, and some combinations of uses generate more interaction and activity than others. Achieving successful synergy between uses is the hallmark of a well-planned mixed-use project.

Developers should also carefully consider the positioning of their project within the market. An understanding of the level of competition for various land uses within the market helps determine which uses are chosen for a given project. For example, because the surrounding area is becoming saturated with retail uses, Tishman Speyer chose to limit the amount of retail at the Sony Center.

Good project management was absolutely key to the success of the project. Especially given the scale and the complexity of the Sony Center, the developer had to have a

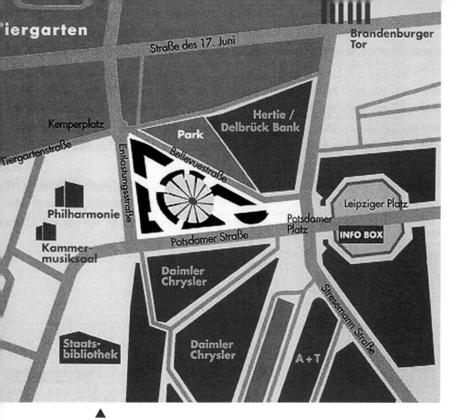

An area map showing the Sony Center am Potsdamer Platz. Cultural facilities, a large park, and the Reichstag (German parliament) are all nearby.

strong grasp of all aspects of the development process (particularly construction) to ensure that the project would be completed on time and within budget.

No urban sites are isolated. It is therefore important to cooperate both with neighbors and with local planning authorities to ensure smooth development. Similarly, especially when using a joint-venture model for development, frequent and open communication between the parties is vital. Right from the beginning of the project, the development team needs to ensure that all its members are on the same page, and that any problems that do arise are dealt with as soon as possible.

Sony Center am Potsdamer Platz

Uses are interspersed in the eight buildings of the Sony Center. Retail and entertainment functions are concentrated at ground level to provide a high level of activity throughout the day and evening.

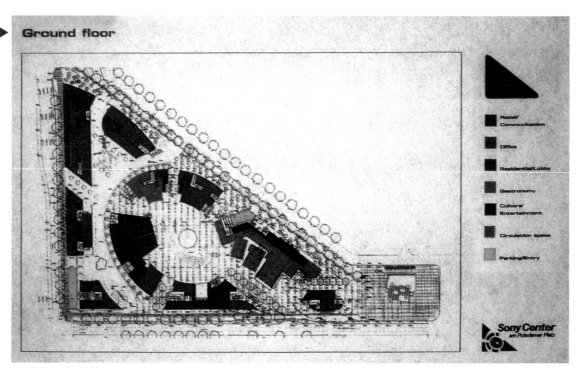

Project Data

Land Use Information

Site area: 26,444 square meters

Gross building area: Approximately 132,500 square meters

Land Uses

Offices (net rentable area): 68,100 square meters

Retail (gross leasable area): 8,100 square meters

Residential units: 26,500 square meters

Other (entertainment): 17,000 square meters

Other (Filmhaus): 17,500 square meters

Parking spaces: 980

Residential Unit Information

Unit type	Unit size (square meters)	Number sold/leased
Apartments	34–105	67
Condominiums	60–210	134

Office Tenant Information

Percentage of net rentable area occupied:
100 percent

Development Cost Information

Total development cost expected at completion:
Approximately DM 1.5 billion

Development Schedule

Sony Berlin founded	1991
Site purchased	June 1991
Helmut Jahn wins the architectural competition	1992
Planning begins	1993
Planning completed	1995
Construction begins	September 1995
Moving of the Kaisersaal	March 1996
Leasing begins	1997
Construction completed	1998
First phases open to the public	January 2000
Grand opening	June 2000

Westend City Center
Budapest, Hungary

For more than a decade, Hungary has undergone a remarkable transformation, turning away from its Communist past and toward a democratic, market-oriented future. The Westend City Center, in Budapest, the Hungarian capital, is symbolic of this dramatic change. Developed by TriGránit Development Corporation, this 192,000-square-meter project combines a hotel, offices, shopping, and entertainment in one of the city's best locations.

Westend City Center formally opened in November 1999, just in time for the holiday shopping season. On opening day, thousands of people jammed into the center to see one of Budapest's most remarkable new real estate projects. With distinctive architectural character, high-quality design and construction, and an attractive mix of uses, the project has already had a tremendous impact on the local market, and has set a new standard for future development in the city.

The project was developed by a joint venture between Canada's TrizecHahn Corporation and Granit Polus R.A., a Hungarian company with extensive development experience in Eastern Europe. TriGránit was formed in 1996 with the goal of developing high-quality office and mixed-use projects in Hungary and Slovakia. Westend City Center represents one of the company's first, and certainly its most ambitious, development efforts. In the case of Westend City Center, TrizecHahn staff assumed the lion's share of responsibility for development work.

**With its strikingly modern design, Westend City Center ▶
has become one of the most important shopping
destinations in Budapest.**

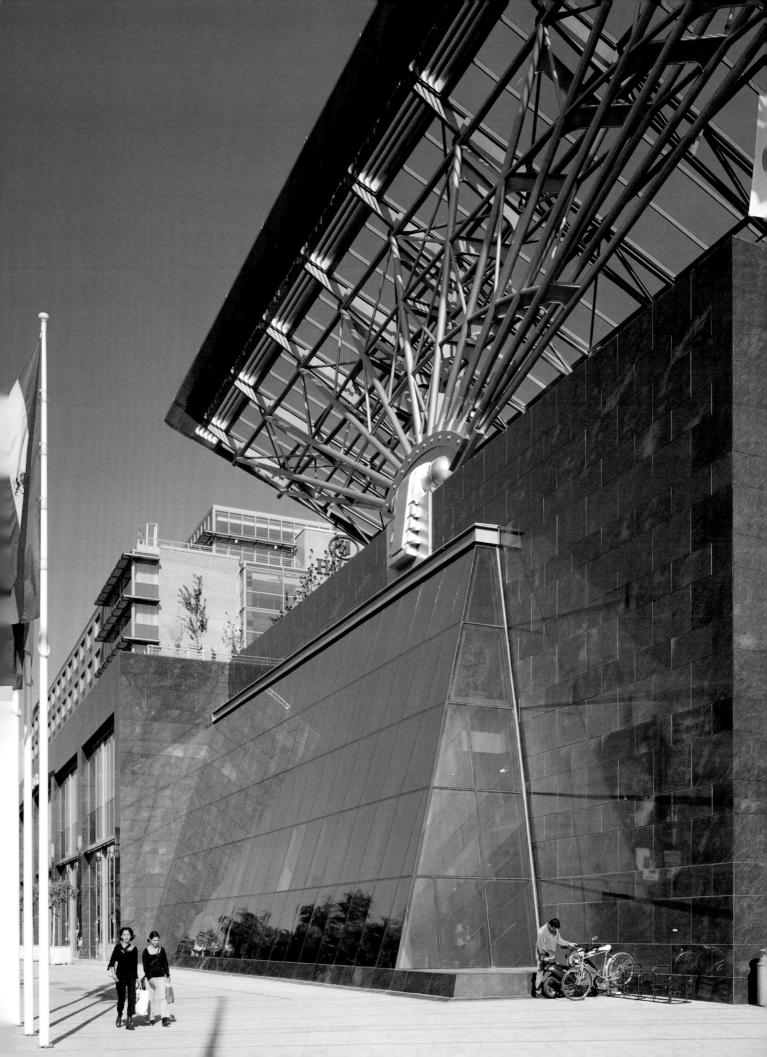

Development Team

Developer
TriGránit Development Corporation
(JV TrizecHahn/Granit Polus R.A.)
Vaci ut. 3
1062 Budapest, Hungary
36-1-238-7738

Retail Concept Architect
The Jerde Partnership International
913 Ocean Front Walk
Venice, California 90291
(310) 399-1987

Project Architect and Planner
Finta Studios
Margit Körut 39
1024 Budapest, Hungary
31-1-374-3374

Other Development Team Members
Brian Jenkins, Project Director
Platz der Einheit 2
Pollux Building, Floor 25
Frankfurt am Main, Germany 60327
49-69-74223-0

Otto Blau, Director of Construction
29 Arjay Crescent
Willowdale, Ontario
M2L 1C6 Canada
(416) 445-3731

The centerpiece of the development is the shopping mall, which features nearly 400 stores in a space of 49,500 square meters, including 33 restaurants and cafés in both a food court and other locations. Apart from the shops, the mall offers a 14-screen multiplex cinema, a variety of water features, and even a 22,000-square-meter roof garden and park. Westend City Center also includes 19,000 square meters of Class A office space; a new, 230-room Hilton hotel; and parking facilities for 1,500 cars. The development scheme also involved the restoration of an historic building on the site, and the reconstruction of a bridge over the railway tracks adjacent to the site. All these facilities are tied together by a distinctive, modern design that nevertheless succeeds in harmonizing with the other buildings in the neighborhood.

The Site
Situated at one of the most accessible points in Budapest, Westend City Center is visited by over 400,000 people each day. Next door to the project is the Nyugati railway station, one of the city's two main stations. In addition to being the city's major destination for commuters, the station is itself a treasured landmark designed and constructed by Gustav Eiffel (best known for his tower in Paris). The site is served by a metro station as well as by numerous bus and trolley lines. Also adjacent is Vaci Road, a major arterial street that connects downtown Budapest with the suburbs to the northeast.

The traditional commercial center of Budapest is only a few minutes away from Westend City Center. Budapest has 2 million residents—including approximately 220,000 within a two-kilometer radius of the site—and receives a remarkable 20 million tourist visits each year. But despite the apparent strength of the local market, no other developments in the city offer the scale or the quality of the shops and services found at Westend City Center.

Given its obvious advantages, one might ask why the site was not developed earlier. The answer is that this was no easy site to develop. Previously occupied by disused railway tracks and assorted railway buildings in various stages of collapse, the 58,000-square-meter site had drawn some interest on the part of other development firms, but none were able to move ahead with the development process. Granit Polus, the Hungarian partner in TriGránit, felt that it could do better; it acquired the site in 1997 and began to prepare plans.

Development Process

A number of obstacles stood in the way of the development of Westend City Center, the most important of which was the need for extensive negotiations with a variety of local authorities to come up with a plan acceptable to all parties. Before TriGránit even came into the picture, the city had been contemplating different uses for the site, including turning it into a municipal park. To get the go-ahead for the project, TriGránit had to agree to a host of concessions to the public authorities,

▲ Located next to the Nyugati station, which was designed by Gustav Eiffel, Westend City Center has one of the best locations in downtown Budapest.

including the restoration of a historic building on the site that had once been a customs house, the reconstruction (in cooperation with the city government) of an adjacent bridge over the railway tracks, the improvement of a commuter railway facility, and the relocation of other buildings associated with the railway station.

TriGránit had to deal with a variety of public agencies during the development process. For example, the Hungarian Ministry of Transportation previously had control of the site and had to be consulted about changes to the railway facilities. The city of Budapest had zoning authority for the site, while a district government within the city was responsible for issuing permits. The national Historical and Cultural Assets Commission had to be consulted throughout the development process, and a local government architectural committee had to approve the initial design and all subsequent changes. In each of these cases, having a knowledgeable local partner was crucial to the success of the project.

Public consultation proved to be an important component in the development process. While the consultative mechanisms in the Hungarian planning process are perhaps not as thoroughly ingrained as they are in the United States, public outreach was undertaken during project planning to gauge local reactions to the proposed design and to help gener-

◀ The centerpiece of Westend City Center, the shopping mall surpasses all local competitors with respect to store selection, amenities, and design.

A distinctive ▶ glass and metal canopy helps to define the architectural character of Westend City Center.

ate the required level of political support. For instance, TriGránit sponsored a public concert at the site as a show of good faith and to give the local population a flavor of the amenities that might be available at the center once it was completed.

Apart from these direct efforts at public relations, however, it was also essential to work within the political system of committees and approving agencies to get the proposal through. In this regard, both the project architect (a highly respected Hungarian firm) and the local partner in the joint venture were indispensable. In fact, without their network of contacts and their deep understanding of the nuances of the local planning and approval process, the project may never have gone ahead at all.

Financing for Westend City Center was handled by local TrizecHahn staff, who worked with four local banks to arrange a financing package worth approximately $127 million. Obtaining financing was easier said than done, however. Because no local banks had ever seen a project of the size and scope of Westend City Center, they had to be persuaded that the project was not only viable but would be a success. To facilitate the later

disposition of the project, its various components are actually on separate parcels—a legal arrangement that does not detract from the functional integration of the center.

During construction, TriGránit used a variety of techniques to ensure that the development would be completed on time and on budget. Compared with those in North America, construction projects in Hungary are sometimes hampered by poor information, low-quality materials, and murky accounting practices. To avoid these pitfalls, TriGránit hired a North American construction manager with extensive experience working in Eastern Europe. Efforts were focused on achieving transparency and reliability in the construction process. Materials were obtained from local sources if possible, but TriGránit did not hesitate to buy materials in other countries if these were more appropriate. Furthermore, TriGránit simply insisted on high-quality construction materials and methods, thereby ensuring the quality of the finished product.

Planning and Design

One of the most intriguing aspects of Westend City Center is its design, which is thoroughly modern, with ample use of steel and glass in the facades, and a highly distinctive, angled, steel-and-glass canopy on the roof near the main entrance. To ensure that the project did not have a monolithic appearance, the center was given a highly differentiated facade, which employs a range of colors and materials and is punctuated by entrances to the various components of the project. As noted earlier, the center's unique architectural character does not prevent it from blending successfully with the other buildings in the area, particularly with respect to its height and massing. It has even set something of a trend: newer development projects being built in the surrounding area echo Westend City Center's design themes.

The shopping mall at Westend City Center would be familiar to any North American consumer. The storefronts have high-quality signage—in fact, TriGránit insisted that the storefronts present an attractive image to shoppers. Thanks to generous proportions and the extensive use of skylights, the public areas of the mall are spacious and bright. Natural plants soften the environment. Like many other recent development projects around the world, Westend City Center has water features: a 20-meter-high waterfall at its main entrance, as well as other fountains, both inside and outside the center, that draw a never-ending audience of children and their parents. As visitors stroll among the three levels of shops, the latest radio hits are broadcast from the mall's sound system.

The shopping mall at Westend City Center opened fully leased in November of 1999. Some tenant turnover has occurred since then, and some design flaws have been revealed. For instance, since the floor plan of the mall looks something like a stretched-out "B," foot traffic naturally tends to flow along the straight part of the layout rather than along the curved part. Some of the smaller

retailers located off the main axis receive insufficient pedestrian flow—an issue that TriGránit is trying to address by creating stores that have frontages on both walkways.

One definite strength of the shopping mall, however, is its hours of operation. Unlike many of its competitors in Budapest, which have short operating hours, Westend City Center is open weekdays from 10:00 A.M. until 9:00 P.M. It is also open late on weekends, and entertainment facilities, such as the cinema, draw people throughout the evening. Giving consumers this added degree of choice and flexibility has helped Westend City Center to succeed.

Naturally, the interior design and facilities of the Hilton hotel are on par with international standards. Three restaurants and cafés offer hotel guests a variety of dining options; the hotel also features ten conference rooms of various sizes. In addition to a state-of-the-art fitness center, the hotel has an executive floor with additional guest facilities, including access to a rooftop terrace with views of the Budapest skyline. Since the hotel's opening in July 2000, occupancy rates have been steadily increasing. As in any good mixed-use development, the hotel is well integrated into the rest of the project.

The office space at Westend City Center is built to the highest international standards. The project offers more than 19,172 square meters of space in three six-story buildings, which are blended architecturally into the rest of the center. In order to be competitive with Budapest's many other recently built office projects, Westend City Center is targeting tenants who want easy access to transit as well as proximity to other concentrations of businesses in the city. Office tenants receive the latest in communications equipment, climate control, and security features. As of

◀ A food court, restaurants, and cafés provide visitors with a variety of dining options.

both underground garages and a multilevel parking structure. (The structure is particularly interesting because it was built above a section of active railroad tracks leading to the nearby Nyugati station.) As it turns out, however, Westend City Center has more than enough parking. The facilities have never been full, and it is unclear when or whether they ever will be. Part of the issue is the cost of parking: patrons of the shopping center have to pay to use the parking structure, which is a somewhat unusual arrangement for the Budapest market. Finding the right pricing level for the parking facilities is an ongoing exercise.

A California-based firm, The Jerde Partnership International, which has worldwide experience in planning and architecture, designed the retail concept for Westend City Center. However, a local Hungarian firm, Finta Studios, served as the project architect and did most of the detailed design work. Having two architects for the same project created both advantages and disadvantages. On the one hand, TriGránit was able to achieve a design that was cutting edge and reflective of international trends in shopping-center design, but that also responded to local sensibilities. On the other hand, tensions sometimes arose between the two architects over the importance of certain project components or over design details. In the end, though, none of these tensions were destructive. The lesson that emerged from the design process was that, as is the case for any partnership, the development of a shared vision and mutual trust is essential to achieving a successful design.

August 2000, 50 percent of the office space at Westend City Center had been leased, and the remainder was under negotiation.

An amenity that all users of Westend City Center can enjoy is the roof garden. Featuring abundant natural grass and an array of trees and flowers, the garden offers a welcome respite from the urban activity below. Futuristic light standards make the garden usable at all hours, and there are many tables and benches where workers and shoppers can have lunch or relax. TriGránit pays careful attention to the maintenance of the roof garden; despite its location, there have been no problems either with the viability of the plantings or with damage to the roof below.

Despite the easy access to public transit, parking was a major concern in the planning and design of Westend City Center. The project currently provides 1,500 parking spaces in

Marketing, Operations, and Management

Being situated on a landmark site with exceptionally high visibility in the local market has certainly helped attract attention and customers to Westend City Center. Moreover, since it was (and is) the largest development of its kind in Hungary, there was no lack of media attention. More traditional methods of advertising the center have also been important. Westend City Center is widely advertised on posters all over downtown Budapest, particularly as a destination for fashion. Because of the importance of the tourist market, advertisements for the center can also be found in hotel rooms and in the free guidebooks given out to tourists.

TriGránit handled all the marketing and leasing in house. North American TrizecHahn staff worked on leasing with international tenants, while Hungarian staff worked with local tenants. Although a number of Western retailers have set up shop at Westend City Center, Hungarian tenants predominate. Unlike some of the other centers in the Budapest market, Westend City Center has only well-established retailers with extensive experience in the market. A number of local firms were used to conduct market studies, and when the shopping mall opened, it was 100 percent leased.

Almost half of the retailers are fashion oriented, making Westend City Center the largest concentration of such stores in Budapest. Compared with similarly sized cities in Western Europe, Budapest has relatively few department stores, and Westend City Center is no exception. Instead, the center is anchored by a 14-screen multiplex theater, a Media Markt electronics store, and a Julius Meinl supermarket, which have been effective in drawing customers to the center. With top-quality seating and sound and a good selection of the latest films,

the movie theaters have attracted more than 2 million visitors, making the Westend City Center cinemas the most successful in the country by a substantial margin.

One of the major concerns in operating in Eastern Europe is security. In some countries, organized crime syndicates prey on small retailers through extortion rackets, and the local police are often ineffective at curbing the problem. Ensuring the safety of both customers and tenants at Westend City Center was therefore a top priority. In the shopping mall, the hotel, and the office areas, uniformed security personnel form a highly visible presence, and all entrances to the project are protected by cameras. These measures, along with a generally proactive approach to safety and security, have been very successful. Since the opening of the project, the center has not had a single major security incident.

Mixed-use developments enlivened with entertainment are garnering increasing attention in the real estate world, and the reasons are vividly illustrated at Westend City Center. Each of the uses generates a level of activity that supports the other uses in the project,

The cinemas at Westend City Center are by far the most successful in Hungary. The colorful lobby (shown) accommodates patrons for all 14 screens.
▼

Site plan.

and the proportions of the project have been correctly gauged to the needs of the local market. Architecturally, Westend City Center demonstrates that different uses can have separate identities within a coherently designed and built whole. But perhaps most important, Westend City Center shows that mixed-use developments generate a level of interest and activity that single-use projects can rarely achieve. Whether they are tenants, shoppers, hotel guests, or simply visitors searching for entertainment—or for nothing in particular—people are drawn to Westend City Center—and, once there, have any number of reasons to stay. The result is good for the health of cities—and, naturally, good for the development team.

Experience Gained

The landmark location, the exceptionally good transit access, and the strength of the high-quality, mixed-use concept made the development of the center a particularly compelling opportunity—one that was well worth the time and effort required to overcome all the obstacles to the completion of the project.

The joint-venture model proved ideal for the development of Westend City Center. Because each of the partners brought different yet complementary skills and knowledge to the development process, both were able to make substantial contributions to the project. However, in the course of the development process, each partner had to learn to recognize the strengths and weaknesses of the other, and to trust the other to further the goals of the joint-venture company.

Developing a project in the Hungarian market created substantial challenges. Some aspects of the development process, such as financing and construction, were particularly tricky. Negotiating successfully required persistence—as well as the local partner's in-depth knowledge. Particularly because of the project's complexity, being able to compromise—whether with the joint-venture partner, with the designers, or with the local approval authorities—was vitally important to success.

Financing the project in Euros, as opposed to U.S. dollars, would have been more appropriate given the location of the project, the financing, and the sourcing of materials. It would also have been helpful to arrange financing sooner in the development process. Although the financing arrangement was sufficient to get the project built, it did create frustration; in retrospect, the developers feel that it may have been better to arrange financing with Western banks, many of whom are showing an increasing interest in the Eastern European market.

As is always the case, controlling the timing of the development process was very important. Delays are always a possibility, but in the case of Westend City Center, it took exceptional effort to ensure that the shopping mall would open in time for the Christmas shopping season. Given the usual construction practices in Eastern Europe, maintaining strict control over the construction process was vital; it was also necessary to introduce high standards of transparency and quality control to ensure the success of the final product. Finally, an active and multifaceted approach to leasing and marketing was important to secure tenants and to attract customers.

Project Data

Land Use Information

Site area: 58,000 square meters (includes 10,000 square meters of air rights over the railroad tracks)

Gross building area: 192,062 square meters

Land Uses

Offices (net rentable area): 19,172 square meters

Retail (gross leasable area): 49,500 square meters

Other (roof garden and park): 22,276 square meters

Hotel rooms: 230

Parking spaces: 1,500

Land Use Plan

Use	Area (square meters)	Percentage of site
Buildings	168,786	88
Landscaping and open space	22,276	12
Total	191,062	100

Retail Tenant Information

Name	Square meters
Ster Century Multiplex	8,942
Media Markt (electronics)	4,300
Julius Meinl (supermarket)	3,706
Play Station West (food and beverage)	2,322
Giacomelli (sports)	1,846
Marks & Spencer (department store)	905
Mango (clothing)	681

Percentage of gross leasable area occupied: 98 percent

Annual rents: Approximately $156 to $1,200 per square meter

Average length of lease: Ten years

Office Tenant Information

Percentage of net rentable area occupied: 50 percent

Number of tenants: Three

Annual rents: Approximately $16 to $18 per square meter

Average length of lease: Five years

Typical lease terms: Net lease with pro rata share of common building space included in rental fee

Development Cost Information

Site-Related Costs

Site acquisition	$14,200,000
Site improvement	500,000
Subtotal, site-related costs	$14,700,000

Construction Costs

Office	$13,400,000
Retail	82,500,000
Hotel	13,600,00
Other (building owner expenses)	11,800,000
Subtotal, construction costs	$121,300,000

Soft Costs

Office, retail, and hotel	$27,900,000
Other (tenant allowance)	17,000,000
Subtotal, soft costs	$44,900,000
Total development cost	$180,900,000

Development Schedule

Planning started	March 1997
Site purchased	December 1997
Leasing started	January 1998
Construction started	June 1998
Construction completed	November 1999 (Phase I)
	July 2000 (Phase II)
	October 2000 (Phase III)

CHAPTER 6

Future Directions

As Mark Twain once said, "the reports of my death are greatly exaggerated." The same is true of retail entertainment development. What some observers have called the decline of a development fad represents, in our view, the birth of a new development paradigm. The search for a new paradigm is never easy, but the retail entertainment industry is evolving quickly: new concepts, projects, and plans are announced as rapidly as old ones are discredited and fade away. Even the terms used to describe this dynamic new form of development have changed since the first edition of this book was published a mere three years ago. What were then called *urban entertainment centers* are now increasingly referred to as *retail entertainment destinations* or simply *destination developments.*

More than a semantic distinction or a marketing ploy, the change in nomenclature reflects a rethinking of how entertainment-related development—or, simply, "entertaining development"—is being successfully introduced, integrated, and sustained as an essential component of a range of development types: new multiuse communities; town centers; strip centers; regional shopping malls; Main Street projects; urban mixed-use developments; sports facilities; museums; amusement parks; casinos; historic and cultural districts; downtowns (urban and suburban); waterfronts; and neighborhood commercial districts. A new entertainment paradigm does indeed seem to have emerged, and it appears to be the real thing.

Westend Plaza, which is being planned in the city center of Frankfurt, ▶ Germany, will be a mixed-use project containing retail, entertainment, office, hotel, and apartment uses. An intimate and energized pedestrian environment will curve through the dense, high-rise urban setting.
TrizecHahn Development Corporation

The success of many first-generation destination developments clearly demonstrated the strength of the market for local and regional entertainment-enhanced development. But many of the industry's initial concepts were flawed because they were based on models that were limited to unique situations in major markets. Over the past few years, recognition of this problem has forced the industry to redirect its creative energy to devise new models that will work in a broad range of situations and locations. The public's demand for entertainment is insatiable—and, as described in chapter 1, is growing stronger. Nevertheless, providing entertainment in ways that are economically and financially feasible, and that also satisfy a remarkably fickle and demanding public, remains a challenge.

Early prototypes were largely freestanding developments in major tourist markets. These locations have unique attributes, including one-of-a-kind anchors. Universal CityWalk in Los Angeles and Orlando is anchored by Universal Studios. Tishman Urban Development's E-Walk and Forrest City Ratner's entertainment center, both on 42nd Street in New York City, are anchored by Times Square. Other projects have different one-of-a-kind advantages. Navy Pier, in Chicago, has a spectacular location on Lake Michigan and was paid for with public funds, and Irvine Spectrum Center, in Irvine, California, is located at the intersection of two of the world's busiest freeways on land that the Irvine Company already owned.

The tenants in early retail entertainment prototypes also foretold a built-in growth limitation for the industry. Tenants in the first successful projects usually fell into neat categories with recognizable names, such as AMC, United Artists, and Loews, for cinemas; Dave & Buster's, Jillian's, and GameWorks, for interactive attractions; and Planet Hollywood and Hard Rock Café, for theme restaurants. How many developments anchored by these big names could be sustained in a typical market? Given the number of customers needed to support them, the answer is not many, even in the largest markets.

Finally, the high cost of constructing and operating destination developments, the difficulty of devising prototypes to which people want to return again and again, and the lack of comparables in an industry where uniqueness is a development goal have made it difficult to obtain financing for freestanding destination projects even in the best locations. The bankruptcies of most of the major cinema operators have temporarily compounded the problem by eliminating, for many projects, what is viewed as the most important anchor for ensuring long-term project success.

Needless to say, an industry dependent on (1) one-of-a-kind locations in major metropolitan areas; (2) tenants that need enormous trade areas; and (3) cinema operators—many of whom happen to be bankrupt—has limited growth potential. This situation was bound to change, and it has.

Retail entertainment development is now viewed in a larger context than it was just a few years ago. Although freestanding centers will continue to be built in some specialized locations, communities and developers alike have come to view entertainment as an essential component of almost all forms of development. Even when it does not constitute the largest part of a development, entertainment may prove to be the most important because it adds value to the other land uses and activities. Entertainment is currently seen as the glue that ties together multiuse and mixeduse developments, providing the spark of excitement that energizes a place around the clock, and creating a memorable destination to which people want to belong—and to which they want to return again and again.

Cities and the places within them have always been successful when they are exciting, diverse, and entertaining, and when they offer the maximum number of places to eat, places to shop, places to visit, and things to experience. In fact, throughout history, these have been among cities' major competitive advantages—a circumstance that is not going to change. The new generation of retail entertainment developments, many of which are profiled in the case studies in chapter 5, are designed to provide all these advantages.

Because of the increasing diversity of the projects, keeping up with destination development activity in cities around the world is now more difficult than it was when the first edition of this book was published. Nevertheless, longer track records and vivid successes and failures are making the trends clearer. The remainder of this chapter focuses on what ULI believes will be some of the most important trends over the next few years. Most of these trends were just emerging when the first

▲
E-Walk, developed by Tishman Urban Development Corporation, is one of two major retail entertainment destinations that opened in 2000 on New York's 42nd Street, in the heart of the revitalized Times Square cultural and entertainment district.
Tishman Urban Development Corporation

edition of this book was written, and they have been updated to reflect changes since that time. In some cases our crystal ball was cloudy, and we have made the necessary corrections. Undoubtedly, new trends and ideas will appear as the industry continues to evolve. ULI believes more than ever that the retail entertainment industry's future is limited only by the imagination of its many talented creators and developers.

Multiuse retail entertainment destinations will be the focus of downtown revitalization efforts. Retail entertainment developments have the potential to create

20/20 Vision: 20 Next-Generation Trends for Out-

For those involved in the out-of-home entertainment business, the future has never been brighter. The companies that have correctly gauged what people want are enjoying tremendous success. Those that haven't—including some of the major entertainment companies and several well-known retailers—are likely to disappear from the out-of-home entertainment business for some time, if not forever. Despite the frustrations experienced by some developers and entertainment companies during the past decade, we foresee an explosion of opportunity as the industry corrects itself and moves forward.

Several factors will contribute to future growth in the industry. First, consumers worldwide, but particularly in the United States, are growing increasingly accustomed to a rich and meaningful experiential quality in their daily lives. Second, we are now witnessing the emergence of Generation Y, the largest generation ever in the history of the United States; this new young-adult population regards shopping as a lifestyle pursuit. Finally, the parents of Generation Y, the aging baby boomers, are reaching a time in their lives—and in their pocketbooks—when comfort,

escape, and indulgence are paramount considerations and rewards.

The evidence for the coming changes is already in. Since 1950, U.S. consumer expenditures on all forms of entertainment have risen 45 percent, after adjustment for inflation.[1] In light of the fact that consumer spending on items such as food, alcoholic beverages, apparel and services, and personal care *decreased* an average of 32 percent during the same period, the level of entertainment expenditures represents an extraordinary willingness on the part of consumers to indulge their leisure desires.

It is important to note, however, that while gross spending on entertainment has increased tremendously, the role of entertainment in consumers' lives has also changed. It has been a long time since the circus came to town to astonish and amaze us. Tastes in entertainment experiences are shifting in the direction of escape, reward, camaraderie, family, and comfort values, and away from bigger-than-life, "plan-ahead" events such as visits to theme parks or amusement facilities. In other words, the demand is there; the question is how to satisfy it.

Here's our 20/20 vision of the future: 20 ideas that we predict will reach the mainstream during the next 20 years:

Lifestyle Showcase Stores.
These will become the primary format for out-of-home retailing. Rising incomes worldwide, increasingly efficient sourcing and distribution, and connectivity provided by the Internet will combine to create a platform for stores with broader stock-keeping units (SKUs), broader sourcing opportunities, and limited (if not just-in-time) inventory methods. This type of store format will particularly appeal to members of Generation Y. Look for more deals like Best Buy and its purchase of Musicland.

Live Performance.
It's coming back, but this time to the masses. One of the big pushes in the past decade was for high-tech gadgetry such as simulator rides (consumers said "Ugh") and video games (works, but mostly for boys). At the same time, live performance—be it musical theater, legitimate theater, concerts, or buskers—remains as vital and engaging as ever.

Watch for new formats, some using technologies to enhance the live performance, ready for insertion in existing urban destinations at affordable (under $20 average) ticket prices.

Hip Communities.
For those in the relaxed time of their lives, new communities will flourish. Notions of what it means to be a "senior" or a "retiree" will shift for at least a generation, as the still-dominant, "refuse-to-admit-they're-aging" baby boomers start to slow down. This "Viagra generation" will enjoy classes in culinary arts and gardening; yoga will be offered at on-site leisure universities.

"Show" Architecture.
Frank Gehry has established the destination pull of a Big Idea place design, and theme parks and Universal CityWalk have established consumer acceptance of super-dense experiential environments. In this busy, noisy world, project curb appeal will be paramount in attracting and keeping customers. Watch for these two trends to be incorporated into many projects coming soon.

Cotenancy Ventures.
Store-within-a-store concepts are a time-honored retail presentation method for specific

lome Entertainment

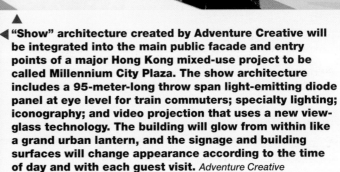

▲
◀ "Show" architecture created by Adventure Creative will be integrated into the main public facade and entry points of a major Hong Kong mixed-use project to be called Millennium City Plaza. The show architecture includes a 95-meter-long throw span light-emitting diode panel at eye level for train commuters; specialty lighting; iconography; and video projection that uses a new view-glass technology. The building will glow from within like a grand urban lantern, and the signage and building surfaces will change appearance according to the time of day and with each guest visit. *Adventure Creative*

brands and products. As the rationale for out-of-home retail facilities shifts, firms with well-defined product lines will team up with other retailers whose wares match the lifestyle attributes of their products; these joint retail pre-sentations will dominate the new retail formats.

Person-to-Person Service. Say goodbye to the continued reliance on minimum-wage staff to represent a store and its brands. As technologi-cal innovations—such as cashiering with your Palm Pilot—free up service staff from cash-wrap duties to focus purely on customer satisfaction and queries, person-to-person service will emerge as the primary means of competitive

Continued ▶

differentiation, allowing more experienced and better trained retail careerists to flourish.

It's All about Me. From day spas and masseurs; to beauty treatments and cosmetics companies; to dry cleaners, florists, and grocers, services for the self will thrive. Look for these at the office, supermarket, shopping center—and delivered to your door.

Destination Resorts. Watch for a new form of local urban resort in a town near you. Daytime escapes—in the form of short leisure trips—will lead the trend. (Club Med has the first of these resorts in Paris.)

Brand Entrepreneurship. Soon to be the talk of the retail industry. Brand impresarios, not unlike today's cosmetics company representatives, will become part of the point-of-sale process.

Performance Studios. Soon to replace movie theaters. As we enter the new millennium, the movie theater remains one of the great "remaining-to-be-reinvented products" of the 20th century. Digital delivery and playback of media will allow cinemas to transform themselves into black-box performance studios (albeit comfortable ones,

with luxurious seats and good sight lines), ready to present great films (hopefully), to simulcast large-screen concerts, and to allow customers to be "digital members" of live television audiences originating from anywhere in the world. Thanks to inexpensive film production equipment, student-produced or independently produced film shorts will come to your local theater as the new form of the cartoon shorts of old.

Flex Platforms. The next generation of common areas in retail centers will be venues unto themselves. These "flex platforms" will become community parks, libraries, town centers, sponsored showcases, performance pavilions, and product-launch centers. More important, as corporate America comes to view these locations as legitimate forums for reaching busy consumers, common areas will cease to be cost centers and will become profit centers. The sponsors are coming!

Authentic Immersive Environments. Consumers love themed environments: the problem is, they love them for a while, and then they get bored. Theming for theming's sake will be replaced by immersive environments based on authentic

products and services, where content will change with each visit. Watch for a brief explosion, though, of ethnic themed restaurants before purely themed venues die away.

Content Is King. The out-of-home facilities that will thrive will be based on the idea that content—that is, what guests "get to do"—is the basis of design. A new type of developer, steeped in the experience of The Mills Corporation and Caruso Affiliated Holdings, will accommodate new entertainment formats that redefine the landlord-tenant relationship and transcend traditional leasing arrangements.

Diversity. The same innovations that allow the emergence of showcase stores with shallow inventory and broad SKUs will also allow diversity to flourish. Major retailers will adapt to provide complete satisfaction for diverse customers, at the same time that narrowly targeted specialty retailers carve niche markets to grow new brands. Generation Y appears to be completely at peace with diversity, and the word is going to be an anachronism in 20 years. What does this mean about the kinds of customers you can expect?

Moments, Memories, Mementos. The "three Ms" will become to out-of-home entertainment what "location, location, location" is to real estate. Consumers will seek experiences that become part of the shared memories of their family, friends, and professional associates. Those who create and operate the facilities that provide such experiences should remember that in the end, they are simply providing the moments, then the memories, of a consumer's life.

Attention Spans and Multitasking. Watch for experiential formats and products that reflect the sensibilities of people who have busy lives, who rely on multitasking to get through the day, and who were raised on MTV and quick-cut film editing. Grocery stores with ready-made meals, gas stations with ATMs: these examples point to the continued packaging of products and services into combined formats that deliver "better" for the consumer (see "Cotenancy Ventures").

The Internet. The Internet will take its place as one of the great conveniences of the modern world, and will be found to have no impact on the time consumers spend in the out-of-home marketplace.

Nevertheless, the motivation for trips will change. With more convenience items being handled at home, through Internet purchases and queries, consumers will be free to focus more on leisure pursuits when they are out in the community.

Women Just Want to Have Fun.
The labor-force participation rate of women is expected to increase to 70 percent by 2020. Brain research indicates that women show decreased blood pressure and increased positive brain-wave activity from doing the "gathering"—especially shopping. Provide out-of-home experiences that satisfy women—the drivers of consumer spending—and the hearts and minds of the rest of the family will follow.

Values-Based Lifestyles.
We've lived through some cynical times. But our new Gen Y group is embracing values as a core attribute of their humanity. Green values, environmentalism, respect for family, are all driving forces that are beginning to influence the out-of-home environment—at least for the young.

The Milkman Returns.
Wow, the Internet is going to allow daily home immersive environments based on authen-

tic products and services, where content changes with each visit, including delivery of produce, convenience goods . . . wait a second, we had that growing up! In many cases, it's not nostalgia that brings back these old products and services: it's that the old way was just better. Watch for many products to bring back solutions from the old days—and watch "what's old become new again."

Today's consumer, from child to retiree, has generally experienced high-quality shows, movies, restaurants, and especially theme parks. Each person in this vast "theme-park generation" is technologically savvy and a sophisticated master of his or her own lifestyle. These consumers are ready for new experiences, and in fact demand them. Are you ready to meet the future? ●

Source: Jill Bensley and Donald Bredberg.

Note

1. Bureau of the Census, *Historical Statistics of the United States, Colonial Times to 1970*, Part 1, 1975; Bureau of Labor Statistics, http://www.bls.gov/cxshome.htm. Calculations by JB Research Company.

new social and cultural centers in urban communities that have lost theirs to blight—and in suburban communities that never had such centers. More than ever, entertainment is seen as a way to energize urban revitalization projects whose character is only partly oriented toward entertainment. Although some cities will not be affected by this trend until some point in the future, for others it is already a reality.

The first example of this trend was Reston Town Center, which was not an existing urban downtown at all, but a new suburban center. Primarily an office development, Reston Town Center also includes a hotel, traditional retail stores, and an entertainment component. The success of this mix of uses in a neotraditional downtown setting led to even more ambitious proposals (both in traditional downtowns and in new suburban communities) to create large-scale, integrated downtown developments that include a major entertainment element.

CityPlace, in West Palm Beach, Florida, the first of a new generation of entertainment-enhanced town-center developments, has created a hub of social activity for the city. Opened in late 2000, the 600,000-square-foot development is adjacent to the city's new performing-arts center and incorporates a historic church that was restored for use as a cultural center. CityPlace is part of a much larger, $375 million mixed-use development that includes residential, cultural, performance, hotel, office, and convention facilities. The developer, the Palladium Company, plans to roll out this concept in other cities, including Bellevue, Washington, and Boston, in the next few years.

The first phase of Silver Spring, Maryland's new town center also opened in 2000 in suburban Washington, D.C. Developed by the Peterson Company and Folger Pratt, this multiuse, neotraditional development is restoring the

CityPlace, developed in West Palm Beach, Florida, by the Palladium Company, opened in late 2000 as the first of a new generation of town-center destinations. The developers restored a historic church, incorporated it into the project as a performing-arts center, and made it one of the focal points of Palladium Plaza, a new public gathering place.
The Palladium Company

commercial and civic heart of an affluent older suburb whose downtown had dramatically declined over the past several decades. Upon completion, the development will include a Muvico megaplex; neighborhood retail, including Fresh Fields, a gourmet organic food market; lifestyle retail stores; public gathering places; and a restored art deco theater that will be used by the American Film Institute as its first regional center for showing classic films and educating the public about the film industry. Attracted by this new retail entertainment destination, the Discovery Channel is constructing its world headquarters across the street.

The Gateway, being developed in downtown Salt Lake City, Utah, by Gateway Associates, a partnership of The Boyer Company and The Jerde Partnership International, Inc., will be a 2-million-square-foot mixed-use development, including 835,000 square feet of retail and entertainment uses, that will provide a centerpoint destination for the city. Sited on three blocks surrounding the historic

Union Pacific Depot, the project will unite retail, dining, entertainment, residential, upscale hotel, and community cultural facilities, and will include a 12-screen megaplex and nightclubs organized around public plazas and gathering places.

The use of retail and entertainment facilities as anchors for downtown revitalization projects is not limited to the United States. Westend Plaza will be a 250,000-square-meter, mixed-use project on five hectares in the heart of Frankfurt, Germany, near the main train station and exhibition fair (Messe). Conceived by TrizecHahn Europe and Eisenbahnimmobilien Management GmbH (a subsidiary of Deutsche Bahn AG), the dense high-rise project will be laced with low-rise pedestrian environments suitable for retail and entertainment facilities. To be completed in autumn of 2003, the project will include almost 100,000 square meters of retail entertainment (including a cineplex, a live-performance theater, and entertainment restaurants) as well as office space, a hotel, apartments, and a wellness center.

These projects, and many others currently under construction around the world, represent the cutting edge of a long-term trend in which retail entertainment destinations will be used to energize broader public redevelopment programs, thereby recreating, for the 21st century, the essential elements of successful downtowns.

Public/private organizations will spearhead the creation of thriving cultural and entertainment districts downtown. Downtowns are favored locations for many large-scale retail entertainment destinations because retailers and entertainment companies want to showcase their attractions in locations with high traffic, visibility, and access, and to link their offerings to the prestige of cities' cultural, civic, architectural, and historic jewels . For their part, cities are eager to accommodate these new developments in order to speed downtown revitalization.

But putting all the pieces together isn't easy; for many cities, the only way to create the necessary preconditions for remaking their downtowns as cultural and entertainment destinations is to take a direct role. At the broadest level, more public/private partnerships will be set up—as, for example, in downtown Los Angeles, where the Los Angeles Conservancy, the city government, and business interests are actively pursuing a strategy to revitalize the district as the region's cultural and entertainment center. Initiatives include finding new uses for the spectacular but currently dilapidated theaters along Broadway, ameliorating the social problems that have blighted the area, developing entertainment activities to complement the many cultural offerings already in place, and converting old commercial buildings into loft and live-work residential space.

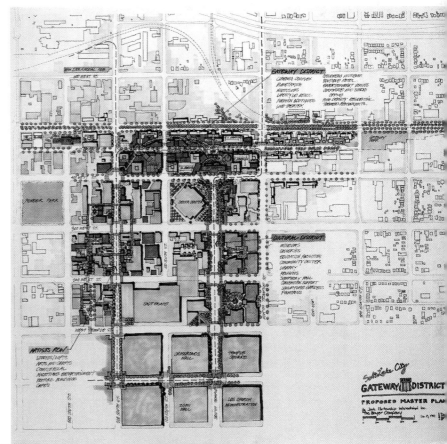

◀ **The Gateway, being developed by Gateway Associates, a partnership of The Boyer Company and The Jerde Partnership International, Inc., in downtown Salt Lake City, Utah, will be a multiblock 2 million-square-foot mixed-use development that will include 835,000 square feet of retail and entertainment uses.**
The Boyer Company

More and more business improvement districts (BIDs) will be set up, as in the downtown entertainment district of Washington, D.C., to improve the designated areas by providing heightened security and sanitation services, infrastructure improvements, direct marketing, and event coordination. BIDs will also work with city governments to devise strategies for finding, siting, and linking new retail and entertainment activities and attractions that can strengthen the district economically and make it more lively. Cultural districts in more cities will broaden their mandate to encourage entertainment attractions as well as the more usual museums and performing-arts facilities.

Retail entertainment destinations will increasingly be anchored by cultural, educational, civic, and sports facilities. Cultural and educational institutions—from museums, performing-arts facilities, and universities to aquariums, zoos, and sports venues, such as stadiums and arenas—are trying to adapt to decreased public funding and to the strong competitive pressures brought about by societal changes. Entertainment offers an opportunity for these institutions to broaden their markets and compete more effectively for consumers' time and attention in a crowded marketplace. In turn, cultural and educational institutions will increasingly act as anchors for retail entertainment destinations, providing the unique local character, cultural context, and educational aspects that are essential for long-term project success.

The technique of colocating entertainment and cultural attractions was pioneered by New York City, and the momentum there is still going strong. Times Square, site of the world's largest concentration of playhouses, now has numerous entertainment destinations, including theme restaurants, such as WWF (Worldwide Wrestling Federation),

Mars 2112, and ESPN Zone; cineplexes; lifestyle stores; and one-of-a-kind attractions, such as the ABC television studios, whose shows can be viewed live from the sidewalk. In addition, Times Square is now home to many of the world's major media giants, including ABC, Bertelsmann, Reuters, and the New York Times (which will soon move down the street to a new headquarters it is building on Eighth Avenue). Several other major cities have followed suit, including San Francisco, whose Yerba Buena Center is the site of the Museum of Contemporary Art, the Moscone Convention Center, and Sony's Metreon retail entertainment destination.

Children's museums are becoming favored anchors for retail entertainment developments. The children's museum in Salt Lake City is being designed as an anchor attraction in the massive Gateway destination project described earlier. In addition, because of the educational and cultural links they offer, many developers are looking to science centers, which have historically been testing grounds for entertainment attractions, as potential anchors for retail entertainment. Virtual-reality attractions, interactive entertainment technology, and large-format films are just some of the features that made the move from science centers to the world of mass entertainment. The recently completed Science City, at Union Station, in Kansas City, Missouri, which occupies a 272,000-square-foot addition to the spectacularly restored historic train station, incorporates entertainment retail and dining along with a live-performance stage, a planetarium, an Iwerks Extreme Screen, and the Kansas City Science Museum as the anchor. David Ucko, president of Science City, said in the January 2000 issue of *Entertaining Places* magazine, "The whole thing is an urban entertainment

Premier Theater at Hollywood & Highland

The 180,000-square-foot Premier Theater, designed by prominent architect David Rockwell, is the centerpiece for TrizecHahn's 640,000-square-foot Hollywood & Highland retail entertainment destination on Hollywood Boulevard in Los Angeles. The $430 million project combines trend-setting clubs, television-broadcast facilities, and studio venues with a collection of world-class retailers, restaurants, and entertainment. The development also incorporates a 640-room hotel, the Renaissance Hollywood Hotel, which will be operated by Marriott International Inc.

The Premier Theater, the future home for the Academy Awards presentations, is being designed with state-of-the-art technology to optimize the venue for audiovisual recordings and live broadcasts in a way that has the least impact on the audience. "This theater is an extension of Los Angeles's status as the world capital for the creation of entertainment products," said Peter Holmes à Court, managing director of Back Row Productions, an international developer and producer of live theatrical productions chosen to program and manage operations for the Premier Theater. "Los Angeles has never had a destination like this before. For the first time, L.A. theatergoers

can park, dine, and see a fabulous show in a world-class venue—all in one location."

Highly regarded for its entertainment product and marketing, Back Row specializes in the development, production, and promotion of innovative artists and new shows, recording and releasing them across multiple media.

"The remarkable vision of this innovative young company has catapulted it into being one of the leading producers of today's most intriguing and highly acclaimed theater productions," said Lee Wagman, president of TrizecHahn Development Corporation. "Back Row's wizardry, coupled with the technological preeminence of Premier Theater, will bring an unsurpassed experience to theatergoers in the heart of Hollywood's entertainment district."

Designed to engage diverse audiences, Back Row's programming plans for the theater include major musical productions, extended concert runs by top musicians, and themed seasonal events such as a Christmas spectacular. Concepts for the opening event include a major television special.

In addition, the company will use the theater to promote outreach programs designed

▲ **The Premier Theater, the future home of the Academy Awards, will be a major anchor of TrizecHahn's Hollywood & Highland retail entertainment destination in Los Angeles. The Rockwell Group used state-of-the-art technology to optimize the venue for audiovisual recordings and live broadcasts.** *TrizecHahn Development Corporation*

to educate adults and children and introduce them to the magic of theater.

"The theater's technology creates an efficient system to both film and record events, as well as broadcast live," said Holmes à Court. "The ability to use the Premier Theater to economically film in a way that

accommodates a range of distribution channels, including the Internet, to meet growing consumer demand is a unique opportunity." ●

Source: *Business Wire,* September 9, 1999.

center that's built around Science City. It's really what we view as a new form of recreational learning that draws from science centers, theme parks, and theaters to create a unique attraction in which visitors explore a city. And in exploring the city they discover things that are fun."

The next great entertainment and cultural district may emerge in Hollywood, California, the symbolic, though not actual, heart of the nation's entertainment industry. The historic Walk of Fame and the existing Chinese, Egyptian, Pantages, Stella Adler, and El Capitan Theaters will soon be joined by the massive Hollywood & Highland retail entertainment destination, the future home of the Academy Awards, and by the Cinerama Dome retail entertainment center on Sunset Boulevard. Smaller communities often have historic and cultural attractions in their downtowns that can be leveraged in the same way.

Retail entertainment components will increasingly be added to stadiums and arenas to create a more continuous customer draw for expensive downtown sites, to leverage the

enormous crowds that are attracted to large-scale events, and to take advantage of these venues as anchors for retail entertainment development. The MCI Center, in downtown Washington, D.C., links retail and entertainment to sports and cultural attractions. Attractions include The National Sports Gallery, a museum of sports memorabilia and interactive virtual sports; the flagship Discovery Store and the Discovery Theater; and a sleek steak house, Nick and Stef's, operated by celebrity chef Joachim Splichal. The success of the MCI Center has dramatically changed the development climate in the east end of the city, creating a frenzy of redevelopment and adaptive use of historic structures in the surrounding neighborhood. Dozens of restaurants have opened, and Gallery Place, a retail entertainment destination that will include large-format lifestyle stores, theme restaurants, a megaplex cinema, condominiums, and office space, is scheduled to begin construction in 2001 next door.

Universities often need gathering places that can provide essential retail and entertainment facilities. Increasingly, large lecture halls will be used for cinemas after classes are over for the day, as they are at the University of California, San Diego, and retail and entertainment uses will be colocated to take advantage of the captive student audience.

The remaking of all types of shopping centers will accelerate, as existing centers create more entertaining environments and add entertainment to attract the new consumer. Overbuilding of retail space continues, and if retail spending slows, the situation will likely get worse. Retail space in the United States is now estimated by the National Research Bureau at more than 20 square feet per person, a historic high. Some of this space is in newer formats, such as off-price megamalls, outlet centers, lifestyle centers, retail entertainment destinations, and repositioned traditional malls and strip centers. But in reality, most of the space is obsolete; thus, the shakeout in the shopping-center industry will continue as some centers reposition themselves to reflect 21st-century lifestyles and others go out of business. The remaking of all types of shopping centers will accelerate, as existing centers create more entertaining environments and add entertainment to attract the new consumer.

How can shopping centers compete? Increasingly, shopping-center owners are adopting a lifestyle and entertainment orientation that transforms the traditional shopping center into more of a gathering place that reflects the uniqueness of its locale and caters to more than shopping needs. Early evidence suggests that these more social environments

Gallery Place, a planned 600,000-square-foot mixed-use entertainment anchor project in downtown Washington, D.C., adjacent to the MCI Center on one side and the historic districts of 7th Street and Chinatown on the other sides, will contain a two-floor retail podium and megaplex, along with condominiums and office space on the upper floors. An existing rapid-transit station will directly serve the project. *KMD*

bring more customers who stay longer, come more often, and spend more money—a retailing grand slam. It is important to note that although the introduction of entertainment can help revitalize many ailing malls as well as assist premium properties in maintaining their competitive positions, it is not a panacea for malls that are poorly located, poorly merchandised, or too small to accommodate the needed changes.

Power centers and off-price megamalls are also increasingly likely to include entertainment in their retail mix. Two of the most advanced examples to date are Arundel Mills, in suburban Baltimore, Maryland, and The Block at Orange, in Orange, California, both of which were created by The Mills Corporation. Arundel Mills contains a massive collection of off-price stores, outlets, and full-priced lifestyle stores; a Muvico megaplex designed around a fantasy Egyptian theme; entertainment restaurants; and specialized

The Block at Orange, developed by the Mills Corporation near Disneyland in Orange, California, is a hybrid shopping center that includes both full-price and off-price stores, 70 percent of which are entertainment oriented. Dramatic pylons, with oversized photos of local residents who have contributed to the betterment of the community, are placed at entrances and along the pedestrian walkways.
The Mills Corporation

entertainment attractions like Vans Skate Park. The Block at Orange, which is even more entertainment oriented (as much as 70 percent of the space is devoted to entertainment) has double-loaded streetfront retailing designed in a racetrack configuration. The outdoor pedestrian walkways are narrow and of varying widths; irregular storefront facades intrude into the walkways. Oversized photos of local residents' faces, mounted dramatically on high poles, are placed at entrances and spaced periodically along the pedestrian walkways. The effect is lively, intimate, stylish, and fun. At Potomac Yards Center, in Alexandria, Virginia, a power center built on land occupied by railroad yards until the 1990s, the addition of a megaplex and new-generation theme restaurants on outpads has extended the center's hours and made it more of a community destination.

Even strip centers are being designed as entertaining destinations to attract more customers. The Commons at Calabasas, in Calabasas, California, a 200,000-square-foot community center developed by Caruso Affiliated Holdings, was built to resemble an Italian village. After years of community opposition to a traditional shopping center, residents approved the entertainment-oriented center—with its elaborate, Italian-style architecture; lake; fountains; sculptures; gardens; Edwards Cineplex; and six restaurants—because it established a unique sense of place for a suburban community that needed it.

In sum, as more entertainment and entertaining features are added to shopping centers, the distinctions between traditional centers and retail entertainment destinations are blurring, and will gradually fade away in the coming years.

New high-technology entertainment concepts, attractions, and anchors will emerge slowly in response to earlier failures. In the first edition of this book, we predicted that new high-technology entertainment concepts would emerge rapidly throughout the retail world. Unfortunately, that hasn't quite been the case. True, the creative ferment in the retail and entertainment industry has never been greater, but the difficulties of rolling out expensive new high-technology entertainment concepts and prototypes have limited their impact in the marketplace. Some sophisticated attractions developed by some of the biggest names in the entertainment industry seemed like sure-fire hits when they were introduced, but once customers had "been there and done that," they didn't return in sufficient numbers to justify the high development and operational costs. Others required such huge population bases to succeed that they could not be rolled out in enough markets and locations to make the concept work. Meanwhile, the turmoil in the cinema industry has made the search for new entertainment attractions even more important.

It is clear that the retail and entertainment industries are still trying to understand the new consumer and figure out what he or she wants. Although the new kinds of social experiences being created are more likely to bring people out of their homes to be entertained in a public environment, these are not likely to be new, high-technology attractions; instead, they are low-technology attractions that have been updated to reflect modern sensibilities. Ultimately, what will drive customers toward retail entertainment destinations are stores, entertainment, restaurants, and environments that appeal to their lifestyles.

No matter how sophisticated the attractions and the technology, what's most important is how entertaining and comfortable the content is; whether the experience is diverse, adaptable, and deep enough to keep people coming back; and how authentically it responds to the consumer's lifestyle, aspirations, and values. Achieving this ideal combination of characteristics, however, is harder than it might seem. Reaching market segments that are easily overlooked—including women; the members of Generations X and Y; and even baby boomers, who are getting older but not "aging"—will determine whether entertainment destinations succeed or fail in the coming years.

Nevertheless, major technological advances will change the experience of shopping and being entertained. For example, film will become digital sometime in the next few years, which means that operators will save money—and that scratchy film prints will become a

The Commons at Calabasas, a 200,000-square-foot community center in Calabasas, California, developed by Caruso Affiliated Holdings, was designed to resemble an Italian village. The entertainment-oriented center, which includes a lake, fountains, sculptures, and gardens, creates a sense of place for a community that needed it. *Caruso Affiliated Holdings*

▼

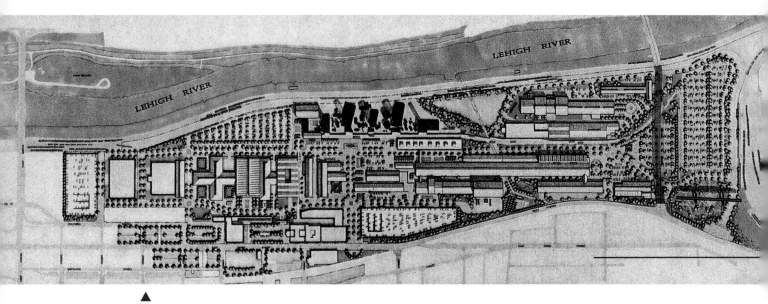

thing of the past. More important, digital technology will permit live, interactive entertainment in movie theaters, as well as a combination of real and virtual entertainment.

Increasingly, shopping center developers will use the power of their own brands to create innovative technological features that will add a new dimension to the shopping experience. For example, Simon Brand Ventures, an initiative of the Simon Property Group, has teamed with Turner Broadcasting, a leading provider of news, entertainment, and sports programming; SFX, the world's leading promoter, producer, and presenter of live entertainment events; and Edward Schlossberg Incorporated (ESI), a design firm that creates interactive experiences. The group is creating the first-ever live retail entertainment network and multimedia platform; the plan is to bring Simon shopping malls alive by integrating the Internet and other technologies to feature original and branded programming from the portfolios of TBS, CNN, TNT, and the Cartoon networks.

In determining the success of retail entertainment developments, developer and local community branding may become as powerful as national retail branding. In the short time since retail entertainment destinations were first introduced, branding has proven to be a powerful business generator. The major entertainment companies have used the power of their own brand images to deepen their penetration of the various entertainment market segments and create new markets altogether. Merchandise, interactive features, events, movies, music, television, publishing, and a range of location-based attractions—from amusement parks to specialized, smaller-scale retail entertainment centers—have been strategically coordinated.

In several cases, efforts on the part of major entertainment companies to create regional entertainment venues failed, forcing those companies to retrench and rethink their local real estate branding strategies. Today, however, major corporations outside the entertainment industry are looking for places with the right image and demographics to market their brands, and sponsorships by such corporations offer great opportunities for new income streams and promotions at retail entertainment centers. These firms are not just paying for access, but for efficient communication with the consumer. Metreon's corporate partners, for example, include Citibank, EDS, Lincoln-Mercury, and Pepsi-Cola. All were carefully integrated into the guest experience through a strategy that maintained the integrity of the project while enabling the corporate partners to achieve their marketing goals.

Through their new MerchantWired technology, shopping center developers like the Taubman Company, Simon Property Group, and others are now busily trying to link their merchants and customers and to exploit their own brand images in order to drive customers toward their centers and Web sites.

Cities with powerful—and not so powerful—images are exploiting them to the fullest as they fight to rejuvenate their downtowns and historic districts. The most dramatic urban branding successes have been centered around major tourist locations like Times Square and the Las Vegas strip, which of course are in a class by themselves, but many smaller communities are now exploiting their identity on a more limited scale. Increasingly, the type and variety of features and attractions that define retail entertainment destinations will be determined as much by the local brands of the cities in which they are located as by the national brands of the tenants that occupy the store space.

Smaller communities, if they are creative, can also take advantage of their brand identity and cultural heritage to create destinations. For example, Bethlehem Works, to be created in Bethlehem, Pennsylvania, is described by its developer, Enterprise Real Estate Services, Inc., as a "mixed-use entertainment/museum/recreation/hospitality development [that will retain] the existing historic character of

Bethlehem Steel Corporation's former plant." The project will include the Smithsonian Institution's National Museum of Industrial History; the Iron and Steel Showcase (an attraction featuring a simulation of the steel-making process); a natatorium; an ice-skating rink; a multiplex cinema; two hotels; a conference center; 175,000 square feet of lifestyle retailing; a 500,000-square-foot retail entertainment complex; and a 75,000-square-foot family fun center. Talk about making a silk purse out of a sow's ear!

New-generation megaplex cinemas have driven customers toward retail entertainment destinations, but they have also driven their operators into bankruptcy. Now what? There is no question that by drawing the enormous crowds that feed the other activities, the new megaplexes have become a driving force in the success of retail entertainment destinations. Offering as many as 24 (and, in a few cases, more) large screens; sophisticated sound and projection systems; comfortable, stadium-style seats; a greater variety and quality of food; dramatic entrances and lobbies; high levels of finish and detail; and strong architectural styles like those found in the movie palaces of the 1930s, the new-generation theaters heighten the entire movie-going experience, creating a strong sense of occasion that is enhanced by their prominent locations and the presence of other nearby attractions, including theme restaurants and entertainment-oriented shops. Because there are so many screens, movies start every few minutes and the same movie is likely to be showing on several screens, thus obviating the need for customers to time their arrival or pick their movie in advance. Families and groups can go to the movies together, split up to watch the movies they want, then rejoin for snacks or dessert.

Warner Cinema

SOUTH ELEVATION

The megaplex cinemas developed by such giants as AMC, Carmike, Edwards, General Cinema, Loews, Mann's, Regal, and United Artists have rendered obsolete thousands of screens across the country, an eventuality that we predicted in the first edition of this book. What we didn't predict was that most cinema operators would be driven into bankruptcy. Customers now routinely pass by older cinema complexes that lack state-of-the-art moviegoing environments to patronize new megaplexes in retail entertainment destinations. Many cinema operators assumed that this phenomenon would affect their competitors but not themselves—which turned out, for some, to be a serious, if not fatal, miscalculation.

While the rapid expansion of new cinema complexes has been great for the moviegoing public, it has become a nightmare for the giant cinema operators, who find themselves in a Catch-22 situation: if they hadn't expanded rapidly with the new megaplex concept, they would have rapidly lost market share to those that did. But by expanding, they cannibalized their own older cinemas and played havoc with their own operating balances.

What is likely to happen now? It seems that it will be 2003 or 2004 before the industry stabilizes and begins to grow at a rate that is in line with consumer demand. In the short term, bankruptcy will wipe obsolete cinemas off the operators' books, leaving shopping-center owners with empty theaters, worthless leases, and uncertain prospects for reuse. In the fall 2000 issue of *Shopping Center Directions,* the National Research Bureau reported on the dimensions of the problem: of the 2,750 cinema complexes in shopping centers, about 1,750 belong to at-risk cinema chains. While many of these cinemas continue to perform strongly and will remain open, others are older facilities in undesirable spaces—in basements, for example, or with little frontage on the common areas of the shopping center. Most likely, the majority of these spaces will never again be used for cinemas, although some may be leased temporarily as second-run houses.

Retail entertainment destinations that are in the planning stages have been left scrambling to find new cinema operators before they can begin construction or lock in financing. Many of these projects will be delayed; some will have to face reality and be scaled back; still others will be forced to substitute other land uses for the cinema space, thus reducing the site's entertainment draw. In any case, cinema construction will not stop altogether: some projects are already in the pipeline, some developers may choose to build cinemas themselves and find operators to run them, and the bankruptcy courts may permit some new construction, if the potential is deemed great enough, by bankrupt operators.

In the long run, the cinema industry will be transformed as it is consolidated by new money. The unequal relationship between cinema operators and movie studios will disintegrate as the few remaining operators—who will be larger and more powerful—succeed in renegotiating, on an equal footing, the unfavorable arrangements they currently have with the studios. Moreover, once movies become digital, film distributors will be unnecessary and new income streams from live events will be feasible, further strengthening the operators' profit potential.

▲
◀ **KMD Architects's concept design for Plaza Pier Show, in Santos, Brazil, demonstrates how retail and entertainment can be integrated in a dramatic modernist environment. The destination will take maximum advantage of its waterfront setting while at the same time providing exciting interior spaces to explore.**
KMD

Specialty cinema concepts will continue to be rolled out for sophisticated urban audiences. New cinema concepts that are ideally suited for specialized locations and markets will continue to be introduced by smaller independent operators. The Landmark and Sundance theater chains, for example, are opening small cineplexes with all the amenities but with fewer than half the number of screens found in the megaplexes. Typically located in downtown or uptown urban locations, these cinemas show art, independent, and international films that are rarely found at the megaplex. Visions, a new, three-screen independent cinema in the arty Dupont Circle

Hotels as Entertainment Anchors

The Economics of Experience

Recent research into the economics of entertainment has confirmed the value-enhancing benefits of integrating an entertainment experience within a standard service offering, and "staging" the service as a memorable special event.

This approach is being effectively applied in a variety of real estate product types, particularly destination developments, retail malls, theme restaurants, and specialty retail shops, many of which have far surpassed their typical nonthemed competitors in various measures of sales and profitability. In addition, theme-park operators and gaming companies have fully embraced the use of architectural theming, interior design, and entertainment elements in their lodging facilities to attract and "transport" guests to other places and environments, enabling them to realize an escapist fantasy or other memorable experience while participating in a variety of hotel service offerings.

However, outside the environment of the theme park and the casino destination, the lodging industry has been slow to understand and appreciate the potential impact that theming and experientially oriented entertainment elements can have on the value of real estate assets.

The Challenge for the Lodging Industry

The hotel industry is highly competitive in terms of the supply/demand equilibrium and capital investment cycles. Whether the economy is expanding or recessionary, examples of underperforming, plain-vanilla hotels abound—a situation that has not only been problematic for their owners but that has also significantly inhibited capital investment both in existing assets and in proposed new properties.

At the institutional level, the standard response to competitive pressures is acquisition or merger; the consolidation of competitors under a bigger corporate umbrella makes it possible to obtain a broader marketing network, a stronger referral and reservation system, greater economies of scale, and a more extensive consumer loyalty program. This "bigger is better" formula, with its requisite focus on brand identity and national quality-assurance programs, may work at the corporate level but is rarely a solution at the individual property level.

Indeed, hotel-company consolidation typically leads to executive reshuffling and management changes, often resulting in *less* attention being paid to property-level concerns and attendant opportunities. Further, while competition among the major chains has certainly raised quality standards to a highly consistent level throughout the industry, it has also institutionalized the lodging experience.

The result is the "sea of sameness" that characterizes the industry today: an overabundance of nondistinctive, chain-dominated properties. Typical hotels within any given market do not differ significantly except in price, a fact that has only added to the industry's competitive challenges rather than diminished them. The real challenge for the lodging industry is to change the product and services provided at the property level in a way that will, at the very least, improve—and at best transcend—the generic need for overnight accommodations.

Approximately 25 years ago, to highlight the standardization of its product and quality and to differentiate itself from the competition, Holiday Inns launched an advertising campaign whose slogan was "The best surprise is *no* surprise." Today, every hotel company offers standardized product and quality, and consumers increasingly desire something more from their hotel experience.

Pioneer hoteliers in both urban markets and tourist destinations are attempting to capitalize on this market opportunity by combining unique theming, architecture, and interior design to yield new or revitalized assets that are competitively distinctive and superior in their performance. Examples include the following:

- The Joie de Vivre Hotels in San Francisco, which are specifically targeted to a magazine-style (that is, highly specialized) customer profile

- The Kimpton Hotel Group properties, which originated from modestly priced boutique hotels with unique restaurants near San Francisco's Union Square

- Loews Hotels's new Portofino Bay themed hotel at Universal Studios Escape in Orlando, and the House of Blues Hotel in Chicago, which integrates lodging with a theme restaurant and a nightclub and music-performance venue

The Renaissance Hollywood Hotel will be part of the glamour, excitement, and entertainment at TrizecHahn's Hollywood & Highland retail entertainment destination.
TrizecHahn Development Corporation

- Elvis Presley's Heartbreak Hotel at Graceland, in Memphis
- Ian Schrager's trendy hotels (designed by Philippe Starck) in major urban centers; examples include the Royalton and Paramount, in New York; the Delano, in Miami Beach; the Mondrian, in Los Angeles, and St. Martin's Lane, in London
- Starwood Lodging's new "W" brand of hotels
- The Hard Rock Hotels in Las Vegas and Orlando (under construction), and the Hard Rock Beach Club resort hotel, in Bali, Indonesia
- Quasi-themed hotels, such as the Four Seasons Hualalai, in Hawaii; the Hyatt Hill Country Resort, in San Antonio; the Opryland Hotel, in Nashville; and Shutters on the Beach, in Santa Monica

- Many of the new ecotourism projects, which feature unique and naturally harmonious designs that emphasize the surrounding environment.

Each of these hotel developments represents the first generation of lodging facilities designed to fulfill the promise and potential of a comprehensive hotel "experience." In each case, the developers and operators are attempting to

- Respond directly to the challenges and opportunities of the local competitive market
- Not only to be distinct from, but to preempt and transcend other existing or proposed hotels
- Establish and sustain a competitive edge
- Increase revenue per available room by (1) capturing a greater share of the lodging market (the occupancy premium); (2) increasing the average length of stay and repeat visitation frequency of hotel guests (product/brand loyalty); (3) increasing per capita expenditures in rooms (the average rate premium) and nonroom departments; (4) attracting incremental (nonhotel guest) customers
- And, in doing all the above, engineer a compelling investment opportunity.

The Future of Lodging: Models for the New Millennium

Hotels are unique among real estate product types in that they are designed to capitalize on the away-from-office and away-from-home requirements of both business and leisure travelers. Accordingly, they have an opportunity to immerse the guest in a public and private environment: future examples of this new lodging genre will undoubtedly expand the definition of the lodging "experience." In our crystal ball, we see some of the possibilities generated by current trends in hotel development:

- More lodging facilities will be planned as anchors for destination developments, whether in urban, suburban, or resort settings.
- These hotels will be integrated into the entertainment complex, not merely located adjacent to it.
- The public services and support facilities (that is, restaurants, bars, nightclubs, retail stores, health clubs, business centers, and conference facilities) will be separated from guest-room towers and located within the destination streetscape in order to capture broader demand segments.
- Hotel lobbies will become smaller, and will be designed with the more intimate ambience of a private club.
- "Urban resorts" will be developed to capture not only the business traveler but also the increasing demand by couples and families for frequent, short-term minivacations.
- These urban resorts will be designed with uniquely themed, entertainment-oriented environments and will provide guests with a total escapist or fantasy experience. ●

Source: Paul DeMyer.

neighborhood of Washington, D.C., shows eclectic art and international films in a facility that combines a restaurant and bar in a renovated theater that previously housed a single screen. A strong market for these specialized cinemas should continue despite the turmoil in the cinema industry as a whole.

Club cinemas will be added to the megaplex moviegoing experience. Limited to adults 21 and over, these luxury cinemas are equipped with oversized leather seats, wider arm rests, café service with full bar, and a first-class ambience. Ticket prices are up to 50 percent higher than for regular screens in the same cinema complex. McCaffery Interests, Inc., repositioned Mazza Gallerie, a high-end mall in Washington, D.C., with a megaplex on the fourth floor containing two club cinemas, in addition to the standard, new-generation cinemas down the hall. The club cinemas have proven to be very popular with the well-heeled customers in the neighborhood, and they fit in well with the image of the center's anchor tenants, Neiman Marcus and Saks Fifth Avenue Men's Store.

Ex-Centris is a three-screen cinema on Montreal's Boulevard Saint Laurent developed by Daniel Langlois, an entrepreneur who founded Softimage, a firm that creates three-dimensional computer animation. The sound quality at Ex-Centris exceeds THX standards, and the air conditioning comes from below and through the seats. There are no concession stands, and no refreshments are allowed in the theaters, since food could spill and gum up the air-conditioning system. One

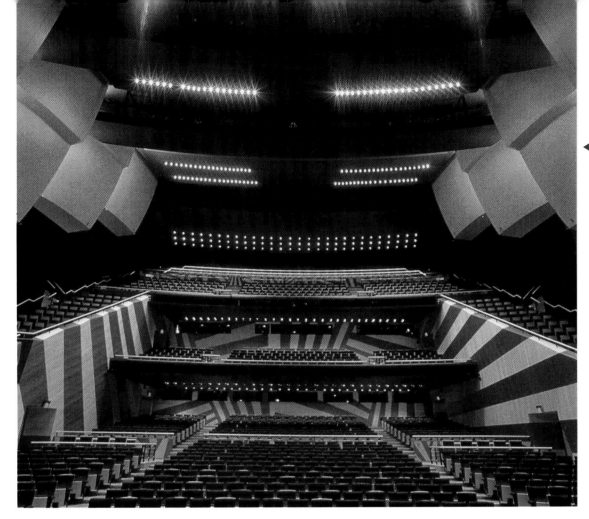

Performing-arts centers, like the one in Dijon, France (left), and sports arenas, like the Philips Arena, in Atlanta, Georgia (facing page), both designed by Arquitectonica, serve as major cultural and entertainment anchors for their communities.
Arquitectonica

theater, with a hinged floor that can be made level, converts to an exhibition space. Another, with a five-ton screen that can roll backward 28 feet to reveal a stage, can be converted for live performances. The posh complex has a two-story café and bar, open until 3 A.M., that draw a hip film-industry crowd. Most remarkable, however, is that the cinema charges the standard ticket price.

Theme restaurants appear to have learned their lesson, and the new generation is offering good food, good service, and lifestyle-oriented environments that customers are flocking to. The theme-restaurant trend that started in the 1970s with Hard Rock Café, and was later reinforced by Planet Hollywood and dozens of other brand-name restaurant chains, has gone through a metamorphosis. When the first edition of this book was published, theme restaurants were thought of exclusively as mini–theme parks with fantasy environments, logo merchandise, and so many different themes that they could be grouped into categories (for example, Hollywood movies, sports, travel, television and radio, computers, music, adventure, and Americana). But for the most part, theme restaurants were not thought of as places with good food or good service—not the most desirable reputation for places where guests plan to dine!

Restaurants based on highly specific themes still exist, of course—and, in many specialized locations (particularly those with large tourist markets), they are doing well because they, too, are paying more attention to the basics. But the theme-restaurant industry has changed dramatically in the past few years. The most off-the-wall concepts have had difficulty rolling out their concept, while some restaurants based on a strong lifestyle or ethnic theme have proliferated widely.

Generations X and Y

Generation X

Generation X, the next cohort to influence national entertainment expenditures, has long been misunderstood. In the early 1990s, public opinion had it that Generation X was nothing more than a bunch of whining slackers who had no ambition other than to get a "McJob." Nothing could be further from the truth.

Gen Xers, who were born between 1965 and 1976, currently number 44.6 million, and there are 13.7 million Gen X households. They are young, with their peak earning years still ahead: in 2000, their median income was $31,000 (the national median is $40,926). Collectively, they earn $425 billion annually—of which almost $21 billion is spent on entertainment products and experiences. More than two-thirds of Gen Xers have gone to college; 70 percent are employed; more than 33 percent are married; and 25 percent already own their own home.

Many Gen Xers complain of feeling mature beyond their years. This feeling stems, at least in part, from their sense of the "debris" left behind by their idealistic baby boomer parents. Forget what the boomers intended, and look at what

they actually left us, Gen Xers say: Divorce. Gangs. Drugs. Latchkey kids. National debt. Environmental chaos. Gen Xers never lost faith in their government; they never had it to begin with.

Still, Gen Xers have proven themselves to be resilient. They are a generation that is determined to be involved, responsible, and in control. In a recent survey done by the young-adult philanthropy magazine *Who Cares,* more than two-thirds of the Gen Xers polled said that they volunteered in their communities, compared with 56 percent of the population at large. Highly motivated to make a difference in the world, Gen Xers are very "green," and consider themselves the "cleanup crew" of previous generations.

Nevertheless, their issues and priorities are very different from those of their parents—a point that must be understood in order to attract Gen Xers to new retail and entertainment experiences. Two retailers who thoroughly understand this generation are Anthropologie and Urban Outfitters. A visit to one of these stores gives a clear picture of the environmentally concerned and

slightly misanthropic view of Gen Xers.

For the members of Generation X, diversity is a simple fact of life: they are more tolerant of differences than any preceding generation and have a less judgmental, more expansive view of lifestyle choices. Xers enjoy a variety of entertainment types, but especially appreciate entertainment that shows the cutting-edge influence of ethnic and cultural minorities.

Because many Gen Xers were latchkey kids, they spent more time alone, entertaining themselves after school, than any other generation in history. Gen Xers are resourceful, accustomed to making do with what they have and resolved to do things themselves. Because they don't know whom else to trust, they often depend solely on themselves.

Xers are the least likely of all of the generations to read or even look at a newspaper. They get their news from the electronic media. However, increasing percentages of Gen Xers are going to movies, galleries, and museums. Having grown up with television and computers, they are visually oriented, extremely computer literate, and very comfortable with high-

tech gadgetry. They are also fast becoming a generation of entrepreneurs: witness the explosion of dot-com businesses whose key management is never over 40.

When Gen Xers control the organizations of tomorrow, they will likely implement a shorter workweek, allowing them more time for their families, and for entertainment and leisure activities—and creating a perfect future market for entertainment providers. They want to have fun—but in a responsible way that makes them feel comfortable. Gen Xers are ready to buy, but they don't want to feel that they're being taken advantage of, and they particularly hate being talked down to. Out-of-home entertainment offerings must take into the account the following trends, which make Gen Xers different from preceding generations:

- They are wired, and tech savvy.
- They want cutting-edge games and experiences.
- They are sophisticated consumers; they enjoy upscale, dress-up restaurants and clubs.
- They are comfortable with computers and the Internet.

- They are more culturally and racially diverse than any preceding generation—a characteristic that must be reflected in music, food, and entertainment offerings. (Think swing dancing, salsa clubs, Latin jazz, independent movies.)
- They are profoundly concerned with the environment. Patagonia is a good example of a company whose stand on the environment has helped make it a favorite of this generation.

Generation Y

The members of Generation Y—also known as echo boomers and millennials, and currently aged seven to 24—make up the next large burst in the American population. Born between 1977 and 1994, Gen Yers number 72 million and make up 26 percent of the U.S. population; they are the largest group of young people in the country's history—larger even than the baby boomers. Gen Y is the most ethnically diverse generation to date: one-third are minorities, mostly African American and Hispanic. Although most of their members are still children, the echo boomers have already had an immense impact on business and society.

Beginning in 1980, a rising U.S. birth rate ended the baby-bust years. Between 1989 and 1993, the total number of U.S. births exceeded 4 million for the first time in almost 30 years. Today, there are almost 57 million children under age 15, and more than 20 million in the four-to-eight age category.

Companies that sell entertainment such as toys, videos, software, and clothing to this group have boomed in recent years. Consider that nine of the ten best-selling videos of all time are animated films from the Walt Disney company. The French vacation company, Club Med, now earns about half its U.S. revenues from family resorts.

As of now, the echo boomers claim less than 4 percent of all household spending in the United States, but in several markets—men's apparel, and women's apparel and footwear—they account for up to 5 percent; they also account for 10 percent of infant clothing expenditures. Echo boomers have above-average consumption of TVs, radios, and sound equipment; computer hardware and software; alcoholic beverages; shelter; and gas and

motor oil. Teens spent approximately $108 billion in 1996, and influenced $300 billion in family spending, voicing their opinions on a wide range of issues—what computer to buy, where to send out for pizza, where to spend the family vacation.

This group is largely responsible for the growth and development of the more than $6 billion home game market (compact discs, game hardware and game software). Gen Yers are very independent for youngsters: a startling 39 percent of 18- and 19-year-olds have their own credit cards. The oldest of the echo boomers are currently forming their first households. As the rest of them come of age and begin to work, their spending power will increase dramatically.

Echo boomers have traditional values reminiscent of those of past generations. They appreciate their families, their country, and the planet. They think things other than money are important for success and happiness, and they feel a responsibility to make the world a better place. They are technologically adept and are growing up to be environmentally conscious and far more tolerant of differences than preceding generations. Even as children, they

are far more politically active than Gen Xers.

The older echo boomers have high educational attainment and see education as a lifelong endeavor that is the key to economic security. They are avid e-commerce users. Sixty percent of households with children seven and younger have a computer, and 67 percent use computers regularly. Echo boomers are the first generation to grow up with a computer at home and often help their parents troubleshoot.

Echo boomers are changing the way many places do business. Hotels and cruise lines offer kids' programs. Malls and supermarkets are providing on-site babysitting. Restaurants are setting out crayons at the table and expanding their take-out menus, all to serve families with small children.

Echo boomers are described as "good scouts." Those in their teenage years are not as angry as teens of previous generations. They are good at multitasking: they can play a video game, listen to a CD, and do homework at the same time. They crave a multitude of stimuli and are avid game and movie consumers.

Continued ▶

Generations X and Y

They seek out cutting-edge, high-impact, technologically advanced entertainment—and push their families to buy it. And, having grown up in the world of malls and cable TV, they have sophisticated tastes.

As the echo boomers grow up, they will change society, and the entertainment being offered must meet their preferences and demands. The following are some of the characteristics of this generation that must be recognized by entertainment providers now and in the future:

- They are more conventional than preceding generations. They love "the oldies" and their parents' cars and clothes.

- They are opinionated and somewhat cynical. They have a strong sense of irony.

- They are "serially monogamous" consumers. They will be fiercely loyal to a brand for a month, then switch to another more current brand.

- Young Gen Yers idolize their parents. According to a Yankelovich survey on men's apparel, women's apparel, and footwear, the number-one objective of preteen children is to connect with their parents. Providing opportunities for Gen Yers to have fun in a multigenerational environment is a key to capturing this market.

- Many come from split families, or families with busy, dual-career households. They will need shorter-term entertainment experiences.

- They are extremely "green," and interested in a company's morality. Marketing and advertising through word and deed are critical.

- They are by far the most wired and tech-savvy generation yet.

Vans Skate Parks, the Disney Magic Cruise Ship, and GameWorks are a few examples of unique entertainment projects that have attracted this group. In the coming years, providers taking note of the unique characteristics of Gen Y will change the face of entertainment offerings. ●

Source: Jill Bensley and Shea Whitney, JB Research Company.

Restaurants such as California Pizza Kitchen, PF Chang's, Il Fornaio, and Wolfgang Puck are among the best-known examples of the new generation of theme restaurants whose reputations rely more on their food than on their decor. These restaurants are moderately priced, serve popular cuisines, cater to local customers more than tourists, and have high design concepts rather than traditional "themes." As a result, they are not perceived as gimmicky or as places to go only when out-of-town visitors arrive. Instead, they have successfully established themselves as local gathering places where people feel comfortable dropping in anytime for snacks, meals, or celebrations. And they have staying power. Because their concepts and price points work well in areas where the demographics are less powerful than in major metropolitan markets, the new-generation theme restaurants are more adaptable to many different types of retail entertainment destinations, and as a result will continue to be rolled out successfully around the country.

Live entertainment and scripted spaces are at the cutting edge of retail entertainment destinations. As we predicted in the last edition of this book, live entertainment—including Broadway shows, off-Broadway shows, touring productions, family shows, theme-park shows, casino shows, concert productions, major events, pageants, and local traditions—offers the opportunity to energize retail entertainment destinations, distinguish them from other places, and characterize them in the minds of the customers as special places to which they want to belong. Tony Christopher, cofounder of Landmark Entertainment, said at that time that all entertainment, including the new interactive media, is based on live theater and that understanding its various forms and using them will make urban entertainment a more compelling experience that brings audiences back again and again. He's still right.

But beyond the special events and major productions, retail entertainment destinations are paying increasing attention to the day-to-day activities that are smaller in scale but perhaps even more important to the ambience and character of a place. The term in use is *scripted places,* which refers to several different aspects of the destination concept: the character of the visitors' itinerary through the place; the experiences that they have along the way; the activities and entertainment that are programmed into the public spaces; the design elements that are encountered, such as fountains, gardens, and architectural elements; and the interplay between the tenants and the public realm.

At the Glendale Marketplace, in Glendale, California, the developer has added strolling musicians, live bands, and clowns to energize the shopping center and encourage people to go up to the second level. The interactive fountains in the central gathering place at Universal CityWalk, in Universal City, California, are the most popular feature. The Moorish archways, courtyards, and fountains at Irvine Spectrum Center, in Irvine, California, draw customers through the outdoor spaces as if they were the rooms in a home.

To appeal to new consumers—especially women—more retail entertainment destinations will take on a lifestyle orientation. Among the diverse and entertaining concepts that seem to be succeeding in retail entertainment destinations are practice areas in stores, where customers can try out goods like sporting equipment; relaxing retailing environments, such as tearooms and coffeehouses; virtual-reality attractions, such as skiing simulations and indoor golf; new-generation megaplex cinemas; motion simulators; museums in the mall; indoor playgrounds; new-generation theme restaurants; live entertainment; and lifestyle-oriented shops of all kinds.

Restoration Hardware, although very light on the basics, has found a way to make hardware merchandise entertaining. Smith & Hawken, an upscale garden center, is trying to do the same for gardening merchandise. Zany Brainy and Noodle Kidoodle have created edutainment products that educate and entertain. Specialty grocery stores are catering to the demand for exotic prepared foods as well as providing on-site and off-site dining in a high-style and entertaining environment. The common thread among these tenants is their orientation toward the lifestyle that educated people aspire to, in which interior decor, gardening, fashion, food and kitchen accessories, books, travel, and learning all play a part. These tenants represent the good life, the comfortable life, the entertaining life; and they represent the types of retailing that will be successful in many retail entertainment environments.

The retail entertainment destinations that succeed in the future will bundle entertaining stores and restaurants into an energized environment that is carefully linked to the consumer's daily life. Whether there are "pure" entertainment attractions or high-technology entertainment features may not be important. But what will be important is meeting the lifestyle expectations and aspirations of the new consumer, especially Generations X and Y, and women, who represent more than 50 percent of the population and make most of the retail spending decisions. Places like American Girl Place, in Chicago, are wildly successful with the women's market. More of

Women and Entertainment for the New Millennium

Sigmund Freud said, "The great question . . . which I have not been able to answer, despite my 30 years of research into the feminine soul, is 'What does a woman want?'" Dr. Freud never answered this question in his lifetime. We are well advised to keep asking, for women will be important consumers of entertainment in the new millennium.

Some facts about this market segment include the following:

- Women hold the national purse strings.
- Young American women are the best-educated market segment.
- Women work, and their leisure time is tight and precious.
- Women are choosing to have smaller families, causing the American economy to grow ever more slowly.
- Entertainment products geared toward women, or designed with women in mind, have shown great success.

National Spending by Women

Consider the first trend in the list. The national population in 2000 was about 281 million, of which 51 percent—about 143 million—were women. National disposable income is estimated at about $6 trillion. *Women are responsible for spending about 80 percent of this total.* Simply put, women spend $4.8 trillion every year in this country on all types of goods and services. With entertainment spending at about 4.4 percent of the national market basket, the female market segment controls $211 billion of entertainment spending in the United States.

Young American Women Are the Best-Educated Market Segment

National spending on entertainment goods and services increases with level of education, with college graduates spending the most in this category. At 59.8 percent, 55.4 percent, and 55 percent, respectively, women now earn the majority of associate's, bachelor's, and master's degrees conferred in the United States.

Women Work, and Their Time Is Tight and Precious

If we are to design and sell entertainment and entertainment retail products to women, we need to understand their lifestyles. First and foremost, women work. The overall labor-force participation rate for women in 1998 was 59.8 percent, up from 35 percent in 1960. But consider the psychographics of this working population:

- Three out of four female college grads (those who spend the most on entertainment of all groups) are employed. Almost 80 percent of women with kids in school are employed, and even those with children under six are more likely to be employed than the general female population.
- These women are busy with work and children. Experiences and facilities must be designed to achieve the maximum efficiency

(shorter stays, more intense entertainment offerings, and no long lines), and some should be designed with the understanding that women may be looking for experiences that they can enjoy with their children. This trend will not reverse itself. Trends over the last two decades show large increases in the participation of mothers in the workforce: the message is, design with the working mother in mind!

Women Are Choosing to Have Smaller Families

Fertility rates vary with the educational and socioeconomic status of women: the higher the level of income and education, the smaller the families. At the time of the first U.S. census in 1790, the average American woman had 7.7 children; by 1890, 100 years later, the average had dropped to 4.4; today, it is just over 2.

The American economy has always counted on large population increases to sustain economic growth. But population growth in the United States is just under 1 percent, and likely to drop further as women become more educated and affluent. In order to sustain market share, entertainment

providers will have to be more competitive, and pay attention to the nuances that attract their core customers—who, in the 21st century, are increasingly likely to be female.

The Most Successful Entertainment Project Geared toward Women: American Girl Place

American Girl Place is the latest entry into what the toy industry is calling a brilliant development and marketing plan. Pleasant Company, with Pleasant Rowland at the helm, has sold nearly 4 million 18-inch dolls and 48 million books since it was launched in 1986. Pleasant Company is now a subsidiary of Mattel, but Rowland still holds the reins and is vice chairman of Mattel.

American Girl Place, developed by Pleasant Company, is a 35,000-square-foot, three-level venue located at 111 East Chicago Avenue, just off tony Michigan Avenue in downtown Chicago. The project is a gentle blend of retail and entertainment that capitalizes on the popularity of the American Girl culture, the catalogue-based line of dolls, clothing, books, and lifestyle

▲
American Girl Place (above and facing page), the most successful retail entertainment project geared toward women and girls, includes a bookstore, a café, a 150-seat live-performance theater, a photo studio, and museum-quality retail space, all in a highly experiential environment that appeals to both children and adults.
American Girl Place

accessories for girls aged five to 12. It is a special place for young girls and their mothers (and fathers) to enjoy a day of fun, food, and shopping.

The store includes a bookstore, café, 150-seat live theater, photo studio, and museumlike retail space that appeals to both children and adults. The professional-quality American Girl Theater offers an hour-long musical revue based on the stories behind American Girl dolls.

Since opening in November 1998, the facility has hosted more than

750,000 visitors. More than 40 percent of the customers are overnight visitors to the Chicago area whose main purpose is to visit the American Girl Store. With such success, a rollout is being studied, with major upscale American downtowns targeted. ●

Source: Jill Bensley, JB Research Company.

these types of places, tailored to emerging markets, will need to be created if retail entertainment destinations are to thrive.

In conclusion: When ULI published the first edition of this book three years ago, the term urban entertainment development was the buzzword of the real estate industry. We asked at that time whether this new form of development had staying power—and, somewhat sardonically, whether it was the wave of the future, the savior of America's downtowns, and the miraculous rejuvenator of shopping centers that some claimed it to be.

The answer is clear today that, in many ways, entertainment development has exceeded the seemingly inflated expectations that it inspired: a dynamic new form of development has indeed been born. But things are not as simple as we envisioned back then. The change in the title of this book reflects the fact that instead of simply creating urban entertainment centers, the retail entertainment industry has created an entire range of project types, ranging from freestanding entertainment projects to multiuse destination developments. Within this range are entertaining strip and power centers; lifestyle centers; entertainment megamalls; shopping malls repositioned with entertainment; cultural and entertainment districts; sports facilities, museums, and convention centers that have been enhanced with entertainment; entertainment hotels; and town centers and mixed-use high rises that include entertainment.

The pent-up demand for exciting, innovative entertainment in safe public environments where people can interact has now been demonstrated. In a few short years, entertainment and entertaining environments have become expected, if not essential, components of almost all forms of develop-

ment. As the experience economy becomes more entrenched, entertainment development will soon be taken for granted.

Although some observers point to the problems of some of the earliest theme restaurants and the current bankruptcy of many of the largest cinema operators and claim that entertainment development was a fad whose time has come and gone, we believe that this is a short-sighted view. As the new face of retailing emerges all around us, entertainment's major role in the transformation of the entire retail industry is indisputable. Retail and entertainment development are clearly merging, and it may soon be almost impossible to differentiate the two. In 1998, the major entertainment companies seemed to be the driving force in the creation of pure entertainment facilities. Today, it is the retail and multiuse developers who are leading the charge, repositioning obsolete developments and creating imaginative new retail entertainment concepts and environments to keep pace with fast-changing consumer demands.

The first edition of this book asked several questions for which we still don't have answers. How many retail entertainment centers and attractions can the market support? What size and combination of features and attractions work best? Will people continue to be interested once the novelty wears off? Perhaps more important, can entertainment providers keep it from wearing off? These questions may never be answered because in most cases, entertainment is no longer associated with a specific, precisely definable type of place. The answers depend on the unique character of local markets, individual locations, and development concepts. What is clear, however, is that entertainment—in all

The Shiodome, in Tokyo, Japan, will be the site of Dentsu Corporation's headquarters as well as a futuristic cultural, retail, and entertainment destination that has been designed by The Jerde Partnership International, Inc., to enhance the corporation's identity and image. *The Jerde Partnership International, Inc.*

its manifestations—has infiltrated mainstream development forms and practices to such an extent that it has opened up countless new development and redevelopment opportunities that were not recognized—or possible—before. The implications for revitalizing cities and creating more livable communities are enormous.

The first edition of this book was the first comprehensive attempt to provide case-study–based information on the issues that are critical to the future of entertainment development. This second edition updates that information and describes an industry that is much wiser. We now have a clearer understanding of the opportunities as well as the limitations of entertainment development, but we still do not have all of the answers.

The case studies in this edition represent second-generation project types that reflect our broader understanding of what constitutes entertainment-enhanced development. Undoubtedly, the lessons learned from these projects will influence how the industry matures in the next few years. But as we said three years ago, the industry is still too new and the experience available is not yet deep enough to make definitive predictions about the future. The book does, however, create a current base of information and insights that the entertainment development industry will need as it evolves.

Where do we go from here? As we said three years ago, stay tuned.